Myth, Media, and the Southern Mind

STEPHEN A. SMITH   Myth, Media,

and the Southern Mind

THE UNIVERSITY OF ARKANSAS PRESS *Fayetteville*

This project is funded in part by a grant from the Arkansas Endowment for the Humanities.

LIBRARY OF CONGRESS CATALOGING IN PUBLICATION DATA
Smith, Stephen A., 1949–
    Myth, media, and the Southern mind.

    Bibliography: p.
    Includes index.
    1. Southern States—Civilization—20th century.   2. Southern States—Popular culture—History—20th century.   3. Mass media—Southern States—History—20th century.   I. Title.
F216.2.S565   1985   975   84-28021
ISBN 0-938626-39-6
ISBN 0-938626-41-8 (pbk.)

To Caleb and Maggie
who can now have their own visions of the South
free from the debilitating influences
of its darker past and particular injustices

Contents

Acknowledgments

This book has been ten years in the making. The list of those to whom I am indebted is longer than most, since I have had more time to steal ideas and borrow insights from more people. Many of my observations and conclusions first developed in graduate classes in history with Walter L. Brown of the University of Arkansas and Robert Gilmour of Princeton University, in anthropology with Mary Jo Schneider of the University of Arkansas, and in sociology with Arnold Feldman of Northwestern University. I am indebted to Carl Kell of Western Kentucky University and Waldo Braden of Louisiana State University for their early encouragement of my interest in the rhetoric of the contemporary South and to C. Vann Woodward of Yale University and George B. Tindall of the University of North Carolina for the inspiration of their scholarship in helping me to recognize the progressive strains of Southern history.

Governor Richard Riley of South Carolina appointed me to the Commission on the Future of the South, and Governor Bill Clinton of Arkansas appointed me to the Southern Growth Policies Board. I am grateful for their confidence and for those experiences which enriched my perspectives on the region. Bill Clinton has been more than a friend for a dozen years, and in my association with him as a hanger-on and a second banana political operative I enjoyed the opportunity to watch as he helped to fashion Southern politics and construct the most recent of the New South myths.

To Irving Rein of Northwestern University, for his wit, patience, friendship, and scholarly guidance, I owe a special debt of gratitude. He not only directed the doctoral dissertation from which this book has been refined, but he also helped me to appreciate the diversity of communication forms in contemporary society and to understand the critical approaches to their study. I am also indebted to the other members of my dissertation committee. Frank Haiman, a good friend and an outstanding scholar and theorist of freedom of speech, not only improved the document but also nurtured my commitment to political freedom. David Zarefsky, a fellow Southerner, saw through my good ole boy façade, offered many detailed and helpful suggestions, required me to rewrite many of my favorite paragraphs, and significantly improved the final draft. Ruth Banes, Willard Gatewood, John Shelton Reed, Raymond Rodgers, and James Whitehead read the study, offered valuable comments, and encouraged its publication

The staff at The University of Arkansas Press has been understanding and supportive. Miller Williams has been both kind and helpful, frequently going far beyond his required duties as Director of the Press. Jim Twiggs and Kathie Villard, my editors, displayed great skill with the English language and with interpersonal communication strategies to demand revisions which I finally thought were my own ideas. Shari Guinn, my friend and World Class departmental secretary, produced the drafts and revisions of the manuscript under impossible deadlines, while at the same time protecting me from students and creditors. I also want to express personal thanks to my first mentor and frequent co-author, Jimmie Rogers of the University of Arkansas, who introduced me to the excitement of communication research and encouraged my graduate education in the field. Had it not been for his friendship, I would have been a rich lawyer by now.

INTRODUCTION A South of the Mind

Before and since Henry Grady used the term in 1886, every generation of
Americans has been told that the South of its day was a New South.
—Edgar T. Thompson, *Perspectives on the South*

Proclaiming the advent of a "New South" centered in a region ripe
for future economic prosperity and social progress, Southern
writers, politicians, business leaders and many other assorted
boosters have uttered their prophecies in succession, from Benjamin Harvey Hill (1871) and Henry Woodfin Grady (1886) to Walter Prescott Webb (1960) and the Sunbelt publicists of the present.
Edwin M. Yoder, in 1972, surveyed the popular fascination then in
vogue and noted the regularity of studies which suggested once
again that the South was supposedly "being supplanted by one of
those 'New Souths' that come and go like French constitutions."[1]
The experience of the past decade, nurtured by media analysis of
the election of a Southern president, has demonstrated that the
proclamation of a New South is still a thriving supply-side industry with strong consumer demand.

In the decade of the 1980s, the controversy over whether a truly
New South has emerged with a new controlling world view or
whether the historically dominant mind of the South will continue
to repeat its inappropriate responses to a changing reality continues to be of interest to journalists, historians, sociologists, po-

litical scientists, communication scholars, anthropologists, and average citizens, especially those living in the South.

No methodology yet discovered can provide a complete synthesis of the whole scope of communication present during any period of time or in any geographical region. Even in the so-called Solid South, there is, and has always been, a great diversity of thought and mythology. During the early nineteenth century, abolition groups were more numerous in the South than in the North, and slaveholding colonels in plantation mansions were a distinct minority group. The populists openly and sometimes successfully opposed the Jim Crow Bourbons after Reconstruction. The Vanderbilt Agrarians and others offered a vision considerably different from the business-progressive heirs of Henry Grady during the early years of the century, and a significant number of Southerners, both black and white, shared perceptions quite at variance with that of the "massive resistance" forces of the 1950s and 1960s. Currently, there are numerous other messages in the contemporary South which cannot be subsumed in the prevailing rhetorical myths explicated in this study.

Anthropologists, sociologists, psychologists, philosophers, historians, political scientists, and communication scholars, often independently, have discovered that mythological analysis is a most productive way to understand the "collective imagination" of a society. Combining and employing the various perspectives of myth and rhetoric, and drawing from related approaches and disciplines, the rhetorical critic can fashion an appropriate approach to the analysis of myths and their function in contemporary society. Such an orientation provides a paradigm for isolating mythic statements, reconstructing public mythologies, and demonstrating the interdependence of communication and cultural values within a group, a community, or a society. This perspective on mythological analysis seems particularly appropriate for application to the study of rhetoric, myth, and culture in the contemporary South.

George B. Tindall has suggested that "the idea of the South—or more appropriately, the ideas of the South—belong in large part to the order of social myth." Tindall saw the tremendous potential for a critical review based upon that fact, but he complained that "the various mythical images of the South that have so significantly affected American history have yet to be subjected to the kind of broad and imaginative historical analysis that has been applied to the idea of the American West. . . . The idea of the South has yet to be fully examined in the context of mythology, as essentially a problem of intellectual history."[2]

Since Tindall's challenge twenty years ago, both historians and rhetoricians have responded, and various periods in the Southern past have been subjected to such an analysis. This book continues the exploration of such traditions as visions of an Old South and the New South, the rhetorical visions of Jefferson Davis and others in the Confederacy, and such myths as the Lost Cause, the Vanderbilt Agrarians, the Dixiecrats, and Massive Resistance, but these visions are placed in a broader perspective and contrasted with the myths of the contemporary South.

My notions of both rhetorical criticism and rhetorical artifacts are less traditional. To comprehend the prevailing cultural myths in the contemporary South requires examination of the diverse forms and symbols through which modern myths are transmitted. I sought the mythic themes wherever they existed and often exceeded the limitations of the oratorical purists who would restrict communication inquiry to the study of formal speeches.

When Tom Wolfe went to North Carolina to observe Junior Johnson playing cultural hero on the stock car circuit, he allowed as how "all the conventional notions about the South are confined to . . . the Sunday radio. The South has preaching and shouting, the South has grits, the South has country songs, old mimosa traditions, clay dust, Old Bigots, New Liberals—and all of it, all the old mental cholesterol, is confined to the Sunday radio."[3] Rather than searching for the essence of the Southern mind on Confederate monuments and in formal literature of the past or in corporate reports and academic tomes of the present, the practical scholar must be prepared to look elsewhere as well for appropriate data and valid conclusions about the nature of communication and mythology in the contemporary South.

I have used formal addresses such as gubernatorial inaugurals and conference keynotes delivered in a traditional public speaking environment, but have also employed a popular culture perspective which includes the study of lyrics of country music and Southern rock music, personal correspondence, tourist advertising and pamphlets, feature articles and newspaper editorials, sporting events, regional cooking, architecture, storytelling, historical essays, personal interviews, television programs, films, fiction, magazines, journal articles, and convention papers. Such a diversity in the selection of rhetorical artifacts for study was necessitated by the nature of public mythology.

The South has indeed developed a new mind that is distinct from that recognized by Wilbur Cash and others in the past. Although the region still harbors a few throwbacks in politics and reincarnations of Henry Grady in various Sunbelt chambers of commerce, the marketplace of mythic dialectic now favors a different vision of reality.

Brandt Ayers, one of the leading proponents of the new vision, once complained that "a viral weed of mythology has been allowed to grow like kudzu over the South, made up of oratory at so many Confederate Memorial Days, of so many Confederate flags waved by college undergraduates and borne by high school honor guards, of so many millions of words spilled on the Senate floor in defense of the indefensible."[4] Mythology will continue to influence behavior through its control of the perception of reality, but in my view it need not have the same limiting effect it has exhibited in the past. It can, if understood, appreciated, and creatively crafted, serve as a rhetorical vehicle for change, progress, and a more just society.

ONE Old Times There Are Not Forgotten

It is all *now* you see. Yesterday won't be over until tomorrow and tomorrow began ten thousand years ago.
—William Faulkner, *Intruder in the Dust*

There are times, argued historian George B. Tindall, when "a myth itself becomes one of the realities of history, significantly influencing the course of human action, for good or ill."[1] For as long as there has been any sense of sectional identity, myths have been among the prominent realities of the history of the South. In fact, it is not coincidental that the first South and the first Southern cultural myth appear to have emerged simultaneously.

T. Harry Williams said, speaking of Southerners, that "more poignantly than other Americans, they realize that the past impinges on the present, and more often than their fellows in other sections they relate the present to something in the past." Compounding the Southern fixation with the past and constituting an essential part of Cash's mind of the South was "the tendency toward unreality, toward romanticism." Evident not only to Cash and his heuristic approach, this tendency, making the region a hotbed of mythology, has also been observed by more methodical scholars studying the early periods of Southern history. "The vogue of romanticism was not particular to the Southern States," observed Clement Eaton, "but it attained a more luxuriant growth below the Potomac than elsewhere in America." This Southern romantic temper, he concluded, was "based primarily on the desire to escape from reality [and] . . . was an outgrowth of an agrarian civilization emerging from the conquest of a wilderness." In such an environment, he said, "the romantic tale, with its melodramatic plot and its focus on the strange and unusual, was a natural concomitant."[2]

Cash, who also attributed much influence to the role of the frontier in the development of the romantic Southern world view, placed greater emphasis on the physical environment of the South, which he saw as "a sort of cosmic conspiracy against reality in favor of romance." It acted to create a mood, he said, "in which directed thinking is all but impossible, a mood in which the mind yields almost perforce to drift and in which the imagination holds unchecked sway, a mood in which nothing any more seems improbable save the puny inadequateness of fact, nothing incredible save the bareness of truth."

Among a population inclined toward both romanticism and identification with the past, one might expect to find fertile ground for the development of shared rhetorical visions and group mythology; however, it took more than two centuries for these conditions to develop in the South. Although Europeans had established colonies in Florida, North Carolina, and Virginia well before the Mayflower landed at Plymouth, there was very little, if any, sectional identity among the Southern colonies, and there is no evidence of the existence of a cohesive group culture. "Prior to the close of the Revolutionary period," wrote Cash, "the great South, as such, has little history. Two hundred years had run since John Smith saved Jamestown, but the land which was to become the cotton kingdom was still more wilderness than not."[3]

John Richard Alden has advanced the idea of a sectional South forming during the last half of the eighteenth century. He contended that "during the period 1775–89, as afterward, heat, geography, racial and national composition, economic pursuits, social order, and even political structure, were ties of unity rather than sources of discord."[4] Alden, however, offered no documentation that these factors had become a salient part of a shared Southern world view or that one even existed.

The South was, in fact, during the last half of the eighteenth century and the first two decades of the nineteenth century, a region of great social and intellectual diversity. In an atmosphere of intellectual skepticism and deism, the region had produced some of the leaders in thought and advocacy for colonial independence, for political and religious liberty, and for abolition of slavery. The foremost historian of the development of Southern sectionalism, Charles S. Sydnor, said that as late as 1819 it might have been "anachronistic to speak of Southerners," and Eaton recognized that even as late as 1860, "there was not one South but many Souths."[5]

Despite the acknowledged diversity of thought and opinion, as well as the differences in geography and culture among the Southern states, the first years of the young republic also saw the beginnings of a pronounced sectionalism. While most scholars date the beginning of the South's transformation from a geographic region to a political unit during the third decade of the nineteenth century, Alden recognized that the process had been in motion for some time. "The election to the presidency of Jefferson at the beginning of the new century and the long-continued ascendancy of the Democratic-Republicans under Jefferson, Madison, and Monroe, soothed the South," he said. "However, as Jefferson walked to his inauguration, slavery was virtually dead in the North; and the census of 1800 revealed that the North was growing more rapidly in numbers than the South." During the Sixteenth Congress the Southern political leadership coalesced around perceived sectional self-interest on the tariff issue and the admission of Missouri to the Union. That leadership made, as John M. Anderson has said,

the fateful tactical error of "a misidentification of the political order with a part of the social order," and the resulting rhetorical
strategy doomed the South to failure and frustration for the next
one hundred fifty years.[6]

While few individuals in 1820 had verbalized or even consciously
recognized the elements of commonality suggested by Alden as
unifying the South, Sydnor contends that "by the 1820s the Southern mind was turned inward to a consideration of its own society."
It was also during this time, said T. Harry Williams, that "Southerners were becoming aware, and often bitterly so, that they were in
some way different from people in the rest of the country."[7]

With the recognition of regional distinctiveness appeared the
basis for sectional identity, the attitude for a group culture, and a
shared vision of reality. In trying to identify and describe the mind
of the South and the cultural mythology which emerged along
with Southern sectionalism, one must proceed with all deliberate
caution.

The process by which a region of great diversity moved toward
rhetorical solidarity is probably more clear to the historian in retrospect than it ever was to any of the tragic players on the scene at
the time it occurred. As the Northern states developed an industrial
economy and experienced greater population growth by immigration, the Southern leadership found itself in a decidedly minority
position, both economically and politically. The psychological result of this recognition was predictable, and, as Sydnor said, "the
mind of the South was transmuted into something very different
from what it had been a generation earlier."

Minority groups often respond to their status by developing
what Herbert A. Miller has described as "oppression psychosis," a
hypersensitivity which leads them to perceive even greater discrimination and persecution than might actually exist. Drawing
on this observation, Lewis Killian has suggested that such a reaction leads a group to develop "a defensive group consciousness that

sets it apart even more and serves to preserve its distinctiveness. This defensiveness sometimes leads to an aggressiveness that seems almost paranoid—a quickness to take offense and a readiness to strike back at forces seemingly on the verge of overwhelming an already persecuted people." When Southern institutions came under attack in the 1820s and 1830s, such a defensive posture drove the South into "a mood of insecurity and isolation," said T. Harry Williams. "Then, as in later crises, external attacks would have the effects of solidifying internal divisions in a region that naturally was one of great contrasts."[8]

Beginning with the tariff issue in 1820, it became clear to Southerners that the degree of national political influence previously enjoyed was declining. The South had, as Cash noted, "begun with control of the national government in its hands, but even there it lost ground so surely and so rapidly that it early became plain that it was but a matter of time before the Yankee would win undisputed sway in the Congress and do his will with the tariff." Forces more related to the Industrial Revolution than to any conscious sectional plot had directed the divergence of political and economic fortunes between the regions. When economic vitality and employment opportunities in the North resulted in greater population growth through immigration, it also gave the North greater representation in Congress. Eaton believed that this "relative stagnation of the older South, in comparison with the rapidly growing Northern states, was one of the factors that rendered Southerners abnormally sensitive to criticism." Whatever its causes, Sydnor observed, "as their influence in national affairs waned, Southerners attempted to invent defenses against what they regarded as Northern political ruthlessness. Feelings of fear, desperation, and bitterness possessed them."[9]

When Southern leaders lost the tariff fights in 1824 and 1828, they again blamed their economic stagnation on the North, and a "feeling of bitterness arose in them as they envisaged profits from their peculiar institution flowing into Northern coffers through the unjust operation of the tariff laws." Business and professional leaders flocked to the Southern commercial conventions, and, "harboring the suspicion that their Northern competitors flourished at their expense," they successfully convinced each other that their failures to develop economically were due to sectional discrimination.[10]

The defenses offered by the South seem almost comic from the perspective of time. In response to the impact of immigration, many Southerners followed socially displaced Whigs in joining the Order of the Star Spangled Banner, with its secret codes and rituals, foreshadowing a later fascination with the Ku Klux Klan and sharing a vision of "plots destined to deprive them of a way of life they considered idyllic." The political manifestation of this group, known as the American Party or Know-Nothing Party, thrived on the rhetorical slander of immigrant groups, which had been one source of significant growth in Northern Congressional power.[11]

On the political front, one result was the debacle of the Nullification movement. Led by John C. Calhoun and his South Carolina political disciples, it remains a landmark of constitutional convolution and rhetorical desperation. Like other contemporary responses, noted Ralph T. Eubanks, "the impulse of nullification was a defensive one. As a cultural impulse it was an expression of the deep-lying anxiety for the future of the mud-sill way." The "mud-sill way" was a widespread contemporary argument for slavery which contended that civilized society rested upon a lower class which performed its physical drudgery. One critic has suggested that the Nullification controversy was only a prelude, "a revealing expression of South Carolina's morbid sensitivity to the beginnings of the antislavery crusade."[12]

The defense of slavery was the rhetorical and logical nadir of the South. It was "the paramount issue that plagued the South and placed the Southern rhetorician in a difficult defensive posture." As Sydnor so aptly said, "The master plan of the South in this war of words called for a defensive instead of an offensive war. It denied the validity of Northern criticisms, and it evolved into a remarkable apologia of virtually every aspect of the Southern way of life."[13]

As numerous historians have noted, the South committed almost every rhetorical and political error in the book. C. Vann Woodward has provided one of the clearest analyses of that public debate:

In the first place the South permitted the opposition to define the issue, and naturally the issue was not defined to the South's advantage. In the second place the South assumed the moral burden of proof. Because the attack centered upon slavery, the defense rallied around that point. As the clamor increased and the emotional pitch of the dispute intensified, the South heedlessly allowed its whole cause, its way of life, its traditional values, and its valid claims in numerous nonmoral disputes with the North to be identified with one institution—and that an institution of which the South itself had furnished some of the most intelligent critics.[14]

Calhoun, the leader of this defense, had earlier gained the reputation of being a rational advocate and an able strategist; however, one study of his speeches defending slavery as a positive good concluded that "so many of his arguments in defense of slavery fail to meet the test of valid logic that Calhoun's reputed skill in logical debating must be seriously questioned." The entire cadre of Southern rhetoricians, not only Calhoun, had become so engulfed by a "feeling of oppression, of defeat, and even desperation" that, as Sydnor said, "from this time onward, it is not always possible to explain Southern actions and attitudes by a rational analysis of the facts in each new episode."[15]

Southerners, as evidenced by their desperate, defensive rhetorical posture, were sorely aware that slavery was "an institution that needed an apology."[16] Realizing the weaknesses in their own defense and recognizing the disapprobation of the rest of the world, the South retreated from debate. Internal and external criticism were vigorously suppressed. As Clement Eaton has documented so well, antislavery pamphlets were banned, the mails were subject to censorship, dissenters were tried for sedition; public opinion frowned upon those who questioned the institutions of the South, and academic freedom was narrowly proscribed. Many called for the prescription of Southern ideals with "proposals to establish Southern publishing houses, to create a committee to examine and approve textbooks, and to establish teachers' colleges and other institutions of higher learning" which would direct the thinking and development of Southern youth. Books on declamation, promoting the South and its institutions, began to replace those containing speeches by Northern orators.[17]

The effect of the decline of open debate and the institution of verbal orthodoxy was to further constrict the ability of the Southern mind to fashion a realistic solution to problems. The Southerner produced in this climate, said Cash, "lacks the complexity of mind, the knowledge, and above all, the habit of skepticism essential to any generally realistic attitude. It is to say that he is inevitably driven back upon imagination, that his world construction is bound to be mainly a product of fantasy, and that his credulity is limited only by his capacity for conjuring up the unbelievable."[18]

The Old South Myth

Being frustrated by repeated and increasingly certain failure to defend its position either politically or morally, beginning to develop a definite group consciousness, and limiting its exposure to rational argument, the collective mind of the South was ripe for the development of a group culture and was in need of a shared mythology to explain and defend itself. The social reality portrayed by the abolitionist attack on the South was most harsh. Southern society and culture had been castigated by such works as Elizur

Wright's moralistic critique, *The Sin of Slavery and Its Remedy* (1833); Theodore Weld's documentary of brutality, *Slavery As It Is: Testimony of a Thousand Witnesses* (1839); Harriet Beecher Stowe's novel, *Uncle Tom's Cabin* (1852); the regular publication of William Lloyd Garrison's *The Liberator*; and the speeches of Wendell Phillips. The South was, said Cash, "beset by the specters of defeat, of shame, of guilt—a society driven by the need to bolster its morale, to nerve its arm against waxing odds, to justify itself in its own eyes and in those of the world." Most of its social and intellectual history from the beginning of the abolitionist crusade had been, he said, "the history of its effort to achieve that end, and characteristically by means of romantic fictions."[19]

The South needed a new mythology to defend its society and its institutions, and the coincidence of this need for an explanatory cultural myth and the vogue of romanticism greatly influenced the nature of the mythic themes which began to appear throughout the region in the 1830s. The artistry of the vision was also fortuitously aided by this timing, for as Eaton noted, "The romantic spirit expressed itself most patently in the arts and social manners." Most prominent among the sources of romantic influence was what Cash described as the "cardboard medievalism" of Sir Walter Scott, who was "bodily taken over by the South and incorporated into the Southern people's vision of themselves."[20]

The first rhetorical myth of the South was based on the theme of cavalier origins, the notion that the South had been settled by the scions of European nobility who came to the southern colonies and established the Tidewater aristocracy. The myth operated to soothe several of the South's immediate psychological problems. First, it rationalized the institution of slavery, for the alleged descendents of the cavaliers could find "a certain satisfaction in comparing their civilization, based on black dependents, with medieval manors, knights on caracoling horses, and humble serfs."[21] They could thus redeem their society in their own eyes as a continuity of tradition rather than admit the guilt and accept the scorn of the rest of the Western world.

Among a group so conditioned by Scott's novels, the fantasy was nurtured, thought Cash, by "writing and reading histories which derived every planter from Cavalier noblemen, and novels which not only accepted the legend, but embroidered on it." The myth was, indeed, developed, embellished and transmitted by such novels as William Alexander Caruther's *The Cavaliers of Virginia* (1834) and *The Knights of the Horse-Shoe* (1845), William Gilmore Simms' *The Partisan* (1835), and Nathaniel Beverly Tucker's *The Partisan Leader: A Tale of the Future* (1836), as well as the works of the cavalier poets Philip Pendleton Cooks and Mirabeau Buonaparte Lamar.[22] Heroic characters in the emerging myth of the Old South included the cavalier gentleman, who became transformed into a planter, and the Southern belle, a reincarnation of the damsel of the castle. Even later historians, captivated by the vision, seemed entranced by these actors in the drama. "It is to the aristocracy—the country gentlemen—of the South," said Eaton, "that one must look for the most marked differences between the North and the South. They cherished a set of values that were different from those of the North." The value allegedly most cherished by these gentlemen was an exaggerated and formalized code of honor. Eubanks has suggested that the emphasis on personal honor was derived from the concept of Norman chivalry and that it became institutionalized in the South as the *code duello*. Eaton, however, believed it to be, in both instances, a cultural concomitant of a feudal social and economic order, noting that ancient Japan had exhibited a similar code of honor. Regardless of the psychological basis for this code, Southerners could see themselves as honorable men and counter the vision of the slaveholder as inhumane barbarian being advanced by Northern abolitionists. Still another function of this myth was to maintain control of the political institutions by the social and economic elites. In the face of a burgeoning democracy, it provided justification for "an aristocracy of public service," the rule by landed, white gentlemen who professed motivation not by money or power but the "love of honor, the tradition of family, and *noblesse oblige*."[23]

The second mythic persona, the Southern belle, was, according to Anne Firor Scott, portrayed as "a submissive wife whose reason for being was to love, honor, obey, and occasionally amuse her husband, to bring up his children and manage his household. She was timid and modest, beautiful and graceful." Cash said, "She was the South's Palladium, this Southern woman, the shield-bearing Athena gleaming whitely in the clouds, the standard for its rallying, the mystic symbol of its nationality in face of the foe."[24]

The development of the mythic role of the antebellum woman has been studied by numerous scholars. Some saw it as the only possible role in patriarchal, slave-based society, while others, such as Anne Firor Scott, thought the myth of the Southern lady "was associated with medieval chivalry." Whatever the cause of its development, the symbol of the Southern belle played a particularly vital role in the mythology of the antebellum South. As another repository of kindness and morality, the image helped to counter the vision of cruelty being advanced by abolitionists. This image, defining the ideal role of women, was also useful in discrediting the women of the North who were active in the abolition movement. Professor McGuffey of the University of Virginia made reference to "those shameless Amazons," and John Hartwell Cocke boasted of once having silenced "this most impudent clique of unsexed females and rampant abolitionists which must put down the petticoats—at least as far as their claim to take the platforms of public debate and enter into all the rough and tumble of the war of the words."[25]

The scene for the drama in the myth was always the plantation. Romanticized in such novels as John Pendleton Kennedy's *Swallow*

Barn, or, A Sojourn in the Old Dominion (1832), it has been best described and scrutinized by Francis Pendleton Gaines in *The Southern Plantation: A Study in the Development and Accuracy of a Tradition*. The plantation fantasy, as depicted by Kennedy, saw life in the South as "the mellow, bland, and sunny luxuriance of her old-time society—its good fellowship, its hearty and constitutional companionableness, the thriftless gaiety of the people, their dogged but amiable invincibility of opinion, and that overflowing hospitality which knew no ebb." [26] Such an image served two purposes for the South. First, it again countered the abolitionist vision of cruelty, and second, it pointed up the contrasts between the industrial North and the agricultural South, idealizing the Southern version of the differences.

While the Romantic movement had a tremendous impact on the development of the antebellum South's controlling mythology, the myth was also influenced by the classical revival of the period. Nowhere, perhaps, was this influence more obvious than in the plantation architecture presumed dominant by those fostering the plantation paradigm. In this myth, every Southern man was a gentleman planter, and he usually lived in a Greek Revival mansion surrounded by magnolias and live oaks draped with moss, a certain contrast with crowded housing conditions in the industrial centers of the North. The emphasis on the classics was widespread in Southern education: orators were quick to make allusions in their speeches or insert Latin phrases to impress their audiences, and regional journals such as the *Southern Quarterly Review* and the *Southern Literary Messenger* were filled with articles on the classics.

The great devotion to the classics, said Eaton, also "meant a greater devotion to tradition." In this context, the myth was especially useful in defending slavery. An integral part of Southern life and the Southern cultural mythology, the institution of slavery had from the beginning presented problems for Southerners who wished to share in the mythic vision of the new nation, based upon the principles contained in the Declaration of Independence and the Bill of Rights. The South passed up the chance to build a compatible regional vision based on the myths generated by Jefferson and Madison, because there was no way to maintain the democratic theme of the independent yeoman farmer in the face of the reality of slavery and the countervision of the abolitionist. Southerners needed to reduce the mythic tension and to find equilibrium in their world view, so Jefferson was "repudiated as a theoretical and dangerous visionary."[27]

Rather than admit the evils of slavery, as Jefferson and Madison had done, Calhoun adopted as his main thesis after 1837 that "slavery is a positive good." To paraphrase Vernon Parrington, he invoked the vision of a Greek democracy, advancing the mythic theme that Southern society, like that of ancient Greece, was the epitome of perfection because it was based on slavery.[28] Calhoun and his "mud-sill" followers now argued that "theirs was an ideal social order and the only permanently founded democracy, all because it had, with God's blessing, slavery. Surely, Southerners had come a long way from Jefferson and a long way out of reality."[29]

The vast majority of the white population was composed of slaveless, independent small farmers who neither shared nor participated in the predominant myth. One might assume that these Southerners held a world view more akin to that of the frontiersman; however, Eaton conceded that "the modern historian finds it difficult to fathom the mind of the Southern yeoman, who constituted the great majority of the people, because they were not vocal; they kept almost no diaries that have been preserved, and their personal papers, except for Confederate letters, are almost nonexistent." Some clues, he said, "can be obtained from editorials, from the sermons of evangelical ministers, and from appeals that politicians made to the electorate," and additional evidence might be found in "folklore, isolated newspaper items, occasional bits of

memorabilia. . . , and the semi-realistic writings of the Southern humorists with a rich vein of social history running through
them."[30]

In reality, the relatively small number of plantations were more
often owned by nouveaux "cotton snobs" than by genteel country
gentlemen, and Annette Shelby, discussing the actual life of the
Southern woman, concluded that "plantation life had been hard
and grueling for most of these women." And even Eaton, who
wanted to find a Southern aristocracy, admitted that "actually not
many Southern women lived according to romantic standards."[31]

The classic façade of the plantation myth hardly covered the social realities, and the Greek Revival mansions were far less numerous than the myth suggested. As Robert Gunderson explained, "Despite the romantic stereotypes of its pillared mansions with high
ceilings and booklined walls, the Old South remained a blighted
area," and Ulrich B. Phillips noted that "Caesar and Cicero were
more often the names of Negroes in the yard than of authors on the
shelves."[32]

Regardless of such inconsistencies with fact as have been noted,
the myth of the Old South has been one of the most powerful and
enduring of American myths. The strength of the myth was due,
primarily, to the fact that it offered an explanatory rationale to
maintain the collective ego. The Southern leadership knew that it
was losing the dominant political and economic position it had
once enjoyed, and it believed its cultural identity and security were
linked to an institution which the rest of the world found to be
morally repugnant. Facing such a situation, it was necessary to
rely upon mythos rather than logos; the Old South myth met that
demand, at least for the antebellum Southern leadership. "En-
abling the South to wrap itself in contemptuous superiority, to sneer
down the Yankee as low-bred, crass, and money-grubbing, and even
to beget in his bourgeois soul a kind of secret and envious awe," said
Cash, the myth "was a nearly perfect defense mechanism."[33]

The Rhetorical Myth of the Confederacy

The nationalistic blooming of Southern sectionalism, as represented by the Confederate States of America, does not appear to have generated a significant controlling cultural myth of its own identity very different from that of the antebellum South. The vocal leaders of secession had hardly finished their Congressional farewell speeches justifying their decision when they were confronted with the necessity of organizing a government, raising public revenues, and conducting a war. The new Confederate leadership, said Jefferson Davis's brother-in-law Richard Taylor, seemed "as unconscious as scene-shifters in some awful tragedy." David A. Thomas's rhetorical study of Davis's speeches revealed that his vision of the Confederacy differed little from that of the antebellum South, and E. Merton Coulter, a noted historian of the Confederacy, suggested that Davis's personal unpopularity was largely responsible for the fact that "the Confederacy never became an emotional reality to the people until Reconstruction made it so after the war had been lost."[34] Davis was never able to capture the imagination of the people. He failed to articulate a public vision of the Confederacy, and he did not represent a heroic figure with whom the people could identify. In fact, no such figure emerged during the period, and this rhetorical void could well have contributed to the South's inability to present a unified front.

Beyond the public forum offered by politics and government, the war dominated civilian communications for the next four years. Hundreds of songs and thousands of lines of verse were written in praise of the Confederate war effort, and the theater survived in Richmond, Charleston, and New Orleans, presenting such stage productions as *The Roll of the Drum*, *The War in Virginia*, and *The Virginia Cavalier*.

Further development of the existing world view, and certainly the full development of a new myth, were severely constricted by the conduct of the war. Actors and writers were drafted, publishing was often suspended by hostilities, and the small literary community seemed to have trouble finding an attentive audience for the works they did manage to publish and distribute. Numerous journals, among them the *Southern Literary Messenger*, ceased publication during the war and were not reopened.[35]

Despite the adversity of wartime conditions, the basic vision which had developed over the past forty years was largely continued during the years 1861 to 1865. The tariff crowd in Congress and the abolitionists were still the villains, distorting the "true" meaning of the Constitution and bent upon destroying Southern agriculture and the Southern way of life. "Ape" Lincoln and his ruthless, unprincipled generals soon joined the constellation of public enemies, while the heroes continued to be the Southern aristocrats striving to protect their noble civilization based on chivalry and slavery, now defended with arms as well as arguments. However, even with the press of unity created by a new nationalism and a consuming war, the mind of the South was far less solid than later mythmakers would suggest.[36]

The Myth of the Lost Cause

While the old mythology had been able to sustain itself even in the face of military conflict and civilian hardship, the experience of war and the impact of defeat soon challenged the validity of the myth and its continued ability to explain the world. The South in 1865 presented a reality which was hard to ignore. Henry Grady's description of the welcome afforded the Confederate veteran was true of many Southerners. "He finds his house in ruins, his farm devastated, his slaves free, his stock killed, his barns empty, his trade destroyed, his money worthless; his social system, feudal in its magnificence, swept away; his people without law or legal status, his comrades slain, and the burden of others heavily on his shoulders. Crushed by defeat his very traditions are gone."[37]

The rhetorical problem created by the new reality has received considerable attention. Not only had the war destroyed the Southern social and economic world, said Stuart Towns, "it had almost crushed the Southern spirit—that is the Southerner's views of himself and his world." Waldo Braden noted that "shattered dreams, ideals, sentiments, beliefs, and lifestyles are not easily recovered or replaced," and Howard Dorgan suggested that "one of the most difficult tasks confronting Confederate apologists had been to build acceptable bridges between what the antebellum South had expected and what the postbellum South knew to be reality."[38]

With no myth to adequately explain the reality, the postwar Southerner faced numerous psychological problems. The region, said Woodward, "suffered from a prevailing sense of inferiority and a constant need for justifying a position." The dreams of a separate nation were gone, the central social institution of slavery had been abolished, the Southern army had been vanquished, the cities and plantations had been burned, and the political leaders had been disenfranchised and branded traitors. As Dorgan has said, the requirements for the new myth were clear: "Defeat had to be softened or changed into victory; causes had to be purified; Confederate fighting men, leaders, and women had to be vindicated; and Southern values in general had to be exonerated. Such steps were necessary before the South could turn an era of humiliation into an era of triumph, and from there into a source of regional pride." Braden suggested that Southerners, already conditioned to accept romantic fantasy, were looking for a new vision, and finding "the present unbearable and the future unpromising, retreated to that romantic past and preferred to live in fantasy."[39]

Performing a remarkable rhetorical feat, the South reconstructed the antebellum myth of the Old South and embellished it to accommodate immediate psychological needs. The myth of the Lost

Cause allowed Southerners to reaffirm the alleged superiority of their culture by declaring that it had indeed been an antebellum golden age of chivalrous gentlemen planters, magnolia-scented ladies, and plantation mansions. With the passage of time, it became easy to believe that the entire South had once conformed to the representation of the old myth, and the rhetorical symbols became even more powerful. If the Civil War had halted the march toward an aristocracy in fact, the new vision allowed it to continue in mythology. As Woodward noted, "The fabled Southern aristocracy, long on its last legs, was refurbished, its fancied virtues and vices, airs and attitudes, exhumed and admired."[40]

Two significant themes emerged during this period to modify the antebellum myth of the Old South. First, the gentleman planter had served as an officer in gray, most likely with the rank of general or colonel and always in the calvary. Second, the South now denied that the Civil War had been fought in defense of slavery, for as Cash said, no one "has ever died for anything so crass as slavery."[41] The old soldiers, fighting instead for liberty, constitutional principles, and protection of the agrarian splendor, had been martyred on the field of battle by the overwhelming numbers of the industrial North or canonized on return by a grateful community at home.

The Lost Cause myth, in all its glory, can be seen in the rhetoric of General Bradley T. Johnson. Writing for the *Confederate Veteran* in 1897, he declared, "I know that the knights of Arthur's Round Table, or the paladine and peers, roused by the blast of the Fuenterrabia horn from Roland at Roncesvalles, did not equal in manly traits, in nobility of character, in purity of soul, in gallant, dashing courage, the men who led." Of the Southern belle, he said, "Of all the examples of that heroic time . . . the one that stands in the foreground, the one that will be glorified with the halo of the martyr-heroine, is the woman—mother, sister, lover—who gave her heart to the cause." With such heroic characters, the South had no need to be ashamed of its heritage, and even the loss in battle had served to secure a victory for true principles. "The world is surely coming to the conclusion that the cause of the Confederacy was right," Johnson continued. "Every lover of Constitutional liberty . . . begins to understand that the war was not waged . . . in the defense of slavery, but . . . to protect liberty won and bequeathed by free ancestors."[42]

This mythic theme, which proved to be a much needed balm for a defeated people, was rapidly accepted throughout the South. Rollin G. Osterweis dates the flowering of the new myth from the death of Robert E. Lee in 1870. The glowing obituaries from the national and world press gave the South a few kind words, and Lee provided the rhetorical symbol around which to develop the new myth and the link between the cavalier ancestors of the old vision and the situation of the present. Describing the myth which matured during the next decade, Osterweis said that by 1880, the symbols of its expression were manifold and familiar.

Confederate museums in Southern towns; statutes of Confederate soldiers in the public squares; tributes and respect for the Confederate veteran and his kin; celebrations on Confederate Memorial Days and at military reunions; renewed devotion to the Confederate battle flag and the favorite war song "Dixie"; pictures of Lee, Stonewall Jackson, and even the once maligned President Jefferson Davis in Southern homes; . . . the chivalric story of the Antebellum South and of the knights in gray who fought for its independence was recreated in a constant flow of newspaper editorials, magazine articles, poems, and books.[43]

The vehicles for expression were, indeed, numerous. The United Confederate Veterans offered a most productive forum in the pages of *The Confederate Veteran*, and the United Daughters of the Confederacy were organized to "perpetuate honor, integrity, valor and other attributes of true Southern character" and "to perpetuate a truthful record of the noble and chivalric achievements of their ancestors."[44]

Other expressions of the myth were found in the poetry of Sidney

Lanier and Henry Timrod, and in such verse as Annie Barnwell Morton's "The Old Jacket of Gray" and Abram Ryan's "The Conquered Banner" and "The Sword of Lee." The New York stage hosted productions of David Belasco's *May Blossom* (1884) and *The Heart of Maryland* (1895), William Gillette's *Held By the Enemy* (1886), and Bronson Howard's *Shenandoah* (1889). The books and articles of George Washington Cable, Joel Chandler Harris, and Thomas Nelson Page were of great influence, as were others such as Lanier's *The Boy's King Arthur*, John Esten Cooke's *Wearing of the Gray* (1897) and *A Life of General Robert E. Lee* (1871), and, later, Thomas Dixon's *The Leopard Spots* (1902) and *The Clansman* (1905). D. W. Griffith's early films *The Honor of His Family* (1910), *The Battle* (1911), and *Birth of a Nation* (1914) continued the tradition. Further reinforcement was found in songs such as James A. Bland's "Carry Me Back to Old Virginny" (1878), and in children's games like the card set "The Game of Confederate Heroes." Such art was, thought Cash, less literature than propaganda. The South's "novels, its sketches and stories, are essentially so many pamphlets, its poems so many handbills, concerned mainly . . . with the Old South, and addressed primarily to the purpose of glorifying that Old South— to the elaboration of the legend."[45]

One recent social historian, James Oliver Robinson, has suggested that "the aristocratic-gentleman idea suffered total destruction in the myths of the Civil War" and held that the symbols and the vision of the antebellum South were "destroyed and dead." Quite the contrary, however, was true. "Once the glorified and purified conceptions of the Old South as a golden age without shadows and the Confederacy as all dash, gallantry, and sacrifice were embraced, they were enshrined in Southerners' hearts," said Henry Savage. "In effect, Southerners had made a religion of the Old South and the Confederacy, replete with unchallengeable tenets, ritual, hallowed saints, and sacred shrines." The old myth generated by antebellum Southerners had been able, according to Osterweis, "by modifying its symbols, not only to survive but to retain its basic qualities and its basic power" and was "triumphant in the restoration of its antebellum social order almost in its original form."[46]

The South seems to have missed a perfect opportunity to re-fashion a new mythology and a world view consistent with the national dream of democracy, progress, and success. Instead, it turned inward and backward, determined to recreate a broken dream which would inevitably fall short in its attempt to organize and explain the events of the future.

TWO Unreconstructed Realities

There is, in very fact, no Old South and no New. There is only The South.
Fundamentally, as it was in the beginning it is now, and, if God please, it
shall be evermore.
—Robert S. Cotterill, "The Old South to the New"

While the vision of the Lost Cause dominated the perception of reality and defined both politics and history for the post-Reconstruction
generation of Southerners, two lesser, competing visions waged ag-
gressive campaigns for mass recognition and the popular imagination. Henry Grady's New South movement tried to speak to the
present by defining the future, and the populist movement tried to
speak to the present by redefining the past—both acceptable strategies for creating and implementing new mythologies.

Much has been written about the New South movement of the
late nineteenth century. Superficial histories and textbooks on the
history of American public address usually select Henry Grady's
speech to the New England Society in 1886 and Booker T. Washington's speech at the Atlanta Exposition in 1895 and assume that the
New South of industry and progress signified a complete break
with the Old South of moonlight and magnolias, plantations and
slavery. Although the casual reader might conclude that Grady and
the other New South propagandists were determined to move be-

yond the myth of the Lost Cause and reject the past to embrace Yankee capitalism, that is not entirely the case. As Cash recognized in the preface to his book, "the extent of change between the Old South that was and the South of our time has been vastly exaggerated."

Paul M. Gaston's book, *The New South Creed: A Study in Southern Mythmaking*, is the definitive study of the New South movement. Despite the surface contradictions between the Old South/Lost Cause mythology and the brash New South view of a bright industrial future for the region, Gaston documented that the two share several common themes. Grady and the other young editors who made up the core of the New South party were very much aware of the power of the Old South myth, and they consciously and carefully crafted a strategy to connect their vision of the future with the prevailing view of the past, always pausing to praise their heritage. Additionally, many of the orators and advocates, typified by former Confederate leaders such as John B. Gordon, J. L. M. Curry, and Daniel Harvey Hill, were equally adept at promoting either vision as the situation demanded.[1]

Gaston demonstrated, however, some real differences between the New South vision of the future and that of the past. The new mythmakers "believed that the antebellum ideal of the leisured gentleman who scorned manual labor was a relic that had no place in the new age. In the stead of the Old South patriarch, the New South spokesmen would substitute as their ideal the hardworking, busy, acquisitive individual."[2] In this vision, the suffering Southern belle Melanie Wilkes lost out to Atlanta businesswoman Scarlett O'Hara, while Uncle Remus and other "happy darkies" concerned themselves with banjo music and trade schools rather than public office and the Fourteenth Amendment.

The New South vision was of a South more urban and more industrial, and Grady urged the University of Georgia to give more attention to management and accounting than to rhetoric and the classics. Such a program for progress did not, however, directly threaten the security of the old myth and its believers, because they shared many common assumptions. They both revered a wealthy leadership elite, they valued military experience, they had little regard for the conservation of natural resources or respect for the rights of labor, and neither allowed the realities of the present to interfere with development of their mythology. Even with regard to the mythic scene of their dramas, the transition from the cotton field to the cotton mill was almost unnoticeable.

One major premise of the New South creed, and the one which protected it most securely from the populist assault, was its dedication to white supremacy. In speaking to Northern audiences, Henry Grady always had a throwaway line about a new day for former slaves or an equitable solution to the race problem; however, in speaking for home consumption, he went to great lengths to establish the fact that the New South vision was for whites only and that blacks now had the freedom to be sharecroppers rather than slaves. Equitable solution did not mean equality in the New South, a view accepted by Booker T. Washington and acknowledged by the Supreme Court of the United States. As Gaston said, "the New South myth, fully articulated, offered a harmonizing and reassuring world view to conserve the essential features of the status quo."[3]

The populist spirit in the South, on the other hand, made a frontal assault on both the Old South myth and the New South creed. The populist movement, organized under a variety of names in the South, tried to redefine the past to re-establish the yeoman farmer as the dominant figure and Jeffersonian democracy as the central theme of Southern history, claiming that John C. Calhoun and Jefferson Davis were merely interlopers in the drama. Such an approach had a potential for success and a much larger audience which could share the vision, because as Henry Savage noted, "for the eighty percent of Southerners who gained their livelihood from the soil, the hope of the day met the unrelieved hopelessness of realities of the day and was cancelled out."[4] A significant majority of both blacks and whites knew that their ancestors were not aristocratic planters and that their children would not be president of Cannon Mills or editor of the *Manufacturers' Record*. The New South was not for them.

Within the confines of the old myth, populist orators and editors also tried to play to the past. By stressing the affinity of the Wall Street capitalists of the 1880s with the tariff clique of the 1830s and by drawing the colonial analogy of an agricultural South thwarted as surely by Northern railroad interests of the day as by Northern shipping interests of an earlier generation, they tried to show that the new South was un-Southern.

Just as the populists were beginning to recruit adherents and achieve electoral success, the New South leadership linked hands with Jim Crow to crush the emerging vision. The rural whites, who had finally recognized class and caste ties with poor blacks and formed a political alliance against the economic powers, were quickly dispersed by the opposition and the power of the controlling mythology which was brought to bear. As Cash said, "The eyes of his old captains were ominous and accusing upon him. From hustings and from pulpits thousands of voices proclaimed him traitor and nigger-loving scoundrel; renegade to Southern womanhood, the Confederate dead, and the God of his Fathers; champion of the transformation of the white race into a mongrel breed."[5]

The Business-Progressives and the Agrarians

As the South moved into the twentieth century, the New South prophets of profits became the promoters of progress—George Babbitt with a Southern accent. Although Senator Robert M. La Follette once remarked that he had been unable to discover any progressive sentiment or progressive legislation in the South, historian Arthur S. Link has assembled a convincing case that the progressive movement received considerable support for its goals and achieved notable victories in the Southern states. It was, however, a progressive movement for whites only. In fact, except for the open obsession with segregation, the South almost seemed to be rejoining the American political mainstream during the first two decades of the new century. Southern soldiers enlisted enthusiastically behind the American flag in both the Spanish-American War and World War I, and the election of Virginia-born Woodrow Wilson resulted in numerous Southerners in the Cabinet. It could also be argued that America was joining the Southern mainstream with regard to racial attitudes. William A. Dunning at Columbia and Ulrich B. Phillips at Yale were issuing neo-Confederate historical studies to support the South's position, and the popular reception afforded the novels of Thomas Nelson Page and Thomas Dixon and the films of D. W. Griffith seemed to settle the question for mass audiences. On the floor of the United States Congress, it required an extraordinary effort by the Southern demagogues to keep pace with the racism of the Republican leaders discussing government of the territories.

By the 1920s business-progressives had captured the governor's office in every Southern state, and their proposals for real estate development, tourism, industrial development, and good roads were pervasive. New three-piece suits were the attire of the day, but this group was quite comfortable using the old time rhetoric to maintain their control. When labor began to organize, demand higher wages, seek better working conditions, and challenge the "cheap, docile labor" theme being used to attract industry, the *Manufacturers' Record* dusted off the defensive Southern mythology to support the boosters of business. It warned against such "outside" influences trying to spread "the communist or Bolshevistic spirit throughout the South to disrupt the labor conditions which have so long existed there for the good of the workers and

the South in general." Sounding like an antebellum Southerner at-
tacking abolitionist groups, the editor also chastised "the women
of New York and other places who are organizing societies to stir
up trouble in the cotton mills of the South." When labor also made
an effort to organize black workers as well as white, Lewis Killian
noted that some employers "made contributions to a revived Ku
Klux Klan, which added 'nigger-loving, communist labor organizers' to its list of targets. Here was a new breed of Carpetbaggers
who sought not just to rob the South of its wealth, but to steal the
souls of its white people."[6]

While the business crowd seemed dominant, they were not without their native detractors. The dialectic between the agrarian and
industrial myths has consistently been among the staple crops of
Southern society, politics, and historiography. The first vision of
the Old South juxtaposed the plantation and the factory, and the
mythology of the Lost Cause attributed the defeat of noble gentle-
men-planters to the superior manufacturing capacity of the North.
The populist movement had charged that the heritage of the Southern yeomanry was being bartered for a mess of industrial pottage,
and now, in 1930, the plaintive cry was raised once again.

Representative of a generation which was threatened by the social changes accompanying industrialization, ridiculed by the columns of H. L. Mencken, exposed by the studies of Arthur Raper,
Frank Tannenbaum, Howard Odum, and Rupert Vance, betrayed
by the novels of Erskine Caldwell, William Faulkner, and T. S.
Stribling, and frightened that their heritage and culture were vanishing, a group of twelve Southerners loosely affiliated with Vanderbilt University issued a manifesto entitled *I'll Take My Stand:
The South and the Agrarian Tradition*. The book proved, as con-
clusively as Margaret Mitchell's *Gone with the Wind* and David O.
Selznick's film version, which shortly followed, that the myths of
the Old South and the Lost Cause were still prominent and powerful forces in Southern life and thought. Unabashedly, the Agrarians

pronounced their book to be a defense of "a Southern way of life against what may be called the American or prevailing way." They declared their struggle to be an ancient battle between agrarianism and industrialism, and they revived the armor and the images of the past to buttress their positions.

At the opening of the volume, John Crowe Ransom called upon Southern leadership "to arouse the sectional feeling of the South to its highest pitch of excitement in defense of all the old ways that are threatened." His essay and those that followed proceeded to do just that. First, they repeated the chants of ancient Greece, feudal England, and the Scottish Highlands, then they blamed the demise of Southern cultural greatness on the events of the Civil War and Reconstruction.

"It is out of fashion in these days to look backward rather than forward," admitted Ransom. "About the only American given to it is some unreconstructed Southerner who persists in his regard for a certain terrain, a certain history, and a certain inherited way of living." As one critic said, however, "To the Agrarians the traumatic experience of the Civil War, the humiliation of Reconstruction, and the effects on the Southern economy were not mere abstractions in history textbooks; they were part of the lives of their own people— of their ancestors and their ancestors' neighbors."[7]

These typewriter Agrarians, a quite different group from the populist leaders, knew that Southerners "lived by images," and they used those images of the past to their full advantage. Nixon labeled the boosterism brigade as merely "Southern Yankees," and Ransom charged that the pursuit of industrialism "is capable of doing more devastation than was wrought when Sherman marched to the sea" and warned that "the carpetbaggers are again in our midst." They idealized the antebellum planter aristocracy, or squirearchy, and knew that to make their point "it might be necessary to revive such an antiquity as the old Southern gentleman and his lady, and their scorn for the dollar-chasers." Davidson suggested that the plantation architecture of the Old South should still hold mythic meaning for Southerners, for it symbolically "expresses the beauty and stability of an ordered life" as opposed to the "complexity, disorder, and fragmentation of the present."

Robert Penn Warren stood as the spokesman for the group on the race issue, and his position, though considered too liberal by some of the members, was little more than a patronizing restatement of Booker T. Washington's "Atlanta Compromise." Such a view, embraced by the rest of the nation a decade earlier, was now out of fashion. The South's position was once again under attack on moral grounds, and the prevailing tenets of religion and morality were under scrutiny as a result of the spectacle of the Scopes trial. The reactionary defense of the South's position was little different from the response of antebellum Southerners to the attack by Garrison and the abolitionists a hundred years earlier. It was an analogy that did not go unnoticed by Owsley, the historian, and Lytle echoed the censors of the last century when he proposed a solution to halt the spread of progress: "Throw out the radio and take down the fiddle from the wall. Forsake the movies for the play-parties and the square dances. And turn away from the liberal capons who fill the pulpits as preachers."[8]

Such a vision did not strain the Agrarians' powers of invention, but neither did it capture the popular imagination of a national audience or have any material effect on the efforts of Southern governments or chambers of commerce in their campaigns to lure Northern capital and industry. It was, said Robert Downs, only "Nostalgia for Never-Never Land," a past that never existed and could not be recreated now. The myths of the Old South and the Lost Cause were acceptable to most Southerners of the period as an explanation of the past, and certainly these myths structured the Southern world view so as to condition regional attitudes, arguments, and behavior. As an overt prescription for economic organization, however, the Agrarian myth was of little interest. "My-

thology which does not solve the problems it is created to solve,"
observed F. Garvin Davenport, Jr., "results in cultural frustration
and increasingly shrill or superficial attempts to make it work
somehow."[9] The Agrarians were unable to make it relevant in the
1930s.

The Dixiecrats and Massive Resistance

The years of the Great Depression and World War II were more
than a minor distraction for mythmakers of all persuasions, but
those times were not completely without tension for the competing
world views of the South. John Dollard published his study, *Caste
and Class in a Southern Town*, in 1937 and Gunnar Myrdal's book,
An American Dilemma, appeared in 1944. Both demonstrated to the
nation that the South had failed to solve its problems and had
failed to allow many of its citizens to share in the American dream.

While the nation was engaged in conflict against Hitler's armies
and his theories of a master race, Southern business and political
leaders were also busy resisting Roosevelt's Fair Employment Practices Committee. The FEPC, said Cotton Jim Eastland, was the
idea of the CIO, "a carpetbag organization that has come into the
South and is attempting to destroy Southern institutions and
Southern civilization." Howard Odum's *Race and Rumors of Race*
suggested that Eastland was expressing a more widespread fear
among white Southerners. In the early forties, said C. Vann Woodward, "the flying rumors of plot and counterplot, of bands armed
with icepick and switchblade, of Eleanor Clubs, conspirato-
rial societies, and subversive Northern agitators often recall the fe-
vered frame of mind that possessed the South in the winter following the Harper's Ferry raid."[10] Only after the war ended in 1945,
however, did the fears receive renewed expression in the continu-

ing saga of mythological defense by the South's threatened political leadership.

Returning black veterans believed they deserved a share of the freedoms they had defended, and the American public had consumed millions of words and reels of film explaining a national vision which was overtly democratic and egalitarian. The realities of racial discrimination in postwar America, especially in the South, did not square with that vision. In October 1947, President Truman's Committee on Civil Rights issued a report entitled *To Secure These Rights*, calling for legislation to prevent lynching, to prohibit employment discrimination, and to protect the right to vote. The following February, Truman submitted a legislative package to Congress to implement the recommendations, and he shortly issued Executive Orders to end discrimination in federal employment and segregation in the armed forces. The rhetorical reaction from the South was loud and familiar.

Governor Fielding Wright of Mississippi set the stage with his inaugural address on January 20, 1948, warning against efforts "to wreck the South and our institutions." Finding a responsive chord, he called a mass meeting in February at Jackson, and four thousand loyal white partisans responded by attending the rally to sing "Dixie," wave Confederate flags, and resolve that the South needed no help or advice from outsiders. In May, again at Jackson, South Carolina Governor Strom Thurmond invoked the images of Reconstruction as he declared, presumably on behalf of the white majority in the South, "All the laws of Washington, and all the bayonets of the Army cannot force the negroes into their homes, their schools, their churches, and their places of recreation and amusement." Opposition to Truman's legislative program was voiced by such planter-business groups as the Associated Industries of Florida and the Arkansas Free Enterprise Association, while their minions in Congress, sounding like the editor of the *Manufacturers'*

Record in 1929, said Truman's ideas sounded "like the program of the Communists."[11]

Not only did the controlling mythology of the past seem to determine the icons and images of the incipient rebellion, reviving the battle flag and martial music of the Confederacy, it was also instructive for the behavior of those Southern politicians who believed their party too soft on the issue of the day. Dissatisfied with the nominee and the platform in 1860, recalcitrant Southern delegates walked out of the Democratic National Convention in Charleston and held their own convention in Richmond to nominate John C. Breckenridge. Again in 1948, dissatisfied with Truman and the adoption of a strong civil rights plank in the platform, the entire Mississippi delegation once again took a walk. The disaffected delegates and others claiming to represent thirteen states convened in Birmingham to nominate Strom Thurmond and Fielding Wright to lead the States' Rights ticket.

The fall campaign saw the "Dixiecrats" vying to capture the South's electoral votes but meeting strong and vocal opposition even in their own region. Loyal Democrats in Mississippi labeled the Dixiecrat effort "an unrealistic, negative, backward looking program suggested by demagogic, bolting politicians and front men for grasping corporations," Alabama Governor Jim Folsom called them "a handful of slickers," and others, reviving the competing myth of the Populists, said the Dixiecrats "actually stood for the interest of millowners, oil magnates, bankers and other members of the Southern Bourbon class and their corporation allies in New York City."[12]

Only in the states of Mississippi, South Carolina, Alabama, and Louisiana, where they had Democratic Party sanction, did the Dixiecrats capture electors. The South gave Truman a larger majority than he received in the rest of the nation, and Thurmond settled for only 39 of the 127 electoral votes from the South. V. O. Key, Jr., in his acclaimed study of Southern politics, said that the revolt had been limited to "the delta of Mississippi, the home of the great plantation planters, few whites, and many Negroes, as well as the last vestige of ante-bellum civilization," and that the vision had been shared only by "the whites of the black belt and little more, at least if one disregards the professional Ku Kluxers, antediluvian reactionaries, and malodorous opportunists." The Dixiecrat debacle, he hopefully predicted, "may turn out to have been the dying gasp of the Old South"; however, acknowledging the power of Southern mythology to resist the forces of change, he concluded that "the regional cast of political attitude has a reality and a being over and beyond all underlying social and economic characteristics that can be pictured in endless tabulations, correlations, and graphic representations."[13]

Key's optimism was soon dashed by the bellicosity of the rhetoric of Massive Resistance—a futile and fatal last stand for the old myth. On May 17, 1954, a unanimous United States Supreme Court issued its opinion in a case styled *Oliver Brown et al.* v. *Board of Education of Topeka, Shawnee County, Kansas, et al.*, 347 U.S. 483 (1954), and the decision meant far more than that Linda Brown could attend Sumner School seven blocks from her home. Within three days, the Louisiana legislature responded with a resolution censuring the Supreme Court decision. It was the first rhetorical volley in a war of words that would dominate Southern politics for the next decade.

The best history of the rhetorical machinations of the Southern response to *Brown* is Numan V. Bartley's *The Rise of Massive Resistance*, which concludes that the movement "rested upon the failure of Southern institutions and Southern society to support a reasonable alternative." Perhaps, had the South not been so conditioned by a hundred and thirty-five years of mythological and rhetorical orthodoxy, it could have fashioned a new explanatory myth. The fact is that it did not, and several reasons have been suggested for that failure. C. Vann Woodward, in terminology applicable to a mind of the South, said that the region, tormented by a "minority psychology and rejection anxiety," was "reliving an old trauma," and was "more deeply alienated and thoroughly defiant than at any time since 1877." Reese Cleghorn, less sympathetically, suggested that "irrationalism has been a public way of life in the South since early in the 19th century when the region had to begin reconciling its devotion to democracy with its denial of democracy to the Negroes. The South thus is vulnerable, by tradition, to nonsense." Although both of these explanations have considerable merit, George Tindall's conclusions seem more relevant to this study. He understood that "in ordering one's vision of reality, the myth may predetermine the categories of perception, rending one blind to the things that do not fit into the mental image." Unfortunately, he said, "the main burden of Southern mythology is still carried in those unavoidable categories set by the nineteenth-century sectional conflict."[14]

The validity of Tindall's contention has been confirmed by Francis Wilhoit's analysis in *The Politics of Massive Resistance*. In this study of the era of intransigence, he identifies the South's defense as being based upon two premises: first, that the practice of segregation was justified; and second, that the federal government had no authority to abrogate state statutes requiring segregation. Since both propositions had been so thoroughly discredited, both in the courts of law and the courts of public opinion, Southern advocates were severely limited in their choice of rational arguments to defend such indefensible propositions. In this instance, as had happened before, the leading Southern spokesmen were forced to fall back on the tired and increasingly strained mythology of the past. Although this approach, which now had little more persuasive force than an inside joke, failed to convince any of the opponents in the national public debate, it did serve a function for some white Southerners. The use of a defensive mythology, which Wilhoit calls counterrevolutionary ideology, "legitimates a given social system; it promotes group cohesion; and it provides its adherents with propaganda ammunition for psychological and political warfare against revolutionary opponents. One may also say that an ideology both describes a special view of reality and prescribes what ought to be."[15]

Both the vision and the strategy of massive resistance sounded like an echo in time. The historical heroes were called forth as they had been before. Nullification and interposition were the first strategies employed, and Calhoun was, of course, the authority for the position. His works were quoted in public speeches, and James J. Kilpatrick, editor of the *Richmond News-Leader*, ran a three-column portrait of the man described as "a kind of Arthurian figure among Southern saints, ever ready to return to the political wars if a new generation of abolitionists should threaten white supremacy and states' rights."[16] Jefferson and Madison, and their positions on the Virginia and Kentucky Resolutions, were also cited, and both Robert E. Lee and Jefferson Davis were held up as heroes by those who were destined to have the same record of success as their saints.

Numerous leaders in the movement also assumed minor hero status by their actions and by their successful re-election. Among members of Congress, Senators Eastland of Mississippi, Byrd of Virginia, Russell of Georgia, and Thurmond of South Carolina were stalwarts. Eastland's speech to a meeting of the White Citizens' Council in 1955, typical of the genre, sounded like that of a Redeemer colonel when he said that public school integration was threatening "the racial integrity, the culture, the creative genius, and the advanced civilization of the white race." He charged that the Supreme Court had "responded to a radical procommunist movement in this country," and he lashed out at the new abolitionists, the "church groups, radical organizations, labor unions, and liberal groups of all shades of red. The South today," sighed the Senator, "is the victim of forces and influences that originated far from its own borders." [17]

At the state level, the movement produced such figures as Leander Perez of Louisiana, Orval Faubus and Jim Johnson of Arkansas, Ernest Vandiver, Marvin Griffin, Herman Talmadge, and Lester Maddox of Georgia, Ross Barnett of Mississippi, and Bull Connor and George Wallace of Alabama. Wallace's 1963 inaugural address is representative of the rhetorical and mythological fare provided by state elected officials during the period. "Today I have stood where Jefferson Davis stood, and took an oath to my people. It is very appropriate then that from this cradle of the Confederacy, this very heart of the Anglo-Saxon Southland, we sound the drum of freedom. . . . I draw the line in the dust and toss the gauntlet before the feet of tyranny. And I say, Segregation Now! Segregation Tomorrow! Segregation Forever!"

Among the dramatic characters in supporting roles were several middle-class professionals. James J. Kilpatrick, who published repeated harangues attempting to resurrect and rehabilitate the doctrines of nullification and interposition, was representative of several Southern editors who attempted to give intellectual respectability to the movement. Educational authorities were represented by Dr. Lindley Stiles of the University of Virginia who once testified that segregation was actually beneficial for black children, casting himself in a role filled so well in the original antebellum production by Professor George Fitzhugh of Virginia.

Just as the saints and heroes depicted in a mythic conflict are illustrative of the values held by those who shared the vision, the villains in the saga are equally useful in understanding the values and actions considered anathema by a society. Foremost in the pantheon of demons were the members of the Supreme Court, especially Chief Justice Earl Warren, author of the *Brown* decision, who became the modern representative of Thaddeus Stephens and Radical Republican Reconstruction, and Justice Hugo Black, who was portrayed as an opportunistic twentieth-century scalawag who had betrayed his region and renounced his Klan heritage.

The *Brown* decision, like every force which has challenged the myth and threatened the security of the racist South, was blamed on outsiders. Senator Eastland blared from the Senate floor that "the decision of the Supreme Court in the school segregation cases was based upon the writings and teachings of pro-communist agitators and other enemies of the American form of Government." Among those enemies, assuming the role of the new abolitionists in the drama, were the members and officers of the National Association for the Advancement of Colored People, especially the attorneys for the NAACP Legal Defense Fund who were storming the Bastille of the segregated South.

One of Wilhoit's major contributions to understanding why the South was unable to generate a new explanatory mythology which would accommodate the social changes portended by the *Brown* decision was his observation that "from the outset the South's counterrevolutionaries suffered from the handicap of having their opponents preempt virtually all the national historic symbols of the United States." With the symbols and themes of democracy and human equality removed from their options, "the South's leaders found themselves at a distinct disadvantage in the vital act of myth-manipulation, for all they had left to manipulate were regional myths and icons discredited by the Great Rebellion."[18]

The irrelevance of the symbols did not, however, diminish their intensity. The Confederate flag and the song "Dixie" gained renewed popularity among the masses, especially in relationship with the rituals of intercollegiate football in the South and the countless ceremonies commemorating the Centennial of the Civil War. The symbolic slogans such as "the Southern way of life" coming from the president of the chamber of commerce or "NEVER!" from Sheriff James Gardner Clark, Jr., of Dallas County, Alabama, were two expressions of the same thought.

Despite the widespread adoption of these symbols throughout the South, reason is not determined by a consensus. "When one approaches the iconography of the Massive Resisters with the objectivity of the scholar instead of the passion of a true believer," said Wilhoit, "one cannot escape the conclusion that it was quite naive, stridently parochial, and hyper-defensive. The segregationists' totemic veneration of the icons of the Lost Cause, their insistence that the South is God's country, their preference for rhetoric over reason, all seemed to suggest a deep malaise in the Southern mind." Such a stance was indicative, he said, "of a kind of spiritual *Angst*, a penchant for romantic escapism, . . . and a growing, gnawing realization of both individual and regional vulnerability. In short, the Southerners' massive resort to symbolism was in itself a kind of sickness."[19]

In 1957, Orval Faubus moved beyond the rhetorical repartee which had been staged in the halls of Congress and chose a new battleground symbolized by the schoolhouse door. The federal response with the 101st Airborne solved the immediate problem, but it gave new meaning to the mythology of a conquered South being reconstructed by a standing army with fixed bayonets. The strategy proved so politically successful for Faubus that it was replayed for local consumption by Leander Perez in the New Orleans public schools in 1960, by Ernest Vandiver at the University of Georgia in 1961, by Ross Barnett at Ole Miss in 1962, and by George Wallace at the University of Alabama in 1963. By the time production was booked in Alabama, it had become pure symbolism, and Wallace's performance proved to be the death rattle of the vision.

Media notice of the election and re-election of rabid segregationist politicians, the official toleration of and participation in racial violence, and the membership rolls of the White Citizens' Councils, organized in Mississippi in 1954, and the Ku Klux Klan, rechartered in Georgia in 1955, might seem to suggest that the South was more solid and more fully committed to the vision than ever before. But despite the absence of an effective, indigenous opposition, numerous Southerners, both black and white, either ignored or opposed the dominating vision of the vocal ruling clique just as had been the case during every period of the past.

Those in control, however, dominated the public forum and the public offices, giving them much more visibility than the opposition underground and the power to effectively suppress internal dissent just as thoroughly as had their predecessors in antebellum times. The dominant mythology was supported by what Wilhoit called "a curious alliance of crackpots, honest conservatives, religious fanatics, visionaries, confused moderates, and simple thugs, often with not much more in common than a shared fear of egalitarian revolution and a belief that the Southern way of life was unique and worth preserving."[20] The manipulation of the symbols and icons of the regional rhetorical mythology gave the temporary appearance of reality for those who shared the mythic vision, and the emergence of a viable alternative myth was temporarily vanquished by the rhetorical hegemony of the old mythology, public political pressure, and private social ostracism.[21]

The Continuity of Consciousness

"The people of the South should be the last Americans to expect indefinite continuity of their institutions and social arrangements," wrote C. Vann Woodward. "Other Americans have less reason to be prepared for sudden change and lost causes. Apart from Southerners, Americans have enjoyed a historical continuity that is unique among modern peoples." Despite these factors which should make the South a seedbed for progressive reforms, it must be remembered, as James Branch Cabell said, that "no history is a matter of record; it is a matter of faith." That is to say, in the words of Davenport, that "history is not so much what happened as what people believe happened. History is a creative form of expression and is politically important to the extent that people use their imaginative understanding of the past to deal with the present."[22]

Rather than accommodating change and moving into the future, the South's mythic vision of the future has been retarded by a mythology which distorted both history and reality. T. Henry Williams noted, "Of all the mind-pictures created by the romantic Southerner, the greatest, the most appealing, and the most enduring is the legend of the Old South." The reasons for that endurance have been suggested by Dewey Grantham, who wrote, "The folklore that helped sustain the Solid South was filled with mythic overtones of white unity and heroic sacrifice in that earlier time of trial and tribulation. The emotional attachment to the idea of 'the South,' constantly reinforced by vague memories, family tales, and endless rhetoric in public places, produced what was surely one of the most remarkable loyalties in American history."[23]

The idea of the South—a particular idea of the South—has been a potent image for both Southerners and non-Southerners, and it has been difficult to overcome, even by those who made an effort to do so. Margaret Mitchell's *Gone with the Wind* was written to provide a new interpretation of Southern culture from a somewhat irreverent Southern journalist. Selznick's film and the audience's response were both different from what she had intended, leading her to accept the fact that "people believe what they like to believe, and the Mythical Old South has too strong a hold on their imaginations to be altered by the mere reading of a 1,037 page book."[24]

During the past one hundred sixty years, the South has experienced more social, economic, and political change than the rest of the nation; however, generations of orators in crisis after crisis have returned repeatedly to the old symbols and the old myth to explain reality for the region. The South's controlling mythology, its rhetorical vision, had become increasingly unrelated to reality and useless as a means of organizing, interpreting, and understanding contemporary events, but the fact that it endured for so long does have meaning for the rhetorical critic and communication scholar. "The Myth of the Lost Cause has relevance for twentieth century Americans," said Rollin Osterweis. "It has flourished longer than any other regional legend; its symbols continue to be visible in all the media by which myths are communicated—on monuments and memorial battlefields, . . . in literature, art, music, and drama, in the ubiquitous use of the Confederate battle flag and battle hymn. More importantly, its great power as a social myth is displayed in the resistance of Southerners to liberal social change in America during the third quarter of the twentieth-century."[25] In trying to comprehend and analyze the force of the myth in continuing and defending the status quo, few have done so as clearly as Paul Gaston, who wrote:

Important though the myth was as bulwark against change, a conscious manipulation cannot fully account for its vitality and effectiveness. Myths are something more than advertising slogans and propaganda ploys rationally connected to a specific purpose. They have a subtle way of permeating the thought and conditioning the actions even of those who may be rationally opposed to their consequences. They arise out of complex circumstances to create mental sets which do not ordinarily yield to intellectual attacks. The history of their dynamics suggests that they may be penetrated by rational analysis only as the consequence of dramatic, or even traumatic, alterations in the society whose essence they exist to portray. Thus, the critique and dissipation of myths becomes possible only when tension between the mythic view and the reality it sustains snaps the viability of their relationship, creates new social patterns and with them harmonizing myths.[26]

THREE   A Vision Gone with the Wind

When a man finds that his interpretation of life—that is, of his experience, his past—does not work, he seeks a new interpretation, molding the theory to the facts.
—James McBride Dabbs, *A Hundred Years Later*

The scholarly works of C. Vann Woodward, George B. Tindall, and V. O. Key, Jr., have clearly dispelled the assumption of any monolithic Solid South, but each has acknowledged the ascendancy of the planter-business alliance and its controlling vision based upon economic conservatism, political reaction, and social and racial discrimination. The vital nexus of these three themes in the dominant vision has been documented quite well, but those wishing to challenge and replace the old myths have been remarkably unsuccessful in their attempts to articulate and popularize a new vision for the region.[1] The antebellum abolition movement, the mountain unionists, the rural Populists, the cotton mill labor organizers, the proponents of interracial cooperation, and the advocates of compliance with federal legislation and court decisions each offered alternative visions of social reality in the South, but each seemed hopelessly overshadowed by the power and pervasiveness of the dominant mythology. The reform movements of the past, said T. Harry Williams, have "failed because they could not overcome the tradition of the past and all the past represented—the Old South, the Lost Cause, and, above all, the race question."[2]

The "race question" and its centrality in the rhetoric and history of the South has been emphasized by numerous writers from Ulrich B. Phillips and Francis B. Simkims to Harry S. Ashmore and Numan V. Bartley. In addition, others have observed another important (and not unrelated) factor—an overtly defensive and hostile reaction to change in institutional arrangements. Edgar T. Thompson recognized and explained the connection between the two themes, noting that "a social order based on slavery or race will, of course, be especially sensitive to behavior and language which touches these nerves and which consequently will be deemed subversive."[3]

The rhetorical recoil of Southern mythology and its continuity through time have been shown in the previous chapter. Unfortunately, said T. Harry Williams, "the South has chosen to stake its destiny on one issue and to defend that issue with one strategy." The old myth, which was always the strategy of first and last resort, has undergone numerous Procrustean adaptations to meet the needs of various crises in the past, and it was able to preserve an almost unchanged relationship among social, economic, and political institutions from 1877 until 1965, with roots extending back to the 1820s and vestiges surviving still.

The prevailing myth had always worked for those in control, and it operated to prevent change in the social order of the South. As Williams noted, "The cherishing of an ideal dream world in the past was both a reflection of the Southerner's capacity for unreality and a cause of his continuing reluctance to face the realities of the modern world; for obviously the myth of a perfect society was a powerful argument against change, against even considering whether there was any need for change." Even as late as 1973 Rollin Osterweis asked how "the Myth, displaying such anachronistic, immature, contradictory qualities, could survive as a formidable influence in the milieu of twentieth-century industrialism now dominating the national tradition and eventually assaulting the legend by all contemporary instruments of mass persuasion." Yet, despite the vast social and cultural changes of recent years, he concluded that the old myth "has defied the erosion of time" and "has continued to dominate the mind of the South, in many ways and on many levels."[4]

The changes observed by Osterweis were deeper and of more consequence than he realized, and their impact has intensified since that time. The contemporary South is now faced with a new set of quantifiable facts with regard to race relations, political conditions, demographic composition, social realities, and communication media. These changes, declared C. Vann Woodward, "are of sufficient depth and impact as to define the end of an era in Southern history." The old myth could no longer serve to explain the South to itself, and, as Thomas S. Frentz and Thomas B. Farrell have noted in another context, the "end of an era is usually marked by the increased incapacity of one dimension of consciousness to solve contemporary social problems." Southerners trying to comprehend and accommodate the changing reality of their world, said Leslie Dunbar, were being "forced to act directly without validating their acts against their history, much of which [was] sinking fast beneath them," and it was increasingly apparent that the new social order was demanding a new mythology to interpret and explain the new realities of the contemporary South.[5]

The Changing Southern World

Just as historians have argued over the date of the beginning of a cultural South, contemporary scholars also disagree on a date for the beginning of the contemporary South. Certainly, the impact of the New Deal cannot be underestimated, for as George B. Tindall said, it shook "the social and economic power structure of the region." Franklin Roosevelt brought Southern blacks and whites together in the same political party, and "his personality and his programs aroused a devotion that ran stronger in the South than in any other region." One North Carolina cotton mill worker expressed the basis for that devotion when he declared, "Roosevelt is the only man we ever had in the White House who could understand that my boss is a sonofabitch."[6] New Deal economic programs provided wages which were more realistic than had been available in the past, blacks and whites were frequently assigned to equal jobs with equal pay, and the pervasive control of the economic elite was challenged.

Many progressive Southerners were hopeful that the Populist coalition could be reassembled and held together for political success and social change. Perhaps Cash expressed that hope best when he said, "Looking at the South in those days, indeed, one might have readily concluded that at last the old pattern was on its way to conclusive breakup, that new ideas and a new tolerance were sweeping the field, and that the region as a whole, growing genuinely social-minded and realistic, was setting itself to examine its problems with clear eyes and dispassionate temper—in a word, that the old long lag between the Southern mind and the changing conditions of the Southern world was about to end."[7] Such a convergence, however, did not occur immediately.

Charles P. Roland and other social historians have emphasized the impact of World War II on the region. The location of defense industries in the South and technical training in the armed forces changed the character of the Southern work force; military travel exposed Southerners to other cultures, and military training brought many non-Southerners to the South, making the region less provincial; and black Southerners had defended freedoms which they now demanded for themselves. Undoubtedly, these changes were beginning to undermine the power of the old myth by removing from reality some of the old props which had supported its credibility.

During the same period, other changes, which would have even greater impact, were taking place in the South. Black political participation, nearly extinguished by Bourbon backlash following the Populist uprising, began to challenge the status quo. Although the first major victory had been achieved in the Texas case of *Nixon v. Herndon* in 1928, the case of *Smith v. Allwright* in 1944, based upon the Fourteenth and Fifteenth Amendments adopted by the Reconstruction Congress, signaled the end of the white primary in the South. Although the Jim Crow party machinery attempted to control black political participation through party loyalty oaths, poll taxes, literacy tests, and other forms of legal subterfuge, it was the beginning of the end. Blacks would begin to play an increasingly more significant role in Southern politics.

The landmark decision of the Supreme Court in *Brown v. Board of Education* in 1954, though neither immediately nor quietly implemented, began the process of school integration and an era of new experiences for a new generation of Southern children. The *Brown* decision was a victory not only for Linda Brown in Topeka, Kansas, but also for Dorothy Davis in Prince Edward County, Virginia, and Harry Briggs, Jr., in Summerton, South Carolina, the appellants in other cases which had been consolidated by the Court. The Civil Rights Act of 1957 and the Civil Rights Act of 1960, adopted over the strident opposition of Southern legislators and with the reluctant support of President Eisenhower, were the first major pieces of civil rights legislation enacted in eighty-two years. Although less forceful than subsequent measures, their impact began to be felt—even in the South and even without a strong federal commitment to enforcement. Changes such as these in the social and political structure were, to paraphrase V. O. Key, Jr., altering the mold that shaped Southern society.

No sooner had the Supreme Court ruled against segregation in the public schools than another challenge to Jim Crow and the "Southern way of life" emerged from within the South. On December 1, 1955, a seamstress named Rosa Parks decided that she was too tired to give up her bus seat to a white man, and her arrest for that decision led to the Montgomery Bus Boycott and marked the beginning of the civil rights movement in the South. The Southern Christian Leadership Conference, formed by Martin Luther King, Jr., in 1958, and the Student Nonviolent Coordinating Committee, organized in 1960, led the fight for the integration of lunch counters, public facilities, and voting booths throughout the region.

Preferring to go out with a bang rather than with a whimper, the proponents of the old myth responded and resisted as never before. Threatened by a changing social environment and challenged by a new vision from the civil rights movement, the Old South's last hurrah became the most grotesque caricature of the old myth ever presented. The strategy was the same as always before—suppress opposition, end rational debate, and substitute common symbols for common sense. This time, however, in the face of changing realities and a communication environment which included television, the power of the old myth was clearly inadequate to explain the South to itself, and assertion only highlighted absurdity.

As in the past, those in control did their best to protect the old myth by stifling competing explanations of social reality. "All over the South the lights of reason and tolerance and moderation began to go out under the demand for conformity," said C. Vann Woodward, describing the climate of the late 1950s. "Books were banned, libraries were purged, newspapers were slanted, television programs were withheld, films were excluded. Teachers, preachers, and college professors were questioned, harassed, and many were driven from their position or fled the South. The NAACP was virtually driven underground in some states." Under such stultifying influences, Woodward continued, "words began to shift their significance and lose their common meaning. A 'moderate' became a man who dared open his mouth, an 'extremist' one who favored eventual compliance with the law, and 'compliance' took on the connotations of treason."[8]

The old symbols used to support the myth were quickly losing their power. The vision, though proclaimed more loudly than ever before, was becoming as worthless as Confederate money. The Confederate flag, which formerly brought tears from members of the United Daughters of the Confederacy and eloquent speeches from the old veterans was, in retrospect, only the "symbol of police brutality, schizophrenic defiance of national efforts toward racial justice, and a paranoic retreat into an illusionary world of simple, violent answers to complex problems." As Garvin Davenport observed, "It is this debased use of the Southern past and of Southern uniqueness which all Americans have had set before them in the headlines."[9]

Unquestionably, the pathetic spectacle of Southern resistance was made even more pathetic by the newspaper headlines and television pictures which displayed the drama for the nation and the world. Even white Southerners were shocked and shamed by the scenes of the South in the early 1960s: the riot at Ole Miss on September 30, 1962; Bull Connor's police dogs and fire hoses in Birmingham in April and May 1963; George Wallace's schoolhouse door charade on June 10, 1963; President Kennedy's national television address on June 11, 1963; the assassination of Medgar Evers in Jackson on June 12, 1963; the march on Washington and King's famous oration on August 28, 1963; the bombing of the Sixteenth Street Baptist Church on September 15, 1963; the killings of three civil rights workers during the "freedom summer" of 1964; and the march from Selma to Montgomery and the murders of Viola Liuzzo and James Reeb in March 1965. Such events might have received little attention in an earlier time, for there were eighty-three lynchings in 1919, and Congress, under threat of Southern filibuster, was unable to pass legislation making lynching a federal offense.[10] With vivid images of Southern violence on the television screens in every home and color pictures in weekly magazines, however, the florid oratory, mythic symbols, self-righteous posturing, and parliamentary tactics of Southern governors, senators, and congressmen were of little effect.

Not only did reason and discussion become difficult, but the impact on the useless public mythology was also evident. Rather than offering the chance to generate new symbols to comprehend the changing reality, insistence upon the retention of the old myth further strained rational response and restrained productive behavior. Stephen Larsen has said that "when the mythic imagination is cultivated, it is the creative source realm of the highest and best in human endeavor, the inspiration of the finest flowering of our culture." On the other hand, the old myth had become inflexible and psychologically brittle, and in such instances, "when neglected, deprived of conscious cultivation, it is equally capable of becoming a choked and tangled garden of weeds. Instead of giving birth to the useful and beautiful, the profound and the sublime, the creative force can produce titans, monsters, and grotesques—as did the Earth Mother in Greek legend, left to herself in a demiurgic frenzy of creation."[11]

The histrionics and hyperbole of the Southern political leadership led Robert Penn Warren to describe the mock confrontations as "an obscene parody of the meaning of . . . history" and to ask, "Can the man howling in the mob imagine General R. E. Lee, CSA, shaking hands with Orval Faubus, Governor of Arkansas?" Another thoughtful Southerner confessed, "It fills me with shame to reflect upon the system I grew up in and gave unthinking approval to until demagogues like Wallace and Faubus, without intending, taught me the errors of my ways."[12] Nothing, it seems, was so impotent as a cultural myth whose time had passed.

Led by the strong rhetoric of an indignant and committed Southern president, who as senate majority leader had refused to sign the Declaration of Constitutional Principles in 1956, the nation supported and the Congress enacted the Civil Rights Act of 1964, the Voting Rights Act of 1965, and the Civil Rights Act of 1968. The new media's piercing of the myth and the implementation of these new federal statutes were the death knell for the old vision and its power to define and control reality for a region.

The Changing Southern World View

William Graham Sumner, in 1907, wrote that "legislation cannot make mores" and "stateways cannot change folkways," and, fifty years later, Dwight David Eisenhower said, "I don't believe you can change the hearts of men with laws or decisions." Events in the South since 1965, however, tend to refute those assumptions. There is clear and convincing evidence that the enactment and enforcement of the Civil Rights Act of 1964 and the Voting Rights Act of 1965 have had dramatic consequences for the old mythology and, hence, the attitudes and behavior of Southerners, the mores, folkways, and the heart of the South.[13]

   The Civil Rights Act of 1964 and the Voting Rights Act of 1965 officially entombed Jim Crow, and it became legally permissible, as well as socially acceptable, for blacks and whites to participate in the same systems of commerce, education, transportation, and government. While Lester Maddox complained of having to serve blacks at his Pickrick Restaurant, others operating commercial facilities welcomed the new laws because they were now free from the threat of white boycotts for serving black customers. Andrew Young told of blacks having hot coffee poured on them at a restaurant in St. Augustine, Florida, and returning one week later, only five days after passage of the Civil Rights Act, to be welcomed as customers. He quoted the management as explaining, "We were just afraid of losing our business. We didn't want to be the only ones to be integrated. But if everybody's got to do it, we've been ready for it for a long time."[14] Furthermore, the fallacies of white supremacy and superiority, formerly enforced and reinforced by the practices of slavery and segregation, were quickly exposed by the demise of forced participation in unequal systems. Blacks began to patronize the same businesses, use the same public facilities, attend the same schools, and hold the same jobs as the white population of the South, and such behavior removed the visible cues which had formerly given credence to the perception of inferiority. Equal status contact reduced prejudice between black and white Southerners, and the drastic reduction, between 1963 and 1971, in the percentage of whites opposed to sending their children to integrated schools represented what George Gallup termed "one of the most dramatic shifts in the history of public opinion polling."

Suddenly, Southerners seemed to be escaping the restrictions of the old myth with its limiting effect on the Southern mind as described by Cash. The "old retarding mythology" had "sustained visions of the past by starving the imagination of government and people alike"; however, Hodding Carter, III, recognized that "Southern legacies are not eternal and need not be accepted when reason suggests their rejection." Likewise, Edgar T. Thompson thought that it was a time of "growing realization that the future holds infinitely more promise than the past," and he said, "we are now in a period of clarification, when almost anything traditional is being questioned." Revisionist historians such as Woodward helped those who were interested to understand that changes had occurred in Southern culture and society in the past and that the belief that social relations were "immutable and unchangeable is not supported by history." Others, such as Leslie Dunbar, saw progress coming to the region now that Southerners were able to release themselves from the shackles of the historical vision of the past. "I believe," he said, "we can see the mind of the white South changing through the action of the black Southerner and the accommodating reaction of the white South." [15]

As Southerners struggled to overcome the past and its myths and began to adjust to the new realities resulting from the Civil Rights Act of 1964, President Johnson, telling Congress and the nation that "we shall overcome," sought and secured passage of the Voting Rights Act of 1965. Nineteen Southern senators had signed the Southern Manifesto nine years earlier, and nineteen Southern senators voted against the act. Little had changed in nine years—or in a hundred—but the Voting Rights Act would create profound changes in the South, its political rhetoric, and its social order.

In 1940 only 2 percent of eligible blacks had been registered to vote in the South, and in 1964 that figure was only 29 percent. By 1972, over 56 percent of eligible Southern blacks were registered to vote, and studies had demonstrated a resulting improvement in social and economic advancement, as well as improved public services and facilities. In 1965, there were only 72 black elected officials in the eleven states of the Old South; in 1979, that figure exceeded 2,000. The impact of the Voting Rights Act on the Southern power structure can also be seen in the rhetoric of Southern senators debating its extension. In 1965, all nineteen votes against the act were cast by senators from the South; in 1975 a majority of Southern senators voted for extension; and in 1982, only four of the eight votes against extension were cast by Southern senators. The act was, said Jimmy Carter, "the best thing that happened to the South in my lifetime. The Voting Rights Act did not just guarantee the vote for black people. It liberated the South, both black and white. It made it possible for the South to come out of the past and into the mainstream of American politics." [16]

The Second Reconstruction of the South, a term often applied to the civil rights movement, also conducted a direct assault on the symbols of the old myth. Martin Luther King, Jr., and other leaders of the Southern Christian Leadership Conference were particularly frustrating opponents for the neo-Confederate defenders of the latest Lost Cause. First, they sought legal equality in direct contravention of the basic tenet of the mythic order. Second, they were native Southerners, several were ordained ministers, and their rhetoric of the streets sounded strangely like their rhetoric of the pulpits. It was quite difficult to brand these dissenters as "outside agitators" or "Atheistic yankees." Finally, the nonviolent protest movement destroyed the Old South images of blacks as either Nat Turner or Uncle Remus. King and his movement presented a new image which could not be described by any symbol in the lexicon of the old mythology.

Other symbols fell just as rapidly. If, as Wilhoit said, the intercollegiate football rivalries were important icons for the forces of segregation and massive resistance, the extent of integration of Southern universities and athletic programs would argue for the surrender of yet another symbol. John Westbrook, the first black football player in the Southwest Conference, recalled insults from coaches, players, and fans at Baylor in 1966, but ten years later there were twenty-two black players on the Baylor team and nine of eleven players on the All-Southwest Conference defensive team were black. At the University of Alabama, George Wallace had moved from the schoolhouse door to the football field to crown the black homecoming queen, and at Ole Miss, black football player Ben Williams was elected "Colonel Rebel" by a vote of the student body and escorted the white homecoming queen in 1975. White planters who are football fanatics and good ole boys from the class of '57 cheer wildly for black athletes on Saturday afternoon, and as a result of that behavior they find it more difficult to maintain the prejudice of the myth on Monday morning. Nowhere is this phenomenon more clearly demonstrated than in *The Courting of Marcus Dupree* by Willie Morris.[17]

Massive Resistance proved to have been the last act in the drama of the old mythology, but few Southerners could agree as to whether it belonged to the genre of tragedy or comedy in the last scene. The old myth had failed to stop the changes—or even to explain them. In a very short time, said Paul Gaston, "white Southerners found themselves in situations they had never believed possible. One after another, old customs and institutions were revised or eliminated and situations abounded for which the myth could by no stretch of the imagination remain instructive."[18]

Some unreconstructed rebels bemoaned the loss of the power of the myth and the continuity of the "Southern way of life." The changes in Southern society signaled, they believed, the end of the South as surely as they meant the end of the myth. Others in the South, however, welcomed the chance to forge a new myth and a new destiny for the region. They endorsed the position of George B. Tindall, who recognized that "to change is not necessarily to lose one's identity: to change, sometimes, is to find it."[19] The South finally had a chance to escape the old mythology and to fashion a new mythic vision compatible with the new realities of the region, one which could be shared by both blacks and whites. As will be shown in the following discussion, Southerners began to struggle with the issues in a more realistic manner, availed themselves of the opportunity presented by the mythic vacuum, and contributed to the evolution of a new rhetorical mythology consistent with and explanatory of the emerging social reality.

Despite the growing distance between rhetoric and reality, rejection of the old myth did not come easily for the South. It had been a part of the region's history and its rhetorical reality since the 1820s, and it had withstood numerous attacks from various competing visions. The rhetoric of Massive Resistance was one last attempt to make it work. "The South," said Henry Savage, "crouched defensively with eyes looking backward, its politics dedicated to little else but the retention of such vestiges of the past as could be fitted into the new framework which the revolution had decreed."[20] Increasingly, though, as each new black voter registered with the assistance of the Voting Rights Act of 1965 and as black citizens exercised their rights which were guaranteed by the Constitution and secured by the Civil Rights Act of 1964, it became obvious that the old symbols were inappropriate. They no longer constituted the necessary "bond of participation" in the emerging biracial and egalitarian society of the South, and they were becoming both "incomprehensible and ridiculous."[21]

For several years in the late 1960s, Southerners were aware that the old myth could no longer serve their region, but they were unable to avail themselves of an appropriate existing substitute. It was a period of mythic confusion, and many found themselves without an explanatory vision of either the past or the future to organize their experiences of the chaotic present. Southern society was without a convenient functioning mythology to provide a "rationale of history and an over-all explanation of change and stability."[22]

In such periods, between the death of a controlling mythology and the birth of its replacement, the communication scholar has an unusual opportunity to observe the reciprocity between mythos and logos. The death of a mythic vision leaves a society consciously seeking definitions of appropriate behavior and unconsciously struggling to find or create a new mythology, to generate new symbols, and to define new goals. As Leslie Stephen observed, "The doctrines which men obstensibly hold do not become operative upon their conduct until they have generated an imaginative symbolism."[23]

Slowly, out of the events occurring between 1954 and 1965, a new myth emerged and began gaining adherents throughout the South. This new vision, born in the 1960s and maturing in the 1970s, was quite different from the mythology which had sustained, instructed, and controlled the South since the 1820s. In the following chapters, I identify and examine the rhetorical implications of three distinct mythic themes found in the rhetoric of the contemporary

South, but I approach that task with obvious caution. In the first place, as Henry A. Murray observed, "recent myths are harder to identify: they are either veiled by the conceptual, discursive language of social ideology and social science, or they are fragmentary, being still in the process of cultural evolution."[24] Second, although these themes now constitute the predominant and most successful mythic vision in the South, they are not the only myths to be found in such a geographically diverse and culturally pluralistic region.

Even the Old South myth, once so dominant and powerful, is still available to those who seek it; but it is now primarily a social relic, preserved by the local chambers of commerce and used as "Yankee bait" by tourism promoters and trinket shop operators. Confederate flag decals, once the badge of white racism, now find a better market at the Dixie Truck Stop in Tuscola, Illinois, than in Tuscaloosa, Alabama; flacked stories about antebellum mansions appear as regularly in markets outside the South as within the region; and it is a New York travel agency which hypes the "Mansions and Magnolias Tours."[25]

The three mythic themes I have discerned as constituting the contemporary mind of the South have been reconstructed from the diverse and voluminous rhetorical artifacts of the contemporary South. The first, the theme of equality, is primarily retrospective in nature, redefining the Southern past to explain the current legal and social status of interracial participation in the regional dream. The second is focused more upon the present, examining the social symbols and cultural rituals of the contemporary South and proclaiming the continuing distinctiveness of Southerners and their regional culture. The third is prospective, developing and displaying attitudes and values about regional economic and commercial development through public scenarios for the future of the South and stressing a new perspective on the sense of place and community traditionally associated with the rural South. All are, in their motives and effects, intrinsically different from the mythology of the Old South and Lost Cause which controlled Southern culture and Southern rhetoric for one hundred fifty years. As will be demonstrated, the contemporary mythmakers constructed a new socio-cultural reality for the region, often drawing symbols from the competing, minority myths of the past but always redefining reality to support the new institutional and social structures of the South which have emerged during the last twenty years. Through conscious rhetorical strategies the new reality was constructed and communicated; through unconscious response to the new reality the mythology of the contemporary South has greatly influenced and directed the rhetorical choice of contemporary Southerners.

FOUR The Theme of Equality

I have a dream that one day on the red hills of Georgia, sons of former
slaves and sons of former slave owners will be able to sit down together
at the table of brotherhood. I have a dream that one day even the state of
Mississippi . . . will be transformed into an oasis of freedom and justice.
. . . I have a dream that one day in Alabama, with its vicious racists, with
its governor having his lips dripping with words of interposition and nullification, . . . little black boys and little black girls will be able to join
hands with little white boys and little white girls as sisters and brothers.
—Martin Luther King, Jr., "I Have A Dream"

The old mythology of the South and the society it depicted were
"for whites only." There were no black planters living in the fabled
white-columned mansions, there were no black belles in hooped
skirts on the verandas, there were no black cavalry officers in uni-
forms of gray, and there were no black industrialists smiling at
their millhands and balance sheets. The old myth had absolutely
no meaning for blacks, and it held meaning for very few whites
when blacks began to have the opportunity to participate in the
"Southern way of life."

Samuel Dubois Cook, President of Dillard University, tells the
story of shocking one white Southerner when he said, "I am a Southerner—just as much as you, and I do not share your views. I am no

segregationist. I am a radical believer in integration and the beloved community of white humanity and black humanity. You do not speak for all Southerners or groups of the South. You do not recognize a large segment of the population." Later, as he began to witness promising changes in the South and its world view, Dr. Cook declared, "I speak not only as a Southerner but, at bloody long last, as a proud Southerner who totally abhors and rejects the utter inhumanity, guilt, and shame of the South's past and who has a genuinely humanistic vision of the New South and of what the South, through a genuine, humanistic revolution can become and contribute to the nation. . . . Blacks are Southerners as well as they are Americans and Afro-Americans." It is a vision for which Cook was still fighting as a member of the 1980 Commission on the Future of the South.[1]

The Old South plantation myth was originally the product of political leaders and literary figures in the antebellum South, rather than being a spontaneous mass creed. Hofstadter has shown that to be the case with the agrarian myth as well, and Paul Gaston demonstrated a kindred genesis in the construction of the first New South mythology. Likewise, the origins of the mythic themes of the contemporary South can be traced to an imaginative, well-educated, vocal, literate, and enthusiastic cadre of middle- and upper-middle-class Southern professionals. Journalists, attorneys, politicians, preachers, historians, sociologists, and educators, both black and white, were primarily responsible for formulating the basic tenets of the emerging mythology and for assuring regional and national exposure to their new vision of social reality. Consequently, the rhetorical mythology of the contemporary South was skillfully developed, redefining the past and projecting the future through symbols and scenarios which clearly reflected the personal views and values of its creators and subsequently determined rhetorical choice and acceptable action for later participants. The myth was artfully designed and psychologically functional, and it was rapidly diffused among a much larger audience of Southerners who readily accepted its basic assumptions about the nature of society.

Redefining the Past

To accommodate the new role for blacks in the Southern world view, it was necessary to fashion a mythic history and mythic vision compatible with the new realities of legal and political equality for blacks. Since the old myth had been so inexorably connected with the praxes of slavery, segregation, and racial inequality, the requirements of the new vision were clear: it required either rejection or redefinition of the past to comprehend the present. Pardon Tillinghast observed that "there is no possibility of making future patterns without past patterns from which to take a departure," and the emerging mythology was based on redefinition of an existing heritage and was thus more palatable to Southerners than would have been a direct and complete rejection of their history. The new myth thus mirrored the form and was almost a mirror image of the old, adapting the familiar chronology but substituting new and more appropriate saints, heroes, villains, icons, and symbols.

Whereas John C. Calhoun had served as the patron saint of the South in the old myth, the proponents of the new myth canonized Thomas Jefferson, author of the Declaration of Independence, and James Madison, champion of the Bill of Rights. The values represented by these new saints were instructive for the new vision. Both Jefferson and Madison predated the influence of Calhoun; both had acknowledged the evils and inhumanity of slavery; and both were unquestionably Southerners. The Jeffersonian ideal of the yeoman farmer seemed far more egalitarian than Calhoun's planter aristocracy, and Calhoun's image was further tarnished by exposure to the restoration of Andrew Jackson, Southern advocate of the Union and symbol of participatory democracy and expanded suffrage. The Jacksonian image was an especially helpful device for the refutation of Southern leaders who advocated resistance to federal authority and restriction of voting rights.

George Fitzhugh, who had given academic respectability to slavery and white supremacy in the antebellum South, was replaced by Hinton Rowan Helper, author of *The Impending Crisis of the South: How to Meet It*, an able critic of slavery, and an observer of its detrimental impact on the politics, economy, and society of the South. Chief Justice Roger Brooke Taney, the border state jurist who authored the *Dred Scott* decision, was countered by veneration of Justice John Marshall Harlan, the border state jurist whose dissent in *Plessy v. Ferguson* declared that "in the view of the Constitution, in the eye of the law, there is in this country no superior, dominant, ruling class of citizens. There is no caste here. Our Constitution is color blind, and neither knows nor tolerates classes among its citizens. In respect of civil rights, all citizens are equal before the Law." Jefferson Davis was largely ignored, and another United States senator from Mississippi, Lucius Q. C. Lamar, a "statesman who had been a fire-brand secessionist but who, in the 1870s became a spokesman for reconciliation between races and regions," became the namesake for an indigenous organization which stressed those same objectives during the 1970s.[2]

In the stead of Henry Grady, the South of the 1880s came to be represented by Walter Hines Page and George Washington Cable. Page was an advocate for universal education in the South, and Cable, who had been openly hostile to Grady, was an outspoken advocate of equal rights for blacks. Such historical support for the emerging mythology, based upon a reinterpretation (rather than rejection) of the South's historical heritage, allowed the new myth to successfully recruit additional participants who would have had difficulty accepting a vision which completely denied the past.

C. Vann Woodward openly criticized the old myth, saying it meant only "juleps for the few and pellagra for the crew, a façade of Greek columns and a backyard full of slums." He was not alone in publicly recognizing the damage done by the old myth and in calling for its rejection. Harry S. Ashmore, editor of the *Arkansas Gazette*, wrote *An Epitaph for Dixie*, and former Mississippi Congressman Frank E. Smith urged his fellow Southerners to *Look Away from Dixie*.[3]

Others, however, were less brash in their approach, suggesting that the mythology of the South in the 1970s was not really that of a new South but, rather, the South which had always been there and was only temporarily obscured by misconceptions. The Old South, said Ralph McGill, "never really was a land of cavaliers and cotton" and the Southern white leadership "never became a class of goateed gentlemen in broad-brimmed black hats, sitting on the verandas of big pillared mansions drinking mint juleps stirred with a silver spoon and served by adoring black servants." As Congressman Ray Thornton explained, it should not be seen as anything particularly revolutionary. "I think really what's happening is not so much a New South—the South is like it has always been. It is that people in other sections of the country are taking the blinders off and looking at the real South and finding what great people and resources we have here."[4]

Governor Reubin Askew of Florida answered the question of whether the contemporary South was actually a "New South" by stating, "I don't think that we're talking about something that's really new. We're talking instead about a humanistic South which always has been there, just below an often misleading surface of racism and despair, struggling for a chance to emerge, to develop and mature, a chance to assert itself, a chance to lead." In the same vein, Terry Sanford, former Governor of North Carolina and president of Duke University, said, "In the early sixties we began to rend the curtain of racial discimination, a cloth woven out of long strands of various mythologies, and glimpsed behind it—for the first time in the century—the real South."[5] In such a context, the history of the region was redefined and accepted, and upon such a base, it became easier to define the contemporary heroes.

As early as 1963, it was becoming apparent that the civil rights movement was presenting a challenge to the old mythology and that Southerners were working to establish a new vision based on events of "the movement." The popular media of the period included movies such as *The Defiant Ones* (1958), *The Cardinal* (1963), *Gone Are the Days* (1963), and *The Intruder* (1963). These films were soon followed by *Black Like Me* (1964), *Nothing But a Man* (1964), *In the Heat of the Night* (1967), *Finian's Rainbow* (1968), *The Heart is a Lonely Hunter* (1968), *Slaves* (1969), and *Tick . . . Tick . . . Tick* (1970). Taken together, they constituted an emerging genre which one scholar has labeled "neo-abolitionist," and presented a graphic critique of Southern society, questioning the basic racial assumptions of the old vision just as clearly as did the rhetoric of the streets. Although not produced by Southerners, these films were distributed in the South, and they nurtured the emerging myth. It might be easy to overlook the impact of such films on Southern society, but their rhetorical influence was very real. "By projecting collective images of a culture, by serving as symptoms of cultural needs, and by symbolizing trends," noted one study, "dramatic media both reflect and create societal events."[6]

Heroic Figures

The leaders of the Second Reconstruction soon became heroes, and, as dramatis personae in the new vision of reality, they are instructive in determining the values and motives of the emerging mythology. "It is not easy to create a myth and emulate it at the same time," said Jerome S. Bruner, but Martin Luther King, Jr., succeeded in that task in the movement and in the mythology of the contemporary South. King's early leadership of the Montgomery Bus Boycott, his organization and direction of the Southern Christian Leadership Conference, his now famous "I Have a Dream" oration at the March on Washington, his march from Selma to Montgomery, and his eventual martyrdom in Memphis helped to create a new social reality and to elevate him to a position of prominence equivalent to that of a contemporary hero—initially for blacks and eventually for whites participating in the vision.

King's advocacy of nonviolent protest, full civil and political rights, and human brotherhood constituted his personal goals, and these became the central themes of the new cultural myth of equality. His books, *Stride Toward Freedom: The Montgomery Story, Where Do We Go from Here: Chaos or Community, Why We Can't Wait,* and *The Trumpet of Conscience,* developed both the strategy and the substance of the movement, and his public speeches translated those ideas to his audience in the South. It has been said that King "had partaken of the myth of Southern history," but it is also true that he was instrumental in developing a new myth for the contemporary South.[7]

Other black leaders became contemporary heroes in the vision. State Senator Julian Bond, John Lewis of the Voter Education Project, and Andrew Young, Congressman, Ambassador to the United Nations, and currently Mayor of Atlanta, were veterans of the civil rights struggle in the South and were among King's lieutenants. Tom Gilmore, once clubbed by the sheriff of Greene County, Alabama, for trying to register black voters, now *is* the sheriff of Greene County, Alabama, as a result of black voter registration. In Mississippi, Medgar Evers has been memorialized in song and books, Mississippi Supreme Court Justice Reuben Anderson served as a member of the 1980 Commission on the Future of the South, and James Meredith's success in Jackson is a symbol of progress in that state. Former Mayor Maynard Jackson of Atlanta and former Congresswoman Barbara Jordan of Texas were also among those who symbolized the new spirit in the South.

The heroes of the vision of equality were not, however, all black, and some would have seemed most unlikely candidates. Among those now honored, though once vilified by the old vision, were some very traditional Southern gentlemen of the federal judiciary. Republicans Elbert Parr Tuttle, John Robert Brown, and John Minor Wisdom were joined on the United States Fifth Circuit Court of Appeals by Democrat Richard Taylor Rives, and together they constituted one of the most powerful forces in bringing about school desegregation in the South after the *Brown* decision. As Claude Sitton, former Southern correspondent for *The New York Times*, said, "Those who think Martin Luther King desegregated the South don't know Elbert Tuttle and the record of the Fifth Circuit Court of Appeals." On the Supreme Court, former Klansman Hugo Black joined the ranks of heroes, and at the district court level Julius Waites Waring of South Carolina, James Skelly Wright of Louisiana, and Frank M. Johnson, Jr., of Alabama became legendary figures in the vision.[8] Reaffirming the South's devotion to the Constitution and its framers and continuing the vision of John Marshall Harlan, their once unpopular decisions became landmarks of courage in the new myth.

Two other figures, though not members of the bench, also figured prominently in the drama of the legal challenge to the old mythology. Morris Dees of the Southern Poverty Law Center in Alabama, who fought valiantly for the rights of blacks in criminal cases across the South, and Charles Morgan, formerly of the active Atlanta office of the American Civil Liberties Union, were both instrumental in establishing new models for lawyers in the South and are now respected for their coverage throughout the region.

They presently hold positions as legal gladiators once occupied by John W. Davis and Robert McC. Figg, Jr., attorneys for segregating states in the early 1950s, in the old Southern vision.

James Jackson Kilpatrick, the newspaper editor and chief popular propagandist for the anti-*Brown* forces of massive resistance, was no longer the interpretive idealogue of the South. The contemporary myth relied upon journalistic support from Harry Ashmore of the *Arkansas Gazette*, Ralph McGill of the *Atlanta Constitution*, Bill Minor of the *Jackson Reporter*, and Hodding Carter of the Greenwood *Delta Democrat-Times* during its formative years, and later relied upon Reg Murphy of the *Atlanta Constitution*, James O. Powell of the *Arkansas Gazette*, Brandt Ayres of the *Anniston Star*, Tom Wicker of *The New York Times*, Reese Cleghorn of the *Charlotte Observer*, Edwin Yoder, Jr., of the *Greensboro Daily News*, and Ronnie Dugger of the *Texas Observer*. All were architects and translators of the new vision of the contemporary South, and their role in its changing cannot be underestimated.

In addition to the editorials and feature articles in progressive newspapers, several films and television movies also assisted in the mass articulation of the vision. *The Autobiography of Miss Jane Pittman* (CBS, 1974) presented a dramatic restatement of Southern historical reality in the fictional life of a black woman who quietly endured "the Southern way of life" as it was interpreted from the 1860s until the 1960s when she decides to drink from a "whites only" water fountain. Then *Conrack* (1974), "a 'white liberal' movie with an unprecedented southern hero," portrayed writer Pat Conroy's experience as a teacher in a black South Carolina school and his efforts to buck the Beaufort establishment's code of conduct.[9] The vision was fully developed on film when Tom Gilmore's election as the first black sheriff in Alabama was dramatized in a television movie, *This Man Stands Alone* (NBC, 1979).

The Voting Rights Act of 1965 and the mythic vision of equality were also responsible for the acceptance and election of a new variety of Southern politicians whose images and rhetoric were consistent with the new mythology. As late as 1968, however, Robert Sherill offered a despairing and disparaging assessment of the future of the South in a book entitled *Gothic Politics of the Deep South: Stars of the New Confederacy*. Pointing to the current leadership of such politicians as George Wallace, Herman Talmadge, Orval Faubus, George Smathers, James Eastland, Strom Thurmond, and Leander Perez, he saw little hope for the emergence of a real New South.

Within the next two years the region was alive with hope. The 1970 gubernatorial elections brought a new and strikingly different group of leaders to Southern statehouses, and their inaugurations were rituals of considerable communal significance for the region. James Hoban has suggested that such events often elevate political leaders to the status of heroes as "the community recognizes their participation in its maintenance, their preservation of its traditions, and their advancement of social order and cohesion. . . . Communal actions, legitimizing the assumption of leadership, mark a transition from a fraternal frame of reference to a paternal one on the part of the leader." The newly elected governors quickly captured the attention of the national and regional press, and the term "New South" soon regained a currency it had not experienced since the late nineteenth century. For Southerners, these new governors were welcome regional symbols of a new identity, sources of pride, and able advocates of a new mythology.

In Arkansas, Dale Bumpers, who advocated the end of racial discrimination, handily defeated Orval Faubus, who was trying to make a political comeback in the gubernatorial primary. Faubus' demise seemed to set a pattern for the old "segs" as Jimmy Swann in Mississippi and Jimmy Davis in Louisiana finished third and fourth in Democratic gubernatorial primaries. Elsewhere across the South, a different rhetoric began to emerge. As Edwin Yoder observed, there seemed to be "a new market in Southern governors—all young, all anxious to put the slogans, the fears, the divisions, the despairs of the sixties behind them." Virginia Governor Linwood Holton said, "No more must the slogan of states' rights sound a recalcitrant and defensive note for the people of the South. For the era of defiance is behind us. . . . As Virginia has been a model for so much else in America in the past, let us now endeavor to make today's Virginia a model in race relations." South Carolina Governor John West promised "a government that is totally color-blind" and declared that "the politics of race and divisiveness have been soundly repudiated in South Carolina."

In Arkansas, Dale Bumpers said, "The people . . . are looking for new approaches, new attitudes and new initiatives. To help in this search our administration will be one of open minds and open doors. The future we envision must be shaped and shared by all Arkansans: old and young, black and white, rich and poor. I appeal to the best in our people to meet this challenge." Reubin Askew exemplified the change in Florida, and, in Georgia, Jimmy Carter vowed that "the time for racial discrimination is over. Our people have already made this major difficult decision." These pronouncements were quite different from the "drum of freedom" sounded by George Wallace in his inaugural address just eight years earlier, and formed the core of the egalitarian myth being articulated in the contemporary South.

In 1971, Mississippi voters added moderate William Waller to the list of progressive southern governors, and in 1974 Arkansas voters once again rejected Orval Faubus in favor of moderate David Pryor. That same year, George Busbee defeated Lester Maddox in the Georgia gubernatorial primary, and in his inaugural declared, "The politics of race has gone with the wind." Edwin Edwards of Louisiana in 1975 and Jim Hunt of North Carolina in 1976 continued the nonracist progressive trend in Southern statehouses. In 1978, another round of gubernatorial elections produced a group of moderate to progressive governors reminiscent of the "Class of

'70." Bob Graham in Florida, Bill Clinton in Arkansas, Dick Riley in South Carolina, Lamar Alexander in Tennessee, Fob James in Alabama, and George Nigh in Oklahoma, joined by William Winter in Mississippi and John Y. Brown in Kentucky in 1979, and Mark White of Texas in 1982, continued to symbolize a new Southern political leadership.

Governor James's inaugural address, delivered from the same location where both Jefferson Davis and George Wallace had thrown down the gauntlet, demonstrated the clever blending of the new vision with the Southern heritage and sounded strangely like a white version of King's "I Have a Dream" oration. "I believe," he said, "if Robert E. Lee and Martin Luther King, Jr., were here today, their cry to us—their prayer to God—would call for 'The Politics of Unselfishness'—a people together—determined to climb the highest plateau to greatness."

Arkansas' Bill Clinton had an impact on the image of his home state and the image of the South that seemed representative of the emerging new leadership. Arkansas' image, noted a reporter for *The New York Times*, "outside the state—when it had an image at all—was of Daisy Mae, Dogpatch, and those exuberant good old boys who gathered on weekends for Razorback football games, calling the hogs and wearing plastic pigs on their heads," but the successes of Clinton and other young political leaders in Arkansas, said a reporter for the *Minneapolis Tribune*, "threatened to push the New South image to extremes and change the prevailing perception of the state."[10]

The changes in Southern leadership—the images they presented to and projected for their region—had an impact on the South which was even greater than on the national press, and these governors were potent symbols in the new mythology. Just as Thurmond, Eastland, Barnett, Faubus, and Wallace had controlled and perpetuated the images of the old vision, the new political elite became contemporary heroes in the emerging mythology. Eschewing the politics of race baiting, white supremacy, and massive resistance to change, they became symbols of confirmation in the mythic vision of equality and provided consensual validation for the reality sanctioned by the new myth.

Popular Forces

The Ku Klux Klan, the White Citizens' Councils, the Defenders of State Sovereignty and Individual Liberties, the State's Rights Council of Georgia, the Patriots of North Carolina, Inc., the North Carolina Defenders of States' Rights, the National States' Rights Party, and White Americans, Inc., which had been the "popular forces" of Southern mythology in the late 1950s and early 1960s, seemed, after the events of 1964–1965, to be groping "piteously toward a past that had now become yet another lost cause."[11] In their stead, a number of groups with interracial membership began to prosper and proselytize for a different cultural myth of the South, gaining new members throughout the region.

Although the success of Southern groups advocating racial equality was new, the tradition was not. The Commission on Interracial Cooperation, organized and directed by Will Alexander in 1919, and the Southern Conference for Human Welfare, organized in 1938 and first chaired by Frank Graham, had both attempted to deal with Southern problems through an interracial perspective. In 1944, the Southern Regional Council, successor to the Commission on Interracial Cooperation, was organized under the direction of Howard W. Odum. During its history, the Council has published the *Southern Frontier* (1944–1946), *New South* (1946–1974), *South Today* (1970–1974), *Southern Voices* (1974–1975), and *Southern Changes* (1978 to the present). Each periodical has been a medium for information, exchange, and advocacy which has reflected the changing goals and direction of the Council, and each has been effective in articulating the myth for the intelligentsia and in providing arguments and ideas for motivating the existing membership of true believers; however, as a means of widely disseminating the vision or converting the unsuspecting, only *Southern Voices* (which folded within a year) can be said to have had much popular appeal. Among its members, a very committed group of Southern activists, the Southern Regional Council has been an indispensable support group and an indigenous source of criticism of Southern institutions. Less accommodating and less concerned with social subtlety than some other organizations, as early as 1951 it had issued a policy statement declaring that "the South of the Future, toward which our efforts are directed, is a South freed from the stultifying inheritance from the past."[12]

Another group, formed by hopeful Southerners just in time to assist in the construction and development of the new mythology, was the L. Q. C. Lamar Society. An association of middle- and upper-middle-class professionals—journalists, college professors, attorneys, politicians, and businessmen—it was organized in 1969 to share information and ideas and to provide "a new definition of the South, by a new generation of Southerners, just as deeply devoted to their region as the Agrarians but more democratic and realistic."[13]

The Lamar Society held a number of conferences in the early 1970s which received considerable coverage and interpretation in the regional editorial pages, issued the *Southern Journal* to circulate the papers and ideas of its members for several years, and published a delightful volume of essays in 1972 entitled *You Can't Eat Magnolias.* The Southern Growth Policies Board, an organization formed by interstate compact among the Southern states and dedicated to sharing data and coordinating regional growth strategies, was formed as a result of the Lamar Society's vision and leadership. This offspring group assumed many of the functions formerly envisioned by the parent organization, so in the mid-1970s, the

Lamar Society relocated its office from Chapel Hill to Washington, D.C., and began to focus upon and assist with desegregation of school systems across the nation.

Another organization of progressive Southerners developing and participating in the mythic vision of the contemporary South is the Institute for Southern Studies, founded in 1970 with offices originally in Atlanta and Chapel Hill. Its active staff described itself as "young, black and white, men and women who were active participants in the struggles of the sixties." Their perceived mission was stated in the first issue of their publication, *Southern Exposure*, which appeared in 1973. "With an appreciation for regional/national interrelations, we seek to offer imaginative strategies for social change. Our goal is to provide ideas, analyses, facts, and programs for groups and individuals building the South of the Seventies and beyond, to translate information into action for progressive change."[14]

The general audience of *Southern Exposure* is younger and more directly experienced in social action than that formerly served by the more academic Lamar Society and its *Southern Journal*. Each issue of *Southern Exposure* is devoted to a particular topic—for example, folk art, energy, women, sports, music, media, politics, labor, justice, or education—which is treated from a particularly Southern perspective. The publication has been quite direct in revealing its hopes of redefining the past and promoting new images of the South. Julian Bond, in a letter to prospective subscribers, said, "If you refuse to accept the tired myths and stereotypes which characterize the outsiders' view of our region, the superficial reporting, continual misinterpretation and plain ignorance, then I'd like to invite you to join the readership of *Southern Exposure*. I believe it will both inform and inspire you, just as it has helped other Southerners rediscover their roots in a populist tradition fed on an intermixture of culture and politics, challenge and hope."[15]

The Institute also sponsors a syndicated column, "Facing South," which appears weekly in more than eighty newspapers throughout the region. Submitted by freelance writers and journalists from the South, the column "aims to dispel some of the myths and stereotypes" by letting people "tell their own version of life in this often misunderstood region."[16] These features on senior citizens, craftsmen, activists, and other contemporary folk heroes are always human in focus and usually upbeat in tone, and they offer hopeful symbols of the contemporary South to the readership of community-oriented weekly newspapers, reaching an audience often overlooked by other Southern organizations.

The Southern Regional Council, the L. Q. C. Lamar Society, and the Institute for Southern Studies have been important popular forces—voluntary organizations dedicated to a new and different vision of the South, offering a catalytic meeting ground for participants and the media forum for expanding their symbols and dreams. In stark contrast with the Ku Klux Klan and the Citizen's Councils of the old vision, these groups are dedicated to quite different mythic interpretations of the Southern past and future.

Less traditional groups have also utilized the more traditional media for similar purposes and with equal effect. John O'Neal, founder of the Free Southern Theatre, described that alternative scene quite well and with considerable rhetorical insight. "There was drama and poetry, exceptional photography and an abundance of good graphic design work," he said. "Tall-tale telling was raised to new heights. . . . This highly developed storytelling tradition in the South serves as the foundation for the remarkable improvisational art of the preacher. . . . And there was music! Organized and spontaneous, professional and traditional. People's music. The people gave form to emotions too deeply felt for speaking by making songs." Bernice Reagon, expressing the mythic power of music, said, "I sang and heard freedom songs and saw them pull together sections of the black community at times when other means of communication were ineffective. It was the first time I knew the power of song to be an instrument for the articulation of our community concerns."[17]

Mythic Events and Sacred Ground

Another key to understanding the rhetorical nature of cultural mythology is the analysis of the important events and special places described in the narrative of the vision. Reciting the history of a society, after reflection upon and redefinition of the past, serves as the dramatic equivalent of the creation myths found in various cultures, and an examination of the major dramatic events and locations in a cultural myth should prove instructive in understanding the motives, values, and behavior which are considered important and appropriate by a group or a society. Just as Plymouth Rock, Independence Hall, and Bunker Hill are sacred places or "sacred ground" representing significant events in the American mythology of liberty, just as the myth of the Lost Cause enshrined Appomattox Courthouse, Virginia, and just as George Wallace rallied the forces of segregation from the Cradle of the Confederacy in Montgomery, the myth of the contemporary South is anchored by symbolic events in its history which help to define its existence and illuminate its values.

In the new mythic vision, no event holds more importance than the decision of the United States Supreme Court in *Brown v. Board of Education* issued on May 17, 1954. It has achieved a status comparable to the "creation myth" found in other societies and religions throughout the world. Even a passing reference, a single phrase, mentioning *Brown* invokes the force of the contemporary mythology. As Pat Watters observed on the twentieth anniversary of the decision, "All Southern time must be measured before and after that date because it so changed history, the fabric of life and the very feel of the institutions of government."[18]

One indicator of *Brown*'s essential role in the contemporary mythology is the regularity of rhetorical re-examination on the dates
of its anniversary. In 1964, Benjamin Muse termed it "a pronounce-
ment second in importance only to President Lincoln's Emancipation Proclamation," and in 1974, the United States Commission on
Civil Rights issued a report entitled *Twenty Years after Brown: The
Shadows of the Past.* Interviewed for the publication, plaintiff Linda
Brown Smith said, "I think the decision was the whole turning
point for black America. From this single decision to open schools
to blacks, this was the key to the beginning of freedom." On the
twenty-fifth anniversary, *Southern Exposure* devoted an entire issue to the history and progress of public school integration in the
South, and President Carter held a commemorative ceremony at
the White House.

The *Brown* decision, in the vocabulary of the vision, symbolizes
a devotion to law and a beginning for a more just society in the
South. Its importance was recognized almost immediately, and its
message spread quickly among the population through the expanded media environment of the period. Tom Gilmore, a participant in and product of the changes brought by *Brown*, said of its
impact in his Alabama homeland, "For the first time, folks in Greene
County, watching television and listening to the radio, became
aware of what was going on in the world around them, especially
in terms of education and the *Brown v. Board of Education* case."[19]

Whereas the Southern political leadership of the South in 1956
had responded to the *Brown* decision by promulgating a "Declaration of Constitutional Principles" and by rallying to preserve the
mythic order for the "Southern way of life" sanctioned by their
Manifesto, Southern political leaders of the 1970s rejected that response and reinterpreted the event. Governor Reubin Askew, in accepting the chairmanship of the Southern Growth Policies Board
in 1975, offered his colleagues a lesson in the new history. "The
Southern Manifesto," he said, "is remembered by most of us today

in the South, when it is remembered at all, with sorrow and regret. It was a covenant with fear and futility, a rejection of both reason and reality."

The exemplary conduct endorsed by the new myth was not that of the nineteen senators and eighty-one congressmen who signed the Manifesto, but, reversing the interpretation of the past, it venerated those who had formerly been vilified. Askew noted that "only a few of those who were asked to sign the document had the courage to refuse. Lyndon Johnson of Texas was one. Sam Rayburn of Texas was another. Albert Gore and Estes Kefauver of Tennessee refused to sign. . . . And there were others, too. But not many." During the emotion of the time, Askew continued, these men "were shunned and scorned by their friends and neighbors. They were branded as traitors to all that they loved. They were told that they had betrayed the future of their states and of the South. And yet . . . they refused to allow the South to stand united behind a Manifesto that manifested all that was bad in the South and ignored or concealed all that was good."

Askew then skillfully wove these themes into the structure of the new myth as he worked to discredit the old vision. "Those who refused to sign the Southern Manifesto," he said, "did not betray the future of the South. They helped make that future possible. By resisting the rhetoric of racism, they helped us to discover, as Southerners, that we are all one people." [20]

Another historic battleground in the mythic history of the vision, a result of *Brown* in practice, was Little Rock Central High School in 1957. The Little Rock school board, moving "with all deliberate speed" (a phrase ironically lifted from Sir Walter Scott), planned to enroll nine black students in all-white Central High School. Orval Faubus, playing to the stands, mobilized the Arkansas National Guard to prevent integration of the school; President Eisenhower nationalized the Guard and sent the 101st Airborne to enforce the order of the federal courts and assure the safety of the students. At the time of the incident, Gloster Current of the NAACP said, "Five years from now, it may well be said that the entire situation was providential and segregation in the south was dealt its gravest blow . . . when Governor Faubus used troops . . . to bar the admission of nine Negro students into Central High School."[21] Such a prediction now seems to have been prophetic, for while the media coverage of the crisis made Faubus a hero to the forces of reaction, it also offered the nation television coverage of mob hysteria and a society without reason. The scene of white crowds taunting a sixteen-year-old girl trying to go to school was sent around the world by television networks and wire services. "Little Rock" soon came to hold the same meaning as "South Africa" in the public mind.

Like *Brown*, the anniversary observances of the confrontation at Little Rock Central High School reinforce its importance in the mythology. In 1975, Daisy Bates was honored by Legislative Resolution, a symbol of the extent of change since she was investigated by the same body for her role, as president of the Arkansas chapter of the NAACP, in supporting the "Little Rock Nine." That same year, Governor David Pryor, who had defeated Orval Faubus in the 1974 primary, addressed the student body at Central High and observed, "We learn from history that the nature of man is to adapt, that the heart of man *can change*." On the twentieth anniversary of the enrollment of Ernest Green, the first black graduate of Central in 1958, newspaper articles reflected on the irony of the present: Ernest Green had just been appointed Assistant Secretary of Labor by President Carter, and Orval Faubus was working as a bank teller in his home town. Green, however, said that "the greatest twist of fate" was that the director of state employment development and the principal at Central were also black. In 1982, on the twenty-fifth anniversary of the crisis, Central High School was designated as a National Historic Landmark.[22]

There were other heroes of Little Rock as well. L. C. Bates, colleague and husband of Daisy Bates, whose newspaper, the *Arkansas State Press*, had been forced out of existence following courageous pro-integration editorials, was sought out by reporters and oral historians who wished to document his role in the crisis. Brooks Hays, the Congressman who had been defeated by a segregationist member of the Little Rock School Board, was honored and remembered for his role in mediation between Faubus and Eisenhower. The *Arkansas Gazette*, which had received two Pulitzer Prizes for its editorials and received an economic boycott by advertisers for its trouble, remains the largest and most progressive newspaper in the state.

Similar mythic significance has been bestowed on the Montgomery Bus Boycott of 1955, the New Orleans public school integration battle of 1960, the integration of the Woolworth lunch counters at Greensboro in 1960, the confrontations at the University of Georgia, Ole Miss, and the University of Alabama during 1961–1963, the Birmingham confrontation with Bull Connor in 1963, the enactment of the Civil Rights Act of 1964, the Mississippi Freedom Summer of 1964, the Selma-to-Montgomery March of 1965, and passage of the Voting Rights Act of 1965.

One of the most tragic and rhetorically powerful scenes of violence occurred in Birmingham in 1963, and both the South and the nation saw Police Commissioner Eugene "Bull" Connor turn fire hoses and police dogs against black demonstrators supporting court-ordered desegregation of Birmingham public schools. At that time, the guardians of the old myth prevailed in Birmingham through manipulation of images, symbols, and stereotypes, but the immediate and long-range impact of the televised violence was to reveal that the mythology of the Old South was dying. Exposed by the new media, the mythic dysfunction was becoming more and more apparent to more and more Southerners. By 1976, blacks constituted 40 percent of the population and 40 percent of the registered voters in Birmingham, holding 3 of 9 seats on the city council. An observer for *Time* magazine surveyed the racial situation and said, "Bull Connor has since died—and so has Birmingham's bitterness. It is significant in the contemporary South that Alabama's largest city has become a model of Southern race relations."[23] Today, Birmingham also has a black mayor.

Perhaps the best planned and most symbolic confrontation battleground was the Selma March of 1965. Martin Luther King, Jr., already a hero of the movement, chose his symbols and his stage quite well. Selma, the Dallas County seat, was the epitome of white repression and resistance to black voter registration; the goal was to reach the steps of the state capitol building where Jefferson Davis had taken the oath of office as President of the Confederate States of America. What happened between these points is now history, and on the tenth anniversary of the march one reporter said, "The event and the place—Selma—have come to symbolize a moment in history when an old order fell and the echoes of the new have leaped the bounds of Dixie and sounded throughout the nation." John Lewis, a veteran of the Selma march and head of the Southern Regional Council's Voter Education Project, organized the "1975 Selma Commemorative March" in which 5,000 people traced the steps of the first journey and held a press conference at Edmund Pettus bridge, scene of a brutal attack by law enforcement officers. This time, as they praised those who made that walk a decade earlier and recounted the effects of the Voting Rights Act which resulted from it, the Alabama Highway Patrol provided an escort.[24]

King had known exactly what he was doing when he planned the original march in 1965. Dallas County, Alabama, had a population that was 57.8 percent black. On March 18, 1965, there were 9,887 registered voters in Dallas County: 9,542 were white, and 335 were black. Those were figures which a television audience could easily understand. In addition, the sheriff of Dallas County was James Gardner Clark, Jr., whose physique has been memorialized in Dodge commercials and numerous "B" movies about Southern justice. King had hoped to generate public support for passage of a voting rights act to remedy the situation; Clark's tactics, and those of George Wallace's Alabama Highway Patrol, gave the nation a public television drama of confrontation and violence like nothing it had ever seen on television news. President Johnson, acknowledging his roots in Southern soil, called for legislation, and Congress responded with the Voting Rights Act of 1965. Scholars have since recognized the value of Selma as a planned media event, and it has become one of the strongest symbols in the contemporary mythology.[25] When a Southerner says he was with King at Selma, it is the mythic equivalent of having been with Washington at Valley Forge. Like *"Brown"* and "Little Rock," "Selma" evokes the entire catechism of the contemporary myth with no need for further elaboration. At Selma, as in other battles of the past, the immediate victims became the later heroes.

Symbolic Redemption

The final symbolic event in the mythology of the contemporary South was the election of Jimmy Carter in 1976. For participating Southerners, the nomination, election, and inauguration of Jimmy Carter signified political redemption of the region and national confirmation of the reality of the myth. It meant that H. L. Mencken had been wrong, that Jeeter Lester and Flem Snopes were dead, and that the national media would no longer equate Southern politics with Orval Faubus, Lester Maddox, and George Wallace. When Carter was nominated, Senator Fritz Hollings of South Carolina sighed, "Now we can rejoin the Union," and sociologist John Shelton Reed predicted, "If Carter is elected the Southern sense of being picked on, of being persecuted will fade." The event, however, also had meaning for others besides the politicians and sociologists. When Jimmy Carter accepted his party's nomination, said

Larry L. King, "Ol' Southern boys around the world . . . lurched to their collective feet, spilling right smart amounts of bourbon and branch water over the rims of their gold goblets or jelly glasses, and with wet eyes huskily proclaimed: 'We ain't *trash* no more.'"[26]

Not every Southerner, not even every Southerner participating in the vision, was enthusiastic about Carter's candidacy. Julian Bond resisted throughout; Reg Murphy, former editor of the *Atlanta Constitution*, and Bob Hall, editor of *Southern Exposure* called him a fraud; and even Larry King knew that many of those ole boys who were whooping it up for Carter in 1976 would cool before 1980; however, few failed to grasp the symbolism of his election and the redemptive impact it had on the self-perception of the mind of the South.[27] Carter, himself, had been aware that the nation's perception of the South as "Redneck Haven" created problems for his candidacy. In a speech at Emory University while he was Governor of Georgia, he said, "One of the greatest afflictions of the South in the past . . . is that . . . politicians have underestimated the Southern people. This has caused the lack of . . . accurate analysis of the quality of the South . . . by the rest of the world." *Time* recognized that Carter was consciously working to correct that image and understood that "one of the most important causes that he identifies his candidacy with is the final, unqualified re-entry of the South into the Union."[28]

With the exception of Lyndon Johnson, active Southern presidential candidacies in the last generation had been represented by Strom Thurmond and George Wallace, spokesmen for racism and reaction, and the image of national leadership in Congress had been typified by the Southern Manifesto and civil rights filibusters. Voters outside the South, who had heard nothing about Southern politics since the head-knocking at Edmund Pettus Bridge, were skeptical of Carter primarily because of his suspect heritage and its implied position on racial issues.[29]

Hodding Carter, III, had offered himself as a candidate for Vice

President four years earlier. A campaign brochure discussed his credentials and activities on behalf of the Southern Regional Council, the Voter Education Project, and the American Civil Liberties Union, and said, "Hodding Carter tackled the social upheaval of the 1960s in the South and was on the cutting edge as the old customs and inequities of life there were pared away."[30] Both Terry Sanford and Lloyd Bentsen made attempts at presidential candidacy in 1972, but none of these efforts captured the nation's attention or imagination as they were upstaged by the familiarity of George Wallace's rhetoric and the drama of his near assassination.

The widespread support which Carter's candidacy received from Southern black leaders such as Andrew Young and Southern white progressives such as Hodding Carter seemed to give more credibility to his campaign, and it signaled a victory for the new vision. Within the South, Carter's appointments and nominations of Young, Hodding Carter, Pat Derian, Reubin Askew, John West, John Lewis, Frank Johnson, Pug Ravenel, Ernest Green, Patricia Harris, Ray Marshall, Michael Cody, and numerous black federal judges added credence to the symbols of change and provided instructive models for contemporary Southerners.

With Carter's victory, however, much of the drive and enthusiasm for change and progress may have been diluted. Those battling for the new mythology had been sustained by successive victories in changing reality, but the election of a nonracist Southern President would be a hard act to follow, and it would diminish the importance of minor victories. Walker Percy, with a bit of disappointment, said, "Now the South appears to have won after all, and both the Southern writer and politician are somewhat at a loss." Brandt Ayres, who had been among the early leaders of the L. Q. C. Lamar Society, said Southerners had been like Sisyphus, fighting for years to push the rock of ignorance, poverty, and prejudice up the hill, but Carter's election put Sisyphus out of work.

Now, he complained, "Sisyphus got a job in real estate, moved to the suburbs, and voted Republican."[31]

Across the South, other ironies were being reflected in the changing rhetoric of the region. In 1978, Strom Thurmond, who had fought and voted against the Voting Rights Act in 1965, 1970, and 1975, and who as late as 1975 had expressed his opposition to the measure as "clearly unconstitutional," was actively and openly soliciting the votes of black citizens who could now exercise their franchise because of the legislation. In 1982, Thurmond voted for extension of the Voting Rights Act, then later supported legislation declaring a national holiday on Martin Luther King's birthday. Even George Wallace, who fifteen years earlier had intoned "Segregation Forever," now realized that "segregation is over and it's better that it's over . . . and it's not coming back." Sounding almost like a charter member of the Lamar Society, he said, "The things the federal government forced upon us, such as doing away with segregated eating places and riding in buses and so forth, turned out for the best. We lost those battles, and we adjusted and went ahead. We are now looking ahead instead of behind."[32] In 1982, Wallace returned to the original Populist roots and rhetoric of his presegregationist days and was elected governor with considerable support from black voters.

While in reality Southern society is far from being totally integrated, there have been positive and dramatic changes. The remarks of Strom Thurmond and George Wallace also indicate that both the rhetoric and the cultural myths have changed dramatically. Along with these changes in reality and the expression of it, there also has been a change in the prevailing defensive rhetorical strategy which dominated the past. The relationship between the old social order of the South and its stridently defensive reaction to change was acknowledged by Garvin Davenport, who suggested, "The South's task in this century has not been merely to rationalize its treatment of the Negro to an indignant nation but to explain in relevant terms to itself its own treatment at the hands of history. When success at this task has been attained, the old defensiveness will no longer be necessary."

There is now ample evidence that the defensive rhetorical posture may be on the wane with the old mythology. "Southerners," said Jimmy Carter in 1971, "now have realized that the solution of our problems is our own, and that we can no longer berate the Federal government, the Supreme Court, or any other 'outside group' for our own problems." It was then, said Brandt Ayers, that he knew the old myth and the Old South were dead. "No longer would Southerners have to feel defensive because they bore the mark of an historic sin. No longer would the South have to starve its talent and imagination by feeding the retarding myths of the past." Charlie Daniels, indicating that the new myth had recruited believers beyond the circle of Southern professionals and professional Southerners in the Lamar Society, confided to a reporter, "Lots of folks in my generation who grew up in the South have a kind of inferiority complex that we're just gettin' out of. I don't feel I have to prove anything to anybody anymore."[33]

Carter's election had confirmed what Southerners had been trying to tell themselves and wanting to believe for the past ten years. David Mathews, former President of the University of Alabama and Ford's Secretary of Health, Education, and Welfare, suggested to the members of the Southern Growth Policies Board that the region could now move forward with a positive agenda for change and serve as a vehicle for national leadership. Carter's election in 1976, he said, was proof that the South had rejoined the American mainstream and that the time had come for the region to abandon the "underdog strategy" and defensive posturing which had controlled the rhetoric of the past.[34] Loosely translated, that's Chamber of Commerce talk for "we ain't trash no more!"

Not only has the South turned away from the desperate defensiveness which it had long substituted for explanation and apology on the issue of racial equality, it now openly discusses the issue and proudly compares its progress toward integration with that of the rest of the nation. In the new mythology, the South's success toward achieving an integrated society has surpassed the rest of the nation, and it appears to be exhibiting a certain smug satisfaction with the result. In 1972, Reubin Askew stated the theme rather politely:

> For many years now, the rest of the nation has been saying to the South that it is morally wrong to deprive any citizen of an equal opportunity in life because of his color. I think most of us have come to agree with that. But now the time has come for the rest of the nation to live up to its own stated principles. Only now are the other regions themselves beginning to feel the effects of the movement to eliminate segregation.
>
> I say the rest of the nation should not abandon its principles when the going gets tough. I do not say this to be vindictive, I say it to be fair. The rest of the nation has sought to bring justice to the South by mandate and court order. Now perhaps it is time for the South to teach the same thing to other regions in a more effective way—by example.[35]

The essence of Askew's position has been repeated by gracious newspaper editors and timid scholars throughout the region during the last decade. The same thought has been expressed from the bar of every beer joint in Dixie by less polished orators who have only recently joined the ranks of those bragging about successful integration yet who now share fully in the vision. Larry L. King seems to have captured the spirit of their version:

> Y'all damnyankee peckerwoods drive on one-way streets in making your judgements, and we're about half tired of it. When *we* go against the grain, then the sky should fall on us and the survivors should be skinned alive or cut up for fish bait. When *you* act equally asinine, then it seems like the cat gets your tongues and there's a conspiracy to look away from what's mean and small and tacky in you. Do you good Boston folk—who once sold slaves on Boston Common—wanna step over here in the pea patch and talk to me about Louise Day Hicks and the violence heaped on your kids

while they were being bussed to school? Naw, I expect you'd rather talk about George Wallace or busing violence in South Carolina a decade ago. Come over here and tell me about Bull Connor's police dogs and fire hoses in Birmingham, so I'll have a chance to drop it on you about the many race riots of Detroit City. The sorry fact is that we've all been white racists, and you deserve as much of the tarnished trophy as the sons of Dixie.[36]

Turning Clio on her head, "Boston" has become another symbol in the emerging mythology. Once the headquarters of William Lloyd Garrison and the abolitionists' attack on the South, a hideout for the pointy-headed intellectuals who angered George Wallace and intimidated Lyndon Johnson, the town where Martin Luther King, Jr., studied the works of Reinhold Niebuhr, the home of Reverend James J. Reeb, who marched with King and was killed at Selma, the former racial conscience of the nation, Boston recently provided an example of hatred, bigotry, and violence and provided a benchmark to show the South how far it had come and how much it could teach the nation. From Vance Packard to Harry Ashmore, from Frank Johnson, a federal judge who should know, to David Hawkins, antediluvian editor of the *Arkansas Democrat*, from John Egerton to Larry L. King, "Boston" became a common theme in the new mythology.[37]

In addition to "Boston," the new mythology was buttressed by the theme of "reverse migration." During the first seven decades of this century, disenfranchised at the ballot box, blacks voted with their feet and went north in search of physical safety and economic security. It was, in fact, a referendum on Southern society. In the late 1960s and early 1970s, the new myth began to include the theme that the South had solved its problems and now offered blacks a piece of the action and a piece of the vision. If blacks were now moving to the South rather than out of the region, Southern mythmakers had yet another symbol of confirmation for the changes in society.

In 1980, the U.S. Bureau of Census documented what the mythmakers had dramatized: the decade of the seventies was, for the first time since the end of the slave trade, one of positive net in-migration by blacks to the South. It was another referendum on Southern society, and the new theme was one confirmed by both blacks and whites. Taylor Wilson, a black Chicago electrician re-turning to the South, said, "I'm moving South for the same reasons my father came here from Mississippi. He was looking for a better way of life." The same theme was echoed by Jack White, a black correspondent in the Atlanta bureau of *Time*, who observed, "The North is still battling things that have already been accomplished in the South. The South's my home, and I would like to raise my children there."[38]

The mythic vision of equality and a biracial egalitarian South slowly emerged from the chaos of the late 1960s and matured dur-ing the 1970s. For the first time in one hundred fifty years, the South had produced a new myth of its own identity which not only refused to recycle but completely rejected the tenets of the old my-thology. Beginning with *Brown* in 1954 and moving through events to the Voting Rights Act of 1965, it became apparent that the old vision of white supremacy could no longer encompass the realities of the contemporary South. "The civil rights movement itself was a great destroyer of the myths of white supremacy, of Southern in-transigence, of other like dread and ugly distortions," said Leslie Dunbar. "It spoke of love and integration and nonviolence and we have an obligation not to give up that vision, not to give it up cheaply, not to give it up at all. We shall need that vision always close at hand as we finish out this twentieth century."[39]

Other participants, too, seemed to be conscious that they were forging a new mythology for the region, one which could be helpful in structuring a better future. Steve Suitts, generally adverse to boosterism and guarded in his assessment of racial progress in the South, recognized the power of mythology. In obvious reference to those who would have denied the power of the new reality to destroy the old mythology, he said, "We should celebrate the vast changes which have come into Southern folkways and stateways." Then, to redefine the past and validate the recent changes, he suggested, "By recollection of the heroes and aspirations of our past we can be reminded of what forces and visions can charter our future."[40]

The first Report of the Commission on the Future of the South, formulated in 1974 and published in 1975, presented a perspective on the future that reflected the optimistic vision of the early proponents of the contemporary New South movement. "Unlike the manifesto of the fifties," said Reubin Askew, "it addresses the real needs of the people. Unlike the manifesto of the fifties, it is a forward-looking document, a document based on the dictates of humanity and reality, and not on the deceptions and distortions of the darkest days in our past." Askew, as always, was careful to draw positive lessons from the past while rejecting the traditional interpretations of the old mythology. "We must build on the best in our past and not on the worst," he said. "There must be no more lost causes for the South. There must be no more sad and wasteful diversions of other days. We need instead an abiding belief in the ability of Southerners . . . all Southerners . . . to rise to the opportunity and the challenge that our future presents."[41]

Likewise, John Lewis, a veteran of the movement and usually a political realist, offered an optimistic view of the future of the South. "There is much evidence that we are building a New South," he said. "It is a very positive example for the rest of the nation that we are making political progress. Here in the South, where racial divisions were once the deepest, I can see the day breaking when this will be considered a region of hope." Lewis' comments, from one who had fought for more than an over-toasted club sandwich at a Nashville lunch counter and had his skull fractured by a policeman's club at Selma, demonstrate that the cultural myth of the contemporary South has bridged the old racial barriers and that both blacks and whites are shaping a new mythology in the region. Terry Sanford, whose experiences of the past are quite different from those of John Lewis, views the contemporary South in equally optimistic terms. "Witness the willingness of people of all classes to seek as well as accept dramatic social change," he said. "This is not the old myth resurrected. It is the fresh wind that should begin to blow across the nation."[42]

In 1963, Martin Luther King, Jr., had shared his vision of the day when, in the words of an old spiritual, blacks and whites would join hands and declare themselves "Free, at last." A decade later, a popular country song echoed that same creed from truck stops and honky-tonks across the South, as another group of Southerners (who had not been at the Lincoln Memorial to hear King's speech) sang a new refrain along with Tanya Tucker, "I believe the South is gonna rise again."[43]

FIVE The Theme of Distinctiveness

Time and television, the two great cultural cuisinarts, have done little . . .
to erode the myth of Southern difference, which for Northerners and Southerners alike always has exceeded even the *facts* of difference.
—Sharon McKern, *Redneck Mothers, Good Ol' Girls, and Other Southern Belles*

Southerners, at least as long ago as the beginning of the nineteenth
century, when comparisons were first made between the Virginia
cavalier and the New England Puritan, seem to have felt that the
South was somehow distinctive, and they have been just as ready
to admit that distinctiveness as others outside the region. During
the last fifty years, however, many of the traditional symbols of difference and distinctiveness have vanished from the social and cultural landscape, yielding to court decisions, modern technology,
and what C. Vann Woodward termed the "Bulldozer Revolution."

The Southerner may not have been very happy about many of those old
monuments of regional distinctiveness that are now disappearing. He
may, in fact, have deplored the existence of some—the one-horse farmer,
one crop agriculture, one party politics, the sharecropper, the poll tax, the
white primary, the Jim Crow car, the lynching bee. But until the day before
yesterday there they stood, indisputable proof that the South was different. Now that they are vanished or on their way toward vanishing, we are
suddenly aware of the vacant place they have left in the landscape and our

habit of depending upon them in the final resort as landmarks of regional identification.[1]

In view of the vast changes in communication, transportation, urbanization, and industrialization, many have proclaimed or predicted the end of the South—both as a distinct region and as a state of mind. The major social commentary in this vein, and a very rhetorical document as well, is John Egerton's *The Americanization of Dixie: The Southernization of America* which bemoaned the homogenization of the nation's cultural diversity. In 1979, five years after publication of his book, Egerton again assessed the state of affairs and told the Conference on Rhetoric of the Contemporary South, "I'm afraid the South has had it." Perhaps not coincidentally, that was also the last of six consecutive conferences on the topic.

Egerton's conclusion, that there is now very little to distinguish between the South and other sections of the country, is shared by polemicists, politicians, and poets. An editorial in the Southern Regional Council's *Southern Changes* suggested that "the South as a marked region is losing currency." Senator Dale Bumpers, in speeches from Maine to Mississippi, said that "sectionalism as we have known it is dying. . . . After a lot of false starts a truly new South is finally emerging, and in many respects, it looks a lot like the old North. . . . The man who walks the streets of New York one day and the streets of Atlanta the next will find only a difference in degree—not a difference in kind. . . . The South as a state of mind, is expiring, and everybody is too busy building skyscrapers and making money to pay much attention." Even James Dickey, poet laureate of the South, held little hope for the future of regional distinctiveness. He told one interviewer that "the increased industrialization and modernization of the South are things that will make the South more like the rest of the country. All those differences—the folkways and mores that distinguish the South—are eventually going to die out."[2]

Despite these prognostications of the South's demise, which seem somewhat like the exaggerations of Mark Twain's death, George Tindall wryly remarked, "The Vanishing South, it turns out, has staged one of the most prolonged disappearing acts since the decline and fall of the Roman Empire." Carl N. Degler agreed that "neither in the realm of social fact nor in the realm of psychological identity has the South ceased to be distinctive, despite the changes of the twentieth century." Harry Ashmore, acknowledging the many recent changes in Southern society, also concluded that "Southerners can still think of themselves, and are thought of by others, as unique—somehow separate and distinct from the general run of Americans."[3]

John Shelton Reed, after plowing through volumes of census data, stacks of computer printouts, and decades of public opinion polls, confirmed the continuing existence of regional stereotypes and found that "Southerners seem more likely than other Americans to think of their region, their states, and their local communities, as *theirs*, and as distinct from and preferable to other regions, states, and localities." That feeling was so pervasive that Charles P. Roland, reviewing and refuting the arguments for the vanishing South, concluded that "the region's unique combination of political, religious, cultural, ethnic, and social traits, reinforced as they are by geography and history, myth and folklore, and convention and inertia, will for a good while keep it distinctive."[4]

Henry Grady had announced the death of the South as he advocated its reunion in the 1880s, and the Agrarians mourned its passing in the 1930s; the debate continues today. One factor that has prevented the resolution of the question is that one view is empirical while the other is emotional. The very belief among Southerners that the South is different has transcended the quantification by the Southern Growth Policies Board; it has, itself, become a rhetorical theme within the mythology of the contemporary South. Aware of Francis Butler Simkins' admonition not to confuse "facts" and "truth," Roland recognized that "this state of mind, the South's perception of itself and the nation's perception of the South, has always been an important element in the actual distinctiveness of the region." Moreover, he said, "the ultimate distinctiveness of the South may lie, not in empirical dissimilarities from other regions, but in its unique mythology: those images of the region that give philosophical meaning to the ordinary facts of life."[5] Indeed, within the rhetoric of the contemporary South, the theme of distinctiveness is quite prominent, and it differs in subtle yet important ways from the old myth; therefore, an examination of the symbols and rituals present in this new mythic vision of distinctiveness could offer an unusual and insightful understanding of the cultural mythology of the contemporary South.

Regional Images and Rhetorical Redefinition

In order to preserve the image of distinctiveness and express regional values, both the South and the nation as a whole have relied upon communication of certain stereotypes which simplify perception and distill experiences, operating in much the same manner that heroic characters in a mythic drama are symbolic of desirable cultural traits and values. The planter, the belle, the Confederate veteran, Sambo, the yeoman farmer, the hookworm-infested clay-eaters, and other mythic figures have been used to communicate the essence of certain perceptions and beliefs about Southern society and to establish the distinctive features of the culture. Through the communication of stereotypes, the nation has come to "understand" the South and Southerners.

In an earlier time, the images of the South and the representative Southerner were communicated through novels of Southern writers ranging from John Pendleton Kennedy and William Gilmore Simms to Joel Chandler Harris and Thomas Nelson Page to Erskine Caldwell and William Faulkner. With the explosion in communication technology, the images have become more complex, and they have often been consciously and rhetorically manipulated to achieve certain purposes. The editors of *Southern Exposure*, themselves exceptionally adroit at creative imagery, complained, "Throughout the country, and even in this region, people view the South through myth and stereotype. It's not surprising. If they turn to newspapers, to television and radio, to popular films and magazines, to most history books and folklore, they encounter these distortions." Their objection was not so much to the practice of image communication as it was to the effect that the old stereotypes were having upon the South. "As long as we allow our past and present to be defined by debilitating stereotypes and comparisons, then we likewise restrict our future. We limit our imagination and ask the wrong questions."[6]

Certainly, the same social changes that generated the new mythic vision of equality were also having an effect upon other themes within the mythology. The aristocratic planter and belle of the old myth were of little use to contemporary Southerners, white or black, trying to find their identity and validate it through the contemporary folklore and mythology of the South in the 1970s. Just as the South was beginning to redefine itself, sifting through the existing and emerging stereotypes and themes at hand, the national media once again became fascinated by the South. Jimmy Carter's nomination and election sent feature writers to find the "real" South, a region which, for the last few years, had been generally ignored except for an occasional movie about a fat Southern sheriff or news coverage of George Wallace's frantic campaigns in 1968 and 1972. As Mike Royko observed in 1976, "Thanks to Jimmy Carter, the journalistic trend-seekers and social scientists have discovered the South. They are now going to explain the Southerner to himself and leave the ethnic in peace."[7]

Southern image-makers, however, wanted to define their own

distinctiveness. Again, *Southern Exposure*, in a pamphlet describing itself to prospective subscribers, said, "The nation, again, has discovered the South. Northern journalists are flooding south curious about our politicians and preaching, football and farming, coal mines and cuisine. They get some good stories. But they miss the South." Claiming that national publications saw only the obvious and missed "the seemingly small but tremendously significant events now taking place in the South," *Southern Exposure* said that "it takes a publication of the South to present the region as it really is . . . and as it can still become." Intent upon offering a homegrown myth, *Southern Exposure*, claimed the image merchants from the Institute for Southern Studies, "covers the South, the people of the South, the interchange of interests and energy that produces the joys and sorrows of living here. It is a sharing, of neighbors and strangers and kinfolk, of experiences and dreams of cultures."[8]

Another regional publication boasting two million readers in the South, *Southern Living*, also asserted its role in building the contemporary vision of a distinctive South. "*Southern Living* is about people," said editor Gary McCalla. "We are dedicated to the premise that there are certain regional differences in the climate, in geography, in the way Southerners live and work, in history, progress, challenges, and opportunities that make the South unique."[9] What both publications seemed to be saying was that the South was a distinctive region with unique people, and both declared their commitment to shaping and sharing the indigenous mythology of the South, a myth of distinctiveness which could be accepted by and instructive for the people of the region.

There is most certainly a strong theme of distinctiveness in the rhetorical mythology of the contemporary South, and it has been enhanced, rather than diminished, by the new media of communication. In fact, the advent of radio and television has allowed the stereotypes and images to become more real and to reach a much larger audience than had read the antebellum novels of plantation life. The South now has an *electronic folklore* with much more egalitarian icons and symbols.

Possibly because there was no real middle class in much of the old South, the old mythology internally revered the symbols of the aristocracy, and the outside image was that created by H. L. Mencken and aided by the Southern Gothic school of novelists. Now, from the middle- and upper-middle-class Southerners profiled in *Southern Living* to the middle- and lower-middle-class Southerners described in the columns of "Facing South," the region finally had a vision of distinctiveness which offered positive and attainable status for the people of the region, one with heroes, symbols, and rituals of the common folks rather than the cotton snobs and Babbitt elite who dominated the myths of the past.

Folklore scholar Andre Dundes concluded that "if one is seriously interested in studying worldview, one will need first to describe some of the folk ideas which contribute to the information of that worldview." Not unaware of the rhetorical implications of folklore, Lynnwood Montell has acknowledged, "Items of expressive folklore can be utilized as tools of persuasion. A folklore item is enacted by a performer who tries to use it to manipulate an audience in one way or another." Examining the popular culture of the region, it becomes evident that the contemporary South has actively redefined many of the old symbols of the past and developed several new media rituals to reconstruct its myth of regional distinctiveness. The symbols may not be obvious, and the complete myth has yet to be presented in a single rhetorical document. Yet, regional distinctiveness can be discovered, as Clement Eaton said, in "the nuances of civilization. These little differences, such as accent in speech, racy colloquialisms, different food, different ways of building houses, different styles of men's hats, are not to be discounted, for the sum total serves to identify regions in America."[10] Few regions, however, have worked as hard as the South to stress those differences.

Myth and Material Culture

Only during the past decade have rhetorical scholars actively joined in the critical analysis of architecture and other artifacts of material culture, but the few published studies have convincingly demonstrated the utility of such criticism in understanding the social and cultural significance of those modes of expression. During an earlier period the mainstay of public monuments in the South was a statue in the town square or on the capitol lawn dedicated to the Confederate dead who had given their lives to protect "the Southern way of life." The market for such monuments has diminished in recent years, but in 1981, reflecting a considerable shift in the public philosophy of Southern political leaders, Southern congressmen voted 109–4 in support of House Concurrent Resolution 153 to provide for a statue of Martin Luther King, Jr., in the nation's Capitol.

Perhaps the most potent and prominent architectural symbol of the old mythology was the antebellum Greek-revival mansion of the plantation. Though much less prevalent than the public has been led to believe, that symbol colored the perceptions of later generations and gave material support to the mythic vision of a "Golden Age" of white supremacy and agrarian splendor. "There has been a great deal of activity in the South in restoring and refurbishing antebellum homes," noted one critique. "In Mississippi, for example, Natchez is renowned for its handsome and well-attended homes. Numerous books have been published on the history and legends of these homes, weaving a romantic sense of past into these buildings. The mansion is a Southern stereotype, but few Southerners could afford such opulence. Natchez mansions do not represent the life most Mississippians knew." [11]

During the last decade a new restoration movement has provided material support for a different historical reality. Growing attention to and appreciation for the vernacular architectural forms such as log cabins, shotgun houses, and other native designs formerly constructed and occupied by lower- and middle-class Southerners, both black and white, have helped contemporary Southerners to gain a new perspective on their heritage, and the finished restorations are symbols of a culture quite different from that represented by the columned mansions. One architectural historian suggested that this "simple, unheralded class of buildings" occurs in such quantity that it "has to be regarded as important." Others contended that "these structures represent an important and basic element of . . . culture: the ingenuity and courage and affirmation of men who built their homes with little money, limited materials, and no formal training as architects and builders." [12]

Sounds and Symbols

Another symbol of distinction is in the use of language, both in its purpose and in its pronunciation. One contemporary Southerner has complained of the stereotypes inflicted upon Southern citizens outside the South whenever they become so bold as to open their mouths and attempt to put a subject and a verb on the same side of a period. Immediately one is greeted, he said, with two questions: "Are you guys from the South?" and "You do wear shoes down there, don't you?" Some have tried to understand the regional accent by tracing its heritage to Scotland, some have predicted and regretted that it will soon vanish, and some have tried to make money from it; but few have denied that the South has a distinctive dialect. [13]

Larry King told the story of the little old lady from east Texas who said, "I ont ker whut they say about Linten Johnson, he's the onliest Pres-i-*dent* we ever had whut didn't have a ak-cent," and King confessed that he, too, thought Jimmy Carter would be the only candidate in 1976 to understand that a "mess" was a unit of

measurement. Another writer, in his search for the essence of the
South, suggested that the only true and lasting mark of the southern region was the use of "Coke," "cola," or "soft drink" as a generic
term for carbonated beverages rather than "soda," "pop," or "soda
pop," and, recognizing the symbiosis between language and culture, concluded that "the day when the boys who hang around the
Red Ace filling station in Cullman, Alabama, walk into Grigsby's
Grocery and order an orange pop, we'll know the South is dead."[14]

Clarence Hall, too, discovered that "the main point of difference
between 'up there' and 'down here' turns on the way we talk. The
problem with having to talk with a 'Yankee' is that he expects us to
make sense with every little word we say." In the South, Hall contended, "communication for the sake of mere understanding has
never been necessary."[15] The communication code described by the
contemporary observer is not that of the mythic "ephemeral and
florid" orators of the Old South or "the high caste Brahmin" novelists of the new South. It is the language of Billy Bob Puckett and Lu
Ann Hampton.

Several empirical studies have demonstrated that regional dialects evoke "a stereotype based predominantly on assumed regional identifications, social status, and attitudes and values" and
that, generally, those with a Southern accent are placed at a disadvantage in communicating with persons outside the region. Within
the South, however, the dialect is often a source of pride, and the
attitudinal connotations are quite different. One group of Southerners argued that "preservation and propagation of our linguistic
heritage does not mean a sacrifice of resourceful, effective speaking. Qualities just the opposite of the insensitive, ungracious, bla-
tant, and intrinsically rude are an advantage, not a disadvantage,
and the more so the higher the level of communication."[16]

In Southern society the spoken word (any spoken word) becomes
a cultural password that allows the speaker to enter the shared social reality as well as the particular conversation with other South-

erners. For example, in assessing Charles Morgan's success in effecting change in the South through his position as director of the American Civil Liberties Union's Atlanta office, John Egerton said, "Morgan used his insider's credentials freely—he had the accent, he spoke the language, he understood the thought processes."

Regional Rhythms

As with the spoken language, the South has developed several distinctive music types which, though national in audience, are regional in their rhetoric. Modern country music evolved from folk ballads and hillbilly tunes in the Southern mountain areas, and today, despite national popular acceptance and commercial success, the lyrics of country music still provide support for the rhetorical vision of Southern distinctiveness. In my study of the lyrics of contemporary country music I discovered that 74.5 per cent of the geographic locations mentioned were either the South as a region or specific Southern states and cities, and another recent study of the subgenre of country music done by Raymond Rodgers revealed that 63.9 per cent of the geographic references were to the South. Both studies also showed that the South was viewed much more favorably in the lyrics than were the Northern states and cities mentioned or compared.

Like the region's language, country music contains the themes of its lower- and middle-class origins—there are more songs about a six-pack of beer than about "Tea for Two." Although the music borrows from both blues and gospel, the performers and the audiences are primarily white. However, just as black artists made major contributions to the region's musical heritage through blues and gospel, they have been a part of the country music scene as well. DeFord Bailey began a sixteen-year career on the Grand Old Opry in 1925, and he is said to have been the first person to record a record in Nashville.[17] Country Charley Pride, the most popular black performer of country music in the contemporary South, draws enthusiastic white audiences, deposits large amounts of green money, and sings of themes which are equally applicable to the white and black experiences in the South.

Another recent phenomenon of the last decade has been the emergence of "Southern Rock" as a distinctive musical and rhetorical genre. Built upon the foundations laid by Elvis Presley, Chuck Berry, Little Richard, and Jerry Lee Lewis, the sound is exemplified on the albums of the Allman Brothers Band, the Marshall Tucker Band, Lynyrd Skynyrd, Charlie Daniels, Alabama, the Atlanta Rhythm Section, the Amazing Rhythm Aces, Wet Willie, Commander Cody, and Black Oak Arkansas. Like its country cousin, Southern rock has produced many lyrical statements about the South and the Southerner—as a distinct place with distinctive people. The music, said Paul Johnson, "contains elements of the often-abrasive braggadocio of many of the region's residents; it incorporates the fears and mythos and chauvinism of the region."[18]

Comestible Communication

"Next to fried foods," said Walter Hines Page, "the South has suffered most from oratory." Today, in the vision of Southern distinctiveness, food (fried or otherwise) is one of the major rhetorical themes in the ritual. Contemporary writers alleged symbolic consubstantiation with such assertions as "Fried chicken is a summer afternoon in the South," and other regional chauvinists have protested the mass sacrilege of Harlan Sanders. Said Bill Terry: "'Southern Fried' used to be a kind of culinary shibboleth pertaining to Southern tastes in comestibles, especially chicken, but the Kentucky colonel and other chicken profiteers, in the interest of haste, standardized the flavor and the texture to an ecumenical blah acceptable from Bangor to Phoenix that has robbed fried chicken not only of its tradition but has made a proud local habitation and a name a national perversity. . . . Chrome and stainless steel cooking baskets are not substitutes for an iron skillet."[19]

On the other hand, Terry sighed, "I am happy to say that Southern fried catfish and the quality that blessed the old days have survived uncorrupted by mass demand and are still safe from the traducers of all things genuine—Madison Avenue and the marketing blitz." That is to say, the South's own myths about catfish are safe from those of the New York ad agencies for the time being, but the Hush Puppy and Catfish Cabin chains are now rapidly expanding. Paul Greenberg, fearful that even catfish were becoming subjected to the influences of mass society, questioned the impact of recent changes upon future generations of Southerners. "Nowadays," he said, "sitting in air-conditioned, mass-fabricated restaurants, eating frozen catfish and processed hushpuppies put on the menu that very day by some thoughtful computer in Cincinnati or Wilkes-Barre, one wonders: Will the next generation know what it was to go out in the heat of summer for a ride in the old Chevy with the windows down and Hank Williams or Garner Ted Armstrong on the radio . . . ? Or to stop at a flyspecked watermelon stand to get a quarter of a melon for two bits and linger there, spitting out the seeds."[20]

When the Carter entourage came to Washington in 1976, one aide was overheard asking, "Where can you buy catfish here? Does any place sell fatback?" Those questions prompted a Southern newspaper correspondent to complain, "When grits are available they are instant. The nearest edible-barbeque shack straddles the North Carolina line, more than 200 miles away. A diligent four-year search by a homesick Southerner has turned up only one country jukebox within the city limits. Grocery store clerks routinely throw away the greens and save the turnips." Such observations, though intended to be humorous, served to reinforce the role of regional foods in establishing the mythic distinctiveness of the South.[21]

While some Southerners have touted "roast possum, gleaming like a greasy baby on a platter, with sweet potatoes," the main mythic fare of non-fried Southern meat is barbecued pork, with a cult and ritual all its own. "Southern people, as everyone knows, take their barbecue very seriously," said one writer in *Southern Exposure*. "The ritual of barbecuing has endless variations from region to region, or even town to town. Yet in each locale, the resident experts will assure you that theirs is the only way, the only method yielding what is termed 'true barbecue.'" Each self-anointed priest of barbecue claims to have special secrets about the type of pit, type of wood, cut of meat (some even prefer beef or chicken), and the recipes for sauce. "Somewhat like religious tenets, barbecue sauces are touted as essential while, at the same time, being declared unknowable."[22]

In addition to the ritual act, noted an article in *Southern Living*, Southerners are also said to "revere legendary barbecue haunts as if they were shrines." Again, confirming the tendency to idealize the vernacular, "some say the best barbecue is found in cafes belonging to an architectural classification that we shall call Barbecue Primitive style. These are often barbecue eateries identified by torn screen doors, scratched and dented furniture, cough syrup calendars, potato chip racks, sometimes a jukebox, and always a counter, producing an ambience similar to a county-line beer joint."[23]

While the lowly grit (or is it grits?) has been one of the most popular symbols in the national media and has even been the subject of a film, at least one Southerner has confessed, "Even when laced generously with red-eye gravy, grits ain't fit to eat." Cousin cornbread, however, is an ever prominent symbol of the South—as long as it is made with white corn meal and without sugar or flour. Such a symbol gives further credence to the egalitarian vision of distinctiveness, for as one fan admitted, "Humblest of the triad of Southern hot breads, cornbread in all its transmogrifications is outranked according to culinary protocol by biscuits and yeast rolls. . . . In general, the corn breads are hearty reminders and properly the accompaniment of fare to suit the appetites of farmers and sportsmen, the Southern equivalent of the peasant breads of Europe." No longer is the South captivated by its own images of the Cavalier's hunt breakfast or the Planter's mint julep; the vision of culinary distinctiveness is one which can be realistically shared and believed by all. As Jody Powell said, "Everybody, black and white, now recognizes you don't have to be ashamed of turnip greens."[24]

Sports as Symbol

Another aspect of the mythology of the contemporary South, which has achieved ritualistic status, is the appetite for sports. Nationally, of course, enthusiasm can be found for sports such as tennis, golf, handball, racquetball, soccer, rugby, baseball, surfing, sailing, hunting, fishing, basketball, and football. In the South, suggested a special issue of *Southern Exposure*, "the relationship of sports to culture is especially strong," and the mythic theme of regional distinctiveness offers a special definition of sports.

While basketball has long been a mania in the Big Ten and Atlantic Coast Conference states, it has recently gained new significance in the South. In 1963, a state senator in Mississippi obtained an injunction to prevent Mississippi State's basketball team from competing in the NCAA tournament because they had been paired with Loyola of Chicago and would be competing against black athletes. From there, editorialized a Jackson newspaper, it was only a short step to recruiting black players for Southern teams.[25] During the next fifteen years, with the successful integration of college athletic departments and with Southern teams holding half the top twenty places in the polls, basketball gained new rhetorical dimensions in the South—both for sports and for society.

Football is also a nationally popular sport, but as one Northern writer observed, "Southern football reached levels of meaning, intensity, and violence entirely foreign to other regions." Alcorn State University football coach Marino Casem, often referred to as the "Black Godfather of Mississippi," offered a different perspective but reached the same conclusion. "In the East," he said, "college football is a cultural attraction. On the West Coast it is a tourist attraction. In the Midwest it is cannibalism. But in the South it is religion." *Time* magazine observed the cultural importance of the sport in a special issue on the South and said, "Football in the south is a social event, fashion show and year-round centerpiece for bragging. Its rituals are as firmly fixed as the firmament on high."[26]

There are other sports which have a particularly Southern flavor and which many Southerners claim as their own. Professional wrestling (not the sterile NCAA matches of skill) draws sixty per cent of its total live audience in the South, and it has a large and devoted television audience as a result of broadcast coverage by WTBS in Atlanta and other locally originated programming. Described as "part athletic competition and part soap-opera," it is a form of entertainment which appeals primarily to the lower and lower-middle classes—both black and white.[27] The "good guys" represent the heroes and display admirable qualities of athletic prowess and fairness. It is worth noting, as has been the case in football and basketball, that Southern audiences seem to be color-blind in choosing champions. Recently Hacksaw Butch Reed, a black wrestler, has been among the favorites on Georgia Championship Wrestling. Cockfighting, from the days of Chicken George, also has been claimed by the South as a regional sport with biracial fans and cockers and three regional periodicals on the sport.

Bass boats far outnumber sailboats, and likewise, hunting takes on special meaning in the South as a symbolic relationship between people and their environment.[28] The game will likely be bear, possum, or coon, and the hunter will more likely be wearing a cap with a Skoal or Mack insignia than English riding pants.

Stock car racing is another major sport claimed by the South. The National Association for Stock Car Automobile Racing was founded in the South in 1948, and today the NASCAR Grand National circuit is still dominated by Southern drivers and Southern tracks. From Darling, South Carolina, to Daytona, Florida, and from Charlotte, North Carolina, to Talladega, Alabama, the cultural significance of stock car racing in the South rivals the role of Indianapolis in mid-American sports culture. The heroes of the sport—Richard Petty, Bobby Allison, Fireball Roberts, Cale Yarborough, Junior Johnson, and especially Wendell Scott—bear little resemblance to the Old South patricians, and the audiences have been described as "a diverse crowd that includes one-gallus retirees, peroxide mountain mamas, and lonely textile workers."[29] Like football, wrestling, and cockfighting, stock car racing provides weekend drama for the audiences, and like hunting and fishing, it is an opportunity for the participants to escape the world of weekday work and exchange tall tales.

Homegrown Heroes

In a vision with such proletarian symbols as the architecture, language, music, food, and sports of the contemporary South, the planter and the belle would seem somewhat anachronistic. The search for new personae has been aided almost accidentally by numerous television series beginning with the Beverly Hillbillies and the Andy Griffith Show in the 1960s and continuing with the Waltons, Carter Country, and the Dukes of Hazzard, all of which have treated Southern society more sympathetically, if less seriously, than did Caldwell, Faulkner, and Tennessee Williams during the 1940s and 1950s.

The characters which emerge in the myth of distinctiveness are not the traditional, heroic figures of invincibility usually found in mythology as exemplified by the omnipotent oligarchs of the plantation or the champions of the civil rights struggle. Rather, the typical hero in the new myth is more akin to what Susanne Langer has described as the "culture-hero," one that "is not seriously 'believed in' as gods and spirits are," but who still represents "man, overcoming the superior forces that threaten him." The hero in this contemporary myth personifies what Ray Browne saw as "America's drive to create the hero as anti-hero, not as superbigman but as verylittleguy."[30]

The principal characters in the myth of distinctiveness are the Good Ole Boy and Ms. Magnolia, two very different characters from any of the Southern stereotypes found between 1820 and 1960. The new personae, like their predecessors, represent clearly defined cultural values, and they have been developed just as intentionally and skillfully.

It is not hard to visualize the contemporary version of Southern belles, and they do, in fact, exist, although they do not receive the same veneration allegedly bestowed in the past. Pat Derian, one who rejects the stereotype and has been instrumental in developing the alternative, can spot them immediately and describes them quite well:

They spring into being at seventeen as respectable Chi O's or Tri Delts, wrestling around on the third tee of every country club south of Maryland. They shimmer, pout, dance in rows, march at the front of bands, diet, make B's without any brains, sometimes if plied with whiskey submit, and always marry. They teach school until the babies come, belong to the Junior Auxiliary, a brand name church, stuff their children with rules and cheese grits until they are forty. At forty they garden, play bridge, fall to drink, and bore their husbands to death. Upon achieving widowhood they travel around the world looking at castles, great gardens, art treasures, and needlework through the ages. They worry their children, work on the grandchildren, and guard our way of life. They are well dressed, very tidy, and anti-intellectual throughout. They always make certain they are treated with proper respect, because they are white and not dirt poor.[31]

These particular ladies, however, have never heard Merle Haggard, tasted baked possum, or smelled a sweaty professional wrestler. The Southern women in the new vision have been characterized by Reynolds Price as "Mack trucks disguised as powder puffs," and by James Whitehead as "Iron Magnolias." They are "calling for change: they have heard all the old myth stories, want some new ones, and are willing to go out and make their own."[32]

The new Southern women are seen in the vision "as breezily impudent backwoods babes fabled for their raw wit, crackerbarrel candor, and constant readiness for a good-natured rebellion," said Sharon McKern. "They're passionate and compassionate, unbelievably candid, fully aware of what it means to be female and Southern in the seventies. They know their rights. They know how to get what's coming to them. But they're not afraid to step back once in a while and have a good laugh at themselves, either." It is a vision that cuts across class and race, and it can be found in black poetry as well as in the lyrics of country music.[33]

The Good Ole Boy, though equally Southern and equally distinctive, is a little less honorable. One should not confuse him with his mean, less polished relative, the Redneck. Billy Carter, who was a Good Ole Boy before he took up with the Libyans and sold out to a mobile home manufacturer, once distinguished between the two by explaining that "a good ole boy . . . is somebody that rides around in a pick-up truck . . . and drinks beer and puts 'em in a litter bag. A redneck's one that rides around in a truck and drinks beer and throws 'em out the window." Larry King, who should certainly know, also makes a distinction between the two and defines a Good Ole Boy as one who "turns his radio down at red lights so other drivers won't observe him enjoying Kitty Wells singing through her nose."[34]

The Good Ole Boy operates on the premise that "life is nothing to get serious about," and was captured in the character played by Burt Reynolds in *W. W. and the Dixie Dance Kings* (1974). He likes country music, his buddies, women, and his automobile, but he has a pronounced disregard for law and authority in general, as well as a cynical attitude toward religious fanatics and big oil companies. He is very much a creature of the South, and he is most definitely not a Southern gentleman of the plantation type. He is a garden variety proletarian, and he is the cultural hero in the contemporary myth of Southern distinctiveness. He and Ms. Magnolia, though quite different, have effectively countered the stereotypes in the vision of the Old South.[35]

The mythic theme of this special difference has served Southern mythmakers quite well in overcoming one of the region's major rhetorical problems. It has been a key element in the strategy of redefinition employed to combat many of the debilitating effects of the old mythology. To a certain extent, the symbols and rituals described in this chapter—the Good Ole Boy, Ms. Magnolia, architecture, dialect, music, food, and sports—constitute intentional efforts to change the regional stereotype from the plantation to the proletariat. Irving Rein has shown how groups ranging from the Dodge Division of Chrysler Corporation to the Gay Liberation movement have employed the strategy of redefinition in recent years, and it has become a frequent strategy of numerous American ethnic groups. "Regardless of the kind of group," George Boss states, "if it fervently wishes to alter its image, then it must consider the characteristics the group prefers to cherish and seek implementation of their reality. If the group desires to modify or eliminate prejudicial and inaccurate stereotypes, it is important to

realize that the major term of the enthymeme, the 'clusters' of attributes, must be reconstructed before any stereotype can be modified or eliminated."[36]

The strategy has moved from the verbal to the behavioral levels
with some degree of national success. Grits was on the menu, and
Willie Nelson was on the south lawn at the White House. Jimmy
Carter wore jeans to survey his peanut patch in campaign commercials, and Hamilton Jordan's wardrobe was designed by Levi-
Strauss rather than Hickey-Freeman. The Southern office of the
National Trust for Historic Preservation began to advocate attention to less refined architectural forms, and Ted Turner sent programming of stock car racing and professional wrestling to satellite receivers across the nation and around the world.

On another level, partially as a result of the success of its internal redefinition, the South was also faced with the rhetorical problem of countering the external views of the region that had been
aided and abetted by Erskine Caldwell, William Faulkner, and the
Beverly Hillbillies. An excellent example of the effort to reverse
these images and refine the themes presented in the new myth of
regional distinctiveness is the Mississippi Travel Department's
"Rethink Mississippi" campaign of 1976. The Department designed
and placed a series of three advertisements entitled "Missinformed," "Missimpression," and "Missunderstood." The ads acknowledged that many people thought Mississippi was "nothing
but watermelon, gumbo, and tarpaper shacks," "nothing but poverty, potholes, and hole-in-the-wall motels," and "nothing but
gators and swamps," and the copy attempted to clear these misconceptions, offering the reader additional information about cultural and recreational resources, a free travel guide, and a "Rethink Mississippi" button.[37]

The mythic theme of regional distinctiveness has been successful
as a strategy of redefinition. In conjunction with the mythic theme
of racial equality it has helped provide a new vocabulary of egali-

tarian symbols and images to supplant the elitist icons of the old myth, and to a lesser degree it has served to moderate the negative stereotypes possessed by persons from outside the South. The strategy must be judged successful for its role in replacing the dysfunctional perceptions of social reality presented by the old myth and in providing instructive models of behavior supportive of the emerging value system.

six The Theme of Place and Community

Southerners have a unique sense of time and place, of belonging, of community. Southerners have roots. They have an identity. A Southerner—whatever his station, whatever his color—has a "home."
—David Mathews, "Coming to Terms with Another New South"

In much the same way that the mythic theme of distinctiveness leads Southerners to feel that their culture and society are unique, the mythic theme of place and community posits a vision of the South as "sacred ground," creating special relationships among the inhabitants and between people and place. Since the days of the colonial search for a mythic "Southern Eden," dating from the late sixteenth century, the Southern sense of place has been a dominant factor in the region's social reality. Frank Smith, a former Congressman from Mississippi and a member of the Lamar Society, said, "Southerners have a sense of identity with place that is only slightly less compelling than our identity with family. It is one of the distinctions that still separates our section from the rest of the country." Reubin Askew repeated and amplified that theme for contemporary Southerners when he said, "We have, in the South, a place where people want to live, a place where they want to work, a place where they want to raise their children. We have, in the South, a place that people can call home."[1]

From the plantation paradigm to Cash's version of Turner's frontier thesis, the sense of place has been a prominent part of the historical and social reality in the South, and the discussion of its role has demonstrated the dialectic of Southern mythology. Henry Grady and his cohorts in the first New South movement called for industrialization, urbanization, and exploitation of the South's resources, both natural and human, with a vision of progress that seemed almost revolutionary; fifty years later the Vanderbilt Agrarians contended that the True South was actually a land of bucolic farmers with small agricultural units divided by pristine wilderness areas, a vision of reality that was labeled reactionary. Today, neither of these visions is controlling in the mythology of place. The contemporary South has developed a new mythic vision which draws from elements of both and which continues the theme of place and community that has always captivated the region's people and engendered a strong attachment to the South.

Despite the suggestion by some scholars that the contemporary rhetoric of whites and blacks reflects different value systems, the mythic theme of community and place, like the themes of equality and distinctiveness discussed in previous chapters, is one shared by both blacks and whites in the contemporary Southern mythology. The theme has dominated the discussions and the publications of the predominantly white mythmakers of the Southern Growth Policies Board; and Alice Walker, a black writer and poet, examined the effect of the contemporary Southern experience and concluded, "What the black writer inherits as a natural right is a sense of community."

The mythic theme can be found in almost every medium of communication in the contemporary South. Carl Kell has suggested that the "dominant value hierarchy of place" permeates Southern rhetoric, and his study of *Southern Living* magazine concluded that the "fundamental rhetorical posture of *Southern Living* is to make the South a more 'desirable place' by producing major investiga-

tive, persuasive essays and feature stories that demonstrate positive solutions to the knotty personal and public *community* problems of the South." In film representations of the South, ranging
from "B" productions such as *Walking Tall* to the more expensive
such as *Nashville*, Kell contends that the theme of "roots in the
land" appears quite frequently and takes on a quality that is mark-
edly Southern. In contemporary literature, Robert Penn Warren's *A
Place to Come To*, Willie Morris's *Terrains of the Heart*, and John
Egerton's *A Mind to Stay Here* are, as suggested by their titles, representative of the Southern sense of place, a theme also found in
the writings of Lillian Smith, Reynolds Price, Ernest Gaines, and
other contemporary Southerners.[2]

In the music of the region, ranging from the rock message of Alabama's "My Home's in Alabama," which declares, "I'm in the heart
of Dixie; Dixie's in the heart of me," to the more traditional lyrics of
country music, the mythic theme of place and community is quite
prominent. My earlier study of country music lyrics found that
among songs containing evaluative assertions about the South,
51.7 percent pertained to positive human relationships and 39.7
percent extolled a sense of place, whereas, in assertions about the
North, that region was "seen as being cold, crowded, hurried, stress-
ful, dirty, impersonal, or all of the above." That perception of reality is not limited to the songwriters in Nashville but is also shared
by the region's political leaders. "In our efforts to improve the
South, we have often seemed to discard that distinctiveness and
make the South a carbon copy of the North," said Reubin Askew in
1975. "It is not too late to correct these mistakes, and it is not too
early to predict what will happen if we do not." The result, he suggested, in imagery similar to the musical message, would be:
"Bleak cities and sterile suburbs. Dirty air and murky water. As-
phalt horizons and neon jungles. Ruined resources and ravaged
land. Empty homes and empty hearts." Arguing for sensitive development of the region, he said, "That is not the South. It is not the

South that we want for our children. It is not the South that we want for ourselves. It is not the vision that we share."[3]

Fathoming the Future

One of the most effective ways of developing a cultural myth is through public discussions of the nature of the future, and that has been a method characteristic of Southern mythmakers almost as strong as their tendency toward discussion of the past. James Dickey, for example, has said he believes the South's sense of place can offer much to the rest of the nation. "The South is the future. It's the future right now," he said in 1977. "It's going to have a marvelous influence on this country because it will teach people to be much kinder to each other and more forgiving and more easygoing and more neighborly and simply more forbearing and genuinely more concerned about other people." Likewise, Governor Bob Graham, in his 1979 inaugural address, told the people of Florida, "We must be hopeful for the future and mindful of the past." His vision of place clearly came through as he said, "Our dream is of a once and future Florida—a Florida in which we can conserve our natural heritage, a Florida in which each of us will be treated with justice, a Florida in which all of us can earn a good living, have a decent home, and educate our children." The mythic theme of community was also evident as he said, "Our dream is a Florida in which we can share a renewed kinship, a Florida in which we will all be friends and neighbors and families."[4]

Terry Sanford, as a founder of the L. Q. C. Lamar Society, had advocated a formalized compact among the Southern states to deal with the problems of the future and the consequences of burgeoning growth in the region, an organization which could help the South avoid repeating "Northern mistakes in a Southern setting." In December 1971, nine Southern states formally organized the

Southern Growth Policies Board, with a staff located in Research Triangle Park, North Carolina, to assist the region in anticipating and dealing with common problems. Composed of the governor, one state senator, one state representative, and two public members from each state, the early leadership came from Governors Dale Bumpers, Jimmy Carter, and Reubin Askew. More recently Governors Hunt, Riley, Clinton, Winter, Graham, and Nigh have been the spokesmen for the group.

The goals and hopes during the early years of the Board were summed up by Askew in 1976. "The South," he said, "is an unfinished frontier. While the cities and states of the North are confined by the consequences of their past mistakes, we have an opportunity in the South to fashion our frontier into whatever we want to make it." The idea that the South was experiencing rapid growth and urbanization, and that because it had been so late in developing there was an opportunity to guide that growth, quickly became a popular theme throughout the region, infecting Chamber of Commerce executives as well as public officials and newspaper editors.[5]

The developing strategy, which was neither one of "no growth" nor a repeat of the "Atlanta Spirit" of the past, accepted the inevitability of, and even the desirability of, economic growth and development. The vision of place and community which emerged from these discussions was more complex than those of the past. Rather than offering a polarized view of the situation, members of the Southern Growth Policies Board began to ask difficult questions. Recognizing the need for new jobs and higher incomes for the region, they asked, "can the South, much of it still struggling to catch up with the level of development and standard of living of the rest of the nation, take a long range view toward its own growth, and especially toward foregoing immediate lower quality growth in favor of future, higher quality growth?" Revealing a vision that was pro-active rather than holding to the Southern tradition of reaction, they also asked, "Can Southern leaders provide the will and strength to enact far-sighted growth management programs, able to prevent problems before they occur, rather than simply responding to them once they have happened?" It was a vision that understood the human impact of change and regional development, and they asked, "Can Southern planners design tools to provide incentives . . . to act so as to enhance the overall public welfare and quality of life of the state, region, and locality?"

Terry Sanford asked the Lamar Society in 1971, "To avoid the blight, to protect the earth, to save the magic of ecology, to enhance the civility of life, what do we do?" Reubin Askew's answer to that question in 1975 provided a basis for the new theme. "The economic development of the South," he said, "need not result in the degradation of our land or the deprivation of our people. We cannot separate the future of our economy in the South from the future of our environment. We cannot allow what has happened in the North to happen here in the South." The questions, the answers, and the theme were still important in 1978 as Jim Hunt, a North Carolina governor in the Sanford tradition, became chairman of the Southern Growth Policies Board and quoted Sanford on the issue.[6]

The questions posed by Sanford and Hunt were not, at least on the surface, unlike those being asked elsewhere in the nation in the decade of the seventies, but the contemporary vision of the South gave special emphasis to the interrelationship between place and community and recognized the possible impact of change upon the values inherent in the Southerner's sense of place. When Governor David Boren assumed the leadership of the Southern Growth Policies Board in 1977, he expressed regional concerns about the nature of growth which ran just as deep as the concern over physical changes in the environment. "How," he asked, "do we retain the community spirit that is so strong? How do we keep alive the values that make our system and our section so vital?"[7]

The realization that changing the "place" could affect the "sense of place" permeates the mythic vision of the contemporary South. The 1974 Commission on the Future of the South, an independently appointed group of prominent Southern leaders charged with reporting to the Southern Growth Policies Board, declared one of the primary objectives of regional growth management to be "to preserve and enhance, in meeting the issues of growth and change, the human sense of place and community that is a vital element of the unique quality of Southern life." The 1980 Commission faced the same question, and one participant said, "Today, the central question is how to extract material value out of modernity without killing our sense of security, community, and place." Senator Dale Bumpers of Arkansas welcomed economic growth in the South, but suggested that "the South doesn't have to have poisoned air, plundered resources, and devastated cities. It doesn't have to allow the congestion that inevitably produces a neurotic insensitivity and indifference to people and institutions." Dolly Parton expressed the same thought just as eloquently and to a larger audience when she said, "It's hard to have deep roots under concrete."[8]

Southern Living magazine, in a special section on the Future of the South, echoed the theme. "If there is a single purpose to this special inventory of facts and ideas, it is to measure the quality of life offered, and threatened, by the growth and prosperity of today's South," said Emory Cunningham. "Can we keep our love of place and family and distinctiveness as a people, and our landscape in its beauty and order, and absorb the growth and density of a more concentrated culture?" The South was saying, both to itself and to the nation, that it held a specific vision of growth, development, urbanization, and industrialization. It was not unquestioning acceptance of progress; it was not rejection of prosperity. It was, said Carl Kell, the idea that growth "must be on Dixie's terms—a sensitive spirit of reform, a sensitive attention to conservationism, a sensitive desire that each man be able to shape his own destiny."[9]

Emphasis on the importance of the Southern sense of place in the face of change became a topic of discussion beyond the offices of the L. Q. C. Lamar Society and the Southern Growth Policies Board. At least one group, with the assistance of the National Endowment for the Humanities, continued to focus upon the questions and expand the range of the audience. This diverse group of scholars, activists, community leaders, and elected officials met in Nashville in May 1976 to consider the future of the region from a humanistic perspective. In a discussion of growth and values in the context of Southern mythology, the participants were divided in their conclusions. Some members acknowledged that "regardless of the validity of the myth of Southern unity and regional identity, the accidents of time and geography have conspired to direct growth into this historically defined region." Others, more aware of the role of mythology in controlling and directing human behavior, felt that "the Southern myths of unity and agrarianism could in themselves be organizing principles to direct and manage the growth of urban problems in more creative and more humane ways than the rest of the nation."[10]

The Southern Growth Policies Board, under the direction of South Carolina Governor Richard Riley in 1980, continued to be concerned with the impact of growth on the tenets of the cultural mythology. The Board's staff did an excellent job of cataloging and statistically measuring the regional trends, then noted that "this process of growth has been a mixed blessing, made all the more so by virtue of its apparent self-sustaining nature." Arkansas Governor Bill Clinton, expressing both the hopes and fears of those sharing the myth, said, "What has not been done very well in the past and what I believe needs to be done now is to gain a better understanding of the relationship between economic, political, and demographic trends and the impact on regional values." Admitting that the question of how to deal with change had been discussed in the past and that the "prevailing opinion has been neither constant nor consistently wise," he said, "I do not pretend that the members of the Southern Growth Policies Board can answer the recurring questions for all time; I do believe that we can and must address ourselves to the facts and trends as they now exist and that we must try to gain a humanistic understanding of the impact of those realities."[11]

A Utilitarian Utopia

Going beyond the realm of academic and polemic discussions of the nature of the future, the myth was also developed daily in more subtle ways by contemporary Southerners. Governor Richard Riley, setting the tone for the administration of state government in his 1979 inaugural address, expressed the belief that "it is not unreasonable to envision a South Carolina of great natural beauty—and great economic strength—at the same time." In a similar vein, Ed Penick, the chairman of the board of Arkansas' largest bank holding company, advocated that business in the South "take full advantage of prospective economic growth while preserving the quality of the lifestyle and the wholesomeness of the environment."[12]

One industry which maintains a symbiotic relationship with the Southern sense of place is tourism. The mystique of place must be maintained to attract customers both from inside and from outside the region. Furthermore, noted Frank Smith, "climate, abetted by scenery and history, is the foundation of Southern tourism, and land use planning is the obvious necessity if the attractions of scenery and history, tied to clean air and water, are to be preserved for exploitation of tourists, and use by natives, for the recreational potential which can be an even greater attraction for Southern life."

Historical sites which attempt to interpret the past and relate it to the present, as well as recreational attractions which rely upon the quality of the natural environment, are motivated to share and perpetuate the vision of place.[13] The Arkansas Department of Parks and Tourism adopted the myth with publications declaring, "Arkansas is a Natural," while the Mississippi Department of Tourism Development offered a booklet entitled, "Mississippi: It's Like Coming Home."[13]

Clare Gunn, a travel writer, demanded that the South be able to shape its own future and said that responsible planning should "provide the businessman with greater overall perspectives for better land-use decision making for his success. . . , better satisfaction to the visitor by giving them a greater sense of place. . . , better protection of all those valuable and special places of the South." While such principles also apply nationally, she said that "the South has special qualities of place—its cities, natural resources, history, lore, and a stronger land ethic than anywhere in the country. With concerned interest by its citizens, the South can demonstrate artful and environmentally sensitive development that emulates the fine qualities of placeness of the South."[14]

Land Lore

The theme of place, with special emphasis on the rural South, was the central focus of a 1979 special section on "The Future of the South" in *Southern Living*: "People in the South are close to the land, whether they make a living directly from it or seek it out for recreation and inspiration. That's not to say Southerners have always treated land in the best way. There have been some hard lessons learned, and there are many more problems today that need attention." Continuing the idea that growth and place are compatible forces in the cultural mythology of the contemporary

South, the editors advocated "using land well without destroying its goodness," and suggested that "you don't have to be against growth and development if you want to see the landscape protected. The South can have both if it will only exercise land use as an art."[15]

Crossing party lines, Bill Workman and Willis Whichard, two prominent political figures, noted that "Southerners have always been a people of the land," and cautiously asked, "Are we selling out the future? We musn't lose sight of the fact that we don't own the land; we only borrow it from our children." The real question, however, went beyond the physical consequences of growth and development in the South. "There's more at stake, of course, than just the loss of farms and scenic woodlands. The very essence of the Southern landscape may be altered in the next few years," contended the authors. "If the character of the land is changing, what about the people? The Southern personality has been shaped by generations of our people living on the land. . . . If we are to maintain this identity, we must first establish ground rules for change."[16] Once again, the voices of the contemporary South were forging a new mythology which borrowed from those of the past, but which approached both the present and the future with a new perspective on creative change.

Other regional publications have also contributed to the development of the vision of place and community, both editorially and through selected feature articles. The editor of *Southern Changes*, looking at the present and to the future, said, "We live in a South where we must now select carefully the changes which we will invite and the ones which we oppose." *Southern Exposure*, in a special issue dedicated to the land as a "foundation of Southern Culture," acknowledged the importance of the vision, saying that "in the South, identity is still bound up with the land." The editors also confirmed their belief in the utility of the mythology as an active

agency for shaping the future of the South. "We view 'Our Promised Land' as a beginning, not as a definitive statement. . . . We encourage our readers to use this issue in creative ways: to preserve
the beauty and power of our Southern land and to change the
methods of control of our primary resources."[17]

The Metropolitan Myth

Despite the South's historical tradition as a rural society and the
essential role of the land in the definition of the mythic sense of
place, the region has become increasingly urban. The 1974 Commission on the Future of the South, recognizing that more than 56
percent of the region's population then lived in urban areas, suggested that "Southerners now live in a society in which the traditional distinctions between rural and urban lifestyles have lost
their meaning." During the decade of the seventies, the South
gained an additional twenty million people, over 63 percent of
whom now reside in metropolitan counties. The importance of the
trend was so pronounced that in 1979 the Southern Growth Policies Board established a task force on Southern cities, and Judge
Reuben Anderson, a member of the 1980 Commission on the Future of the South, concluded that "the Future of the South cannot
be separated from the future of Southern cities."[18]

Early in the 1970s, Joel Fleishman, Vice-Chancellor of Duke University and a member of the board of the L. Q. C. Lamar Society,
recognized that "the choice for the South is not whether it will
have cities, but what kind of cities it wants to have. The choice for
the South is whether to remain agrarian in values while becoming
urban in form, or take hold of the energy of urbanization and shape
it into more graceful, more humane, and more livable cities than
those in other regions." That same theme was repeated and refined

by the editors of *Southern Exposure* in mid-decade when, conscious of place, they said, "We should ask . . . not whether we can avoid the Northern urban crisis, but how can cities be shaped so people feel at home in them? The answers, of course, are incredibly difficult, but we must at least begin where we are, get connected to our roots and our neighbors so we can judge what is good from a common base, a common language."[19] The challenge to Southern policymakers and mythmakers was clear; they were to attempt to preserve the mythic sense of place and adapt it to the realities of the increasingly urban South.

While the vision of place and community moves toward accommodation of urbanization in the South, the dialectic of development continues just as strongly in the cities as it does in the rural landscape. Cognizant of the trends, the director of the Southern Growth Policies Board predicted in 1978 that "the next half-decade will determine whether we are capable of handling our material progress so that it protects our heritage, traditions and culture, thus assuring all of us of livable cities and a vibrant economy." Some contemporary Southerners feel that "too much of the urban development is merely an imitation of the Northeast. The traditional assets of the South—our sense of place, smaller population centers, more open space—are sacrificed for the glittering symbols of 'progress.' More importantly, the strength of our cities—our people—are ignored." Whether it concerns the location of a freeway in Memphis or construction of downtown convention complexes in Norfolk and Charleston, objections are heard from those who believe in the community values of residential neighborhoods, think human scale is important, and question the process by which public development decisions are made.[20]

Pat Watters believes that regional distinctiveness and the Southern sense of place will continue to be immune to the social influences of the McDonald's arch, but Alice Walker, in discussing the importance of this feeling to black Southerners, said, "if I leave Mississippi . . . it will not be for the reasons of the other sons and daughters of my father. . . . It will be because the pervasive football culture bores me, and the proliferating Kentucky Fried Chicken stands apall me, and the neon lights have begun to replace the trees." Some have praised John Portman's Peachtree Center in Atlanta as a symbol of the modern South, contending that Southern charm, friendliness, and hospitality continue unabated in the new environment of glass and chrome commercial architecture; others doubt it. James Reston, sensing a degree of sameness between Atlanta and the rest of the nation's cities said, "what has been gained and what has been lost we will leave to the fertile, creative mind of the writers of the South, but for now, Atlanta seems to have the same sights and sounds, hopes and problems as the rest of America."[21]

The small town was, and still is, important in the contemporary Southern vision. "The home town's values, perceptions, even its personal style of politics define in many ways the Southerness of the South," observed one reporter. "Ultimately there grows a deep sense of belonging, of defining one's life through one's place in the community." The most successful fusion of the reality of urbanization with the vision of place and community can be seen in the strength of the neighborhood movement during the last decade. Almost as if the ambience of a small town in the rural South had been transported through time and space, the contemporary urban neighborhood serves as a symbol of community in the South. Just as the "town" fathers and mothers of many rural Southern communities have realized that "the best future will be one that includes the physical charm and a sense of belonging traditionally found there," many city planners and community activists have concluded that "a down-to-earth future for our cities, rooted to the land and to the past, may be better than a fantastic one."[22]

External factors, too, have acted to nurture the mythic theme of place. Many Southern cities experienced their major growth during the seventies decade of Community Development Block Grants, Historic Preservation grants and loans, and awareness of energy shortages, rather than during the sixties decade of urban renewal, thus guiding Southern urban neighborhood development and redevelopment in different directions from that taken by the older cities in the North and Midwest. The 1980 Commission on the Future of the South, in suggesting perspectives and activities for planners in the eighties, said, "Local pride and citizen participation are strengthened by a strong identification with the city and the neighborhoods. A city or an entire urban area is only as strong as its neighborhoods. Urban programs must recognize the neighborhood concept of a community and encourage the continued vitality of the neighborhood movement."

The concept of place in integrated neighborhoods of the contemporary urban South is supported by Ansley Park and Inman Park in Atlanta, the Oakleigh District in Mobile, Coliseum Square in New Orleans, Riverside-Avondale in Jacksonville, the Quapaw Quarter in Little Rock, Trinity Park in Durham, Oakwood in Raleigh, and similar areas in almost every major Southern city. One couple in Atlanta's Inman Park neighborhood said one of the most important benefits of living there "is the sense of community spirit, of people working together and forming a cohesive community." In an article on the neighborhood movement in the South, Philip Morris of *Southern Living* commented on the impetus for the trend. "Not to be overlooked, though rather hard to pin down, is the sense of place and community that most residents of reviving districts comment upon. They like the diversity of ages, of interests, of architecture, of viewpoint, that come together as an urban place. . . . The last thing they want is to have their districts resemble suburbs."[23] Not unexpectedly, the myth of community was further articulated in a specialized periodical entitled *Southern Neighborhoods*.

Rhetorical Resolution

The myth of a Southern sense of place and community has survived the passing of the plantation and the blooming of the "Bulldozer Revolution." The symbolic relationship between people and the land remains important in the contemporary South, even in the urban South. It has survived changing systems of settlement, transportation, and communication, and, though somewhat less provincial than in the past, it remains important in the South's perception of reality. The meaning of the experience for the region was expressed quite well by the editors of *Southern Exposure* when they said, "We have learned much about the limitations and potentials of using our roots and region as a point of reference for grasping larger realities. We have come to take the South almost as a metaphor for everybody's home—for a place that possesses a peculiar, yet imperfect, integrity stemming from a rich history—and we see Southerners as archetypes of people who move into the future while affirming their connections to the past."[24] That is the theme of place in the contemporary South.

Nowhere has this particular mythic theme been better defined or more necessary than in the developing frontier of the contemporary South, for the competing visions of uncompromising opponents of growth and adamant proponents of unbridled development still operate within the cultural and philosophical milieu of the region. Against voices calling for more real estate developers in Florida, advertisements for a mobile home park boasting "Real Southern Living," and the recent fascination for Sunbelt boosterism, the myth offers perspective and a more cautious reality; against the modern Agrarians, it recognizes the inevitability of change while advocating a more humane and less obtrusive direction for that change.[25]

The heroes in the vision are the groups and individuals acting to preserve the revered sense of place and further the values of community; the villains are greedy developers, real estate hucksters, and insensitive promoters and planners who ignore the sense of place or exclude the members of a community from decisions affecting their lives. Once again, the dialectical nature of mythology becomes clear in the articulation of social and cultural values. The conflict is one between the worshipers of mammon and those who believe that the South, like the mythic giant Antaeus, can maintain its strengths and virtues only through communion with the earth. So far, of course, the tension has not been completely resolved; but the emerging myth is stronger than it ever has been in the past, it has a powerful and organized coalition of proponents, and it offers a realistic synthesis of the more worthy goals espoused by both the Agrarians and the New South boosters. The hopefulness of the proponents was expressed well by Askew when he said, "There is courage now in the South. And there is grace. There is warmth and compassion and wonder in living. There is a hope for a tomorrow that will not be tainted by the misgivings of today."[26]

SEVEN

The Meaning of the Myth

> The myth must be judged as a means of acting on the present; any attempt to discuss how far it can be taken literally as future history is devoid of sense.
> —Georges Sorel, *Reflections on Violence*

After experiencing and enduring a regional mythic continuity dating back to the 1820s, the South in the late 1960s and early 1970s was compelled to seek a new mythology to interpret and explain the new social and cultural realities of the contemporary South. The mind of the South, as described by W. J. Cash and others, finally yielded to change when it could no longer serve effectively, or even marginally, as a guide to understanding social reality in the post-*Brown* South. Initiated by the United States Supreme Court in 1954, demanded by Southern blacks from Montgomery to Little Rock to Greensboro and back to Montgomery via Selma, and codified by the Congress with the Civil Rights Act of 1964 and the Voting Rights Act of 1965, the transformation of Southern society so rearranged the essential "realities" of the past that the power of the old mythology was destroyed. The events of the last three decades toppled "so many foundations of the old order that we now live in a post-New South that nobody has yet given a name," said George B. Tindall, speaking at a symposium at the University of Alabama in

1976. David Mathews, during the same program, joined in that assessment. "By 1970," he said, "it was clear that the South had to get on with its future and that neither the antebellum past nor the era of the old New South was a completely adequate guide. Indeed, for Southerners in the 1970s the search for a new blueprint is of paramount importance."[1]

In a region as large, diverse, and dynamic as the South in the seventies, there were many voices and many potential mythic themes. In the preceding chapter, I have surveyed the rhetoric of the region, found and reconstructed one particular mythology struggling for and ascending to dominance in the contemporary communication environment, and identified the heroes, symbols, rituals, and sacred ground contained in three distinct rhetorical themes within the mythology. The three major themes are the myth of racial equality growing out of the civil rights movement, the myth of continuing regional distinctiveness found in the popular media of the region, and the myth of place and community which persists in the face of dramatic demographic and technological change in the South. Each mythic theme is an integral part of the new rhetorical mythology, the new blueprint for the South, and each holds special meaning for those participating in the redefinition of the past, action for the present, and projection of the future.

The mythology of the contemporary South was not entirely the product of carefully planned persuasive strategy by a formal alliance of modern mythmakers, but neither was it the completely accidental result of unconscious public rhetoricians. Many of those responsible for development of the contemporary mythology were well aware of the potential power of collective cultural myths, and they were also cognizant of the limits of those myths. As they described their scenarios for the future of the South, they often revealed their hopes as well as their strategies. The future, said Emory Cunningham, publisher of *Southern Living*, is "not a destination, but rather a process, a becoming. The future never really arrives, but it is always there on the mind. A way of thinking, really." Aware of the fallacious future offered by the first New South vision and the problems it encountered when, unsupported by reality, it declared that the future had arrived, he said, "As a region, the South has long thought about itself and has at various times proclaimed a New South, sometimes stretching the point. But the process is valid: to consider where you are and where you want to be." [2]

David Mathews, too, sounded that same hopeful theme about the South and its mythological processes. "Our efforts to describe a 'New South' can never be complete," he said. Aware of the conational dialectic within the mythology, he added, "this time we must choose causes that are just and have a future. We must choose them deliberately and realistically. We must . . . create our future not by abandoning our past but by realizing that all our traditions are two-sided coins and that the very tendencies that have made Southerners reactionary could, indeed, have at times made them progressive." [3] This rhetorical stance, redefining the past and reorienting the visionary process to the future, has acted to significantly strengthen the effectiveness of the emerging mythology.

Unlike the New South proponents of the last century, the contemporary Southern mythmakers also seem to be aware that the *ultimate goals of the myth* and the *realities of the present* are not necessarily identical and that the influence of mythology must be active and continuing if it is to remain relevant. As Willard Gatewood suggested, "We in the South . . . have abundant reason to subject all regional images, including the latest ones, to close and critical scrutiny. Our past demonstrates only too graphically how images lend themselves to manipulation and how often we have been seduced and catastrophically misled by those at greatest variance with reality." A contemporary awareness of the tragic Southern past may, however, "well serve as a useful antidote to some of the extravagances of the ahistorical mythmakers, adept at convincing themselves and others that what ought to be is what actually exists." David Mathews, speaking for the contemporary architects of the new mythology, seemed to share Gatewood's view. In setting regional goals, he said, "we must use myths, but we must not do what we have done time and time again—turn from reality to romanticism. The people of the South are keenly aware that they must once again influence their own destiny."[4]

Rhetorical Reality

An understanding of contemporary mythology is important for reasons other than merely being able to appreciate the artistic technique employed in describing particular visions of reality. Real people, not mythical heroes, psychologically adopt these mediated messages about the nature of their culture and society as significant elements of their world view, thereby exerting considerable influence upon their subsequent behavior. Fortunately for the critic, recent developments in communication theory have helped to explicate the rhetorical nature and persuasive consequences of public myths. Melvin DeFleur and Sandra Ball-Rokeach have offered a sociocultural model of mass media persuasion, drawing upon George Gerbner's cultivation theory as well as their own work, which has explanatory value for understanding how cultural myths are developed through public communication and how they function as persuasive strategies to influence the behavior of members of the societies in which they exist.

The communication process is essential to the construction of cultural myths and a shared social reality. In an effort to illuminate the process by which public communication contributes to creating and supporting public world views, DeFleur and Ball-Rokeach suggest that "as people communicate intensively over the years, selected assertions become regarded as true or correct metasymbolic representations of specific aspects of reality. Because of this process, our interpretations of reality, as well as folkways and other social norms, are *constructed* as by-products of the biosocial process of communication." From such a perspective, the process by which cultural myths are generated and constructed becomes more clear. Public speeches from respected figures, song lyrics by popular singers, and feature articles in trusted publications, as well as exposure to and repetition of other value-laden symbols and rituals, contribute to the contemporary Southerner's construction of social reality, and dramatic forms of public communication containing mythic themes about the nature of the past and of the future are especially powerful means of constructing perceptions of reality. Social participation and a feeling of group membership are strengthened as members of a society "imprint and recall socially constructed cultural beliefs about the factual nature of reality and the evaluation of that reality. . . . Such beliefs also make it possible for people to form groups with complex organizational rules and ultimately to develop the social institutions of society itself."[5]

Rhetorical Redefinition

The myths of the Old South, the Lost Cause, and the New South, generated during the nineteenth century, had dominated the Southern past and had held the region's imagination and better instincts captive for twice three score and ten years. Those myths and the social and legal institutions which they supported defined social reality for generations of Southerners. When the cathartic events between 1954 and 1965 transformed the social and institutional structures of the South, the old myths failed. The rhetorical and behavioral excesses of the South during that era of social and cultural chaos were due, at least in part, to the anxieties of participants in a threatened and obsolete cultural myth, frustrated by the inability of the familiar mythology to adequately explain the changes and determined to somehow make it work once again.

Within the epistemological void left by an inadequate mythology and in the face of new social and institutional arrangements mandated by Congress and the Supreme Court, the contemporary mythmakers found it easier than had their progressive predecessors to fashion a new mythology. Rather than reviving the old symbols to embellish another Lost Cause or transforming them from an agricultural to an industrial setting as had been done in an earlier New South, the new generation of communicators chose new symbols to redefine the past and project the future as guides for comprehending reality in the present. The new symbols and the values which they represented helped to construct a new mythology and a new definition of reality. The new myth provided a workable and acceptable definition of the new institutional realities and allowed Southerners to accept and adapt to the dramatic social and cultural changes which had taken place in their region.

As had been the situation with the construction of the first New South creed, most of the new mythmakers were from a younger generation than the guardians of the old myth and most were upper-middle-class professionals with some degree of access to the public forum and the prevailing media of mass communication. The mythic theme of racial equality was consistent with and supportive of the removal of the old legal barriers, and the new leadership venerated the heroes of the civil rights movement and hallowed the battlegrounds of that social and constitutional struggle. The symbols they chose projected their own values and defined a new reality which enshrined those values. The mythic theme of distinctiveness, likewise, substituted new heroes and rituals which were much more egalitarian than those of the old mythology, emphasizing new values and allowing a much larger segment of Southern society to confirm the reality of the myth. The mythic theme of place and community redefined the ancient struggle between rural agrarianism and urban industrialism, suggesting that the sense of place and the ties of community so important to Southerners can coexist with the forces of demographic change and economic development being experienced by the region. These were the values and symbols offered by the new mythmakers, and their access to the media allowed them to share their newly constructed reality with others across the South.

Rhetorical Response

Having seen how public communication is essential in the construction of reality and a society's controlling mythology and having seen how a group of contemporary Southerners constructed a new explanatory mythology for the post-*Brown* South, we must also understand how such cultural myths function rhetorically and persuasively to gain new participants and influence the attitudes, values, and behavior of other members of the society. Once again, the model developed by DeFleur and Ball-Rokeach is instructive. They suggest that "mass-communicated messages can be used to provide individuals with new and seemingly group-supported interpretations—social constructions of reality—regarding some phenomenon toward which they are acting. By doing so, it may be possible to mediate the conduct of individuals as they derive definitions of appropriate behavior and belief from suggested interpretations communicated to them."

Thus, when Reubin Askew, Pat Derian, Julian Bond, Terry Sanford, Philip Morris, or some other credible figure with access to a public forum and the channels of mass media provides a public vision of reality in the South, the receivers of the message assume that the message is a reflection of "the Southern way of life." DeFleur and Ball-Rokeach explain that *"persuasive messages presented via the mass media may provide the appearance of consensus regard-*

ing orientation and action with respect to a given object or goal of persuasion. That is, such messages can present definitions to audiences in such a way that listeners are led to believe that these are socially sanctioned modes of orientation their groups hold toward given objects or situations. The communicator thus provides social constructions of reality shortcutting the process of consensual validation, particularly with respect to objects or practices concerning which groups do not have fully institutionalized cultural interpretations."[6] Such a perspective also helps to explain why the contemporary mythology, being presented in a mythic vacuum, became more successfully established than previous competing myths which had tried to challenge the old myth while it was functional and secure.

The power of cultural myths, then, is demonstrated by their ability to define reality. Since individuals usually form their self-perceptions and pattern their behavior within a social context, the generally held perceptions of social reality become instructive in determining the individual's attitudes about events and institutions, the values which they cherish, the terms on which they interact with and respond to other members of the society, and the social and political discourse in which they engage and to which they respond. The mythic narrative presents normative roles which serve as models for appropriate behavior by demonstrating approved group values, maximizing individual rewards, and achieving group integration. The new Southern mythmakers thus gained new adherents and supporters while simultaneously discrediting their opponents who clung to the old vision by suggesting that disciples of the old order were nonconforming deviants.[7]

In evaluating the rhetorical impact of the cultural mythology of the contemporary South, it is important to understand, as Joseph Campbell advised, that myths "are not to be judged as true or false, but as effective or ineffective, maturative or pathogenic." The effect standard was also of primary importance to Kenneth Boulding, who held that "the meaning of a message is the change which it produces in an image."[8] By this standard the rhetorical mythology of the contemporary South must be judged to have been effective in constructing a new and different social and cultural reality for the region. While the old mythology, in its manifestations as the myths of both the Old South-Lost Cause and the first New South creed, was decidedly elitist, the contemporary mythology is clearly egalitarian. The mythic theme of racial equality provided new heroes, including black heroes for the first time in Southern history, and new values which undermined the ideology of white supremacy and the social structure which it had supported. The mythic theme of regional distinctiveness offered new middle- and lower-class heroes and rituals to demonstrate the uniqueness of Southern culture, and it also reversed the caste system suggested by the symbolic heroes of the planter and the industrialist found in the old myth. The mythic theme of place and community has served to arbitrate the demands of the competing myths of the past, and it stresses the need for broad and active community involvement in future development decisions.

The prevailing rhetorical mythology of the contemporary South is unquestionably different from that which dominated the late 1950s and early 1960s. It posits a past and a future which can appeal to a much larger audience, it offers both a greater opportunity for participation and tangible symbols of a new reality, and it stresses more egalitarian values than did the myth which dominated the past. As a result of these accomplishments, the new mythology has yielded and will continue to yield significant results in action. Emory Cunningham, expressing the editorial philosophy of *Southern Living*, said that "the basic strength behind this regional awareness and projection is that people do care; and when shown a reasonable goal and a fair way to proceed, they will act. We have many individual futures to face; thankfully, the South continues to seek a shared one as well."[9] Just as the old myths dictated defensive and reactionary behavior in the past, the contemporary cultural mythology serves to guide action in directions compatible with the values of the new social reality. As a result, blacks and progressive whites are being elected and appointed to public office, all Southerners have a greater opportunity to participate in the myth and enjoy the benefits of society, and both rural and urban development are being influenced to retain and encourage a sense of place and community.

Multiple and competing myths have coexisted in the past; for example, the myth of the Lost Cause and the vision of the New South espoused by Henry Grady and his associates, and the results of this survey of contemporary myths do not suggest that there is unanimous participation in the realities constituted by the three mythic themes which were analyzed. As George Tindall has observed, "there is still a lot of shade in the Sunbelt," and likewise, there are still other competing realities in the South, including that of the Sunbelt itself. White racists still lurk in small town cafes and big city bank spires, although they are probably no more numerous in the South than in the rest of the nation. Not yet everyone shares the myth of place and community, and even some who do are often lured into commercial strip and suburban residential tract development by a vision of quick profits. Even the good ole boys are frequently duped by the homogenizing pleasures of modernity and the chance to escape their double-wide mobile homes. They can often be found, said Paul Hemphill, "out in the suburbs now, living in identical houses and shopping at the K-Mart and listening to Glen Campbell (Roy Acuff and Ernest Tubb are too tacky now) and hiding their racism behind code words. They have forfeited their style and spirit, traded it all in on a color TV and styrofoam beams for the den."[10]

That the three major mythic themes of the contemporary mythology do not constitute a completely objective description of Southern society and that the myths cannot serve as a factual projection of future history (although they may well serve as a rhetorical guide to planning the future) is of only secondary importance and concern to the rhetorical critic. The contemporary mythology can be judged effective in constructing a new, viable, and widely shared sociocultural reality, in gaining access to and becoming the dominant world view in the contemporary media, in recruiting new participants in the vision, and in rhetorically fostering new behavioral responses to contemporary social problems and public affairs.

It is hoped, however, that as a result of thoughtful criticism, contemporary Southerners will better understand their emerging mythology, will be able to manipulate and reinforce it, will achieve its goals more quickly and more effectively, and will maintain the myth and transmit it to an even larger Southern audience. One participant in a symposium on the South, reflecting upon the presentations and discussions, found that "the mythology and actuality of the Southern past, present, and future that used to float in the ether of day to day unimportance, now stands objectified and demanding attention." I hope that this book will also make some contribution to understanding and improving the society of the contemporary South. Perhaps the sense of Southern history and mythology presented here can, as Willard Gatewood suggested, "not only help us to understand that myths and images, however transitory, do have a life of their own, but also enable us to comprehend the degree to which they are rooted in reality and the degree to which they function as motivating forces in history."[11]

My cautious optimism for the future of the region is shared by many, including George Tindall, who hedged his hopes for the South by warning that "before this begins to sound like Henry Grady warmed over and spiced up with a dash of Pollyanna, let us not forget that if experience is any guide, the South will blow it." Perhaps an understanding of the nature and function of the contemporary mythology will assist Southerners, black and white, to avoid repetition of those past mistakes; however, that alone will not be enough. In working to implement the myth and improve the reality, they should be aware that, as Joel Fleishman said, "if we have a better vision of our future, we must use all of our imagination and more than all of our energy to bring it to pass."[12]

The Media and the Myth

While Southerners today have recognized that their rhetorical past has been controlled by myths and have expressed a commitment to shaping and manipulating new myths for the future, some believe that the greater task will be in adapting the symbols and language of myth to the grammar of the post-McLuhan communication environment. "If we, as public address scholars and students of our sub-cultural communication systems, would take another look, I believe that we would find our work just beginning," said Carl Kell at the 1978 Conference on the Rhetoric of the Contemporary South. "New communication systems are being generated. We can study them as they develop." Indeed, with the contemporary mythology passing through such different chains of transmission as the lyrics of country music on a truck-stop jukebox and the slick pages of the *Economist* on the desk of international financiers, neither practitioners nor critics can ignore the relationship between the form of media and the function of messages. As David Berg noted, "virtually no aspect of public address remains unaffected by mass media. Rhetorical criticism, consequently, if it is to remain a viable instrument for social analysis, must take cognizance of the media's influence on human communication behavior."[13]

The influence of mythology in the nineteenth-century South owed much to the romanticism of the literature of the period, but it was also nurtured by the dominant oral traditions of storytelling and public oratory which translated the symbols and transmitted the drama for the mass audience. James Dickey, in an interview with *Time* magazine, acknowledged that debt. "The South has a long tradition of slow-moving, of standing and watching, of having the time—of giving ourselves the time—to sit, on country porches and courthouse Confederate monuments and on green benches in public parks and tell each other stories, gossip, and use words," he said.[14] Although this characteristic time orientation might be attributed by some to the heat and humidity of the Southern climate or to the debilitating lethargy of hookworm infestation, Southern culture did operate to sustain the influence of the oral traditions. The social pressures to display polite manners in conversation and to conform to the regional ideology only strengthened the importance of communication through stories to make a point while avoiding direct confrontation between friends.

There is a contemporary recognition of the importance of folk orators in the South, and among the programs at every Conference on the Rhetoric of the Contemporary South were admonitions to capture and preserve that tradition. Kathryn Windham, of Selma, Alabama, has authored a book on storytelling entitled *Alabama: One Big Front Porch*, and she helped organize the National Association for the Preservation and Perpetuation of Storytelling in 1975. Located in Jonesboro, Tennessee, the association maintains the National Storytelling Resource Center and hosts the annual National Storytelling Contest. Other organizations, such as the Center for Southern Folklore in Memphis and Appalshop in Whitesburg, Kentucky, have actively recorded folk communication on film and videotape, believing that many of these talents are important to Southern culture and should be preserved and shared.

The heritage of the oral communication system is also reflected in much of the literature of the South. Dickey, in a 1977 interview, said, "People are so garrulous down here. They love to tell stories and anecdotes. Most Southern literature comes right off the front porch. People sitting and talking, long-windedly, but always willing to listen to each other's stories because they've all got good ones to tell." The transition to the printed page was not too difficult. He continued, "look at the Southern writers—Faulkner, Eudora Welty, Flannery O'Connor, Erskine Caldwell, Mark Twain even—they're all essentially storytellers, yarn-spinners. And the poets, too; they have that kind of gift of honey on the lips. Not so much the gift of gab, but a touch of eloquence. That's just the way things have always been down here." Erskine Caldwell shares that same view of the relationship between the region's oral tradition and its literary heritage. "In the South the small town is always alive, not only with gossip, but with stories and anecdotes and talk and conjecture about other people—next door, across the street, around the corner, on the other side of town. . . . All these things I think are conducive to Southern writing," he said. It is a tradition which influences not only fiction and poetry, but history and criticism as well. Cash's *Mind of the South* purports to be a combination of history and analysis, but his style is unmistakably that of the rhetorician and the storyteller. Judge Willis Whichard chose to make a keynote address on the contemporary South in story form by reading an imaginary letter to a fellow North Carolinian from the nineteenth century. Reese Cleghorn wrote of changing Southern society by telling a story about his grandfather, and Roy Reed did the same in a hypothetical letter to his grandfather. The form may well, as some suggest, be fading, but it is not yet gone.[15]

Southern journalists are also adept at preservation of the storytelling art on newsprint. "Southerners do seem to have a certain romance with the written and spoken word. There is a relish for sounds, unique expressions, and the embellished story," said the editors of *Southern Exposure*. "Reporting—like conversation—has always demanded more than the exchange of a few facts, and many of our brethren have been only too willing to turn their preoccupation with language and penchant for irrelevant detail into successful careers." As examples they listed Tom Wicker, Walter Cronkite,

David Brinkley, Clifton Daniel, Willie Morris, Robert Sherill, Nelson Benton, Charles Kuralt, Larry King, Marshall Frady, and Frank McGee, to which list should be added Reese Cleghorn, Pat Watters, John Egerton, Fred Graham, Bill Moyers, Hodding Carter, Roy Reed, Ernie Deane, Roy Blount, Florence King, Sharon McKern, Shirley Abbott and Paul Hemphill.[16]

Among newspaper spellbinders, Johnny Popham has been called "the undisputed king of loquacity and garrulity and verbosity." Claude Sitton, who followed Popham as Southern correspondent for *The New York Times*, described him in action: "After his competitors have surrendered in silence, Popham comes alive. Eyes popping, eyebrows arching, knuckles cracking—all in furious concentration on the tale at hand—Popham launches into a soaring soliloquy," he said. "His delivery and Tidewater accent approximate nothing so much as dollops of sorghum syrup spat from a Gatling gun. This tidal wave of sound has been known to levitate a listener who, transfixed by the onrush of oratory, rises up on tiptoes, wide-eyed and open-mouthed. Not even strong men fortified by strong drink can stand against Dixie's crackerbarrel Demosthenes," concluded Sitton, revealing himself to be a fair storyteller himself. Another friend, Ella Brennan of restaurant fame, remarked of Popham, "The stories he told! And they usually had a subtle message. He has a way of making people understand without preaching." He managed, and still manages, to do the same in his newspaper writing.[17]

There are, however, those who feel that the form is vanishing with the forum. "I can't imagine the Southern style lasting more than another generation," said Harry Ashmore. Blaming the forces of change in part on the South's economic revival and the rhetoric of the nonracist politics of the region, Ashmore also recognized, "beyond that is the communication revolution: broadcasting, radio, and television. We're all part of the same communication system. We all have to see Barbara Walters whether we want to or not.

That's bound to have an impact. I think a lot of the old Southern traditions existed because the communities were isolated." The South is moving, like the rest of the nation, from a culture of "primary orality" and "literacy" to one of "secondary orality." In such a culture "television quickly becomes a society's number one storyteller," and those seeking to understand the regional rhetoric must recognize that, from Barbara Walters to network soap operas, "entertainment is not neutral but an active force in the communication of values."[18] The South's future mythology might well be vulnerable to new messages over which local mythmakers will have little control.

The persuasive nature of storytelling and the importance of its control in a society has long been recognized. Plato, in the *Republic*, had one of his characters say, "first . . . we must supervise the makers of tales; and if they make a fine tale, it must be approved, but if it's not, it must be rejected. We'll persuade nurses and mothers to tell the approved tales to their children and to shape their souls with tales more than their bodies with hands. Many of those they now tell must be thrown out." While there is presently no concentrated effort to shape television programming to reflect the "approved" Southern myths discussed here and reject those in conflict, there is an awareness that the network gatekeepers in New York and Los Angeles have significantly more control over the selection of plots and the televised constructions of reality than do Southerners themselves. In the future, however, regionally originated programs broadcast by satellite from stations such as WTBS in Atlanta, as well as the phenomenal growth of local access cable channels and the potential for new Low-Power Television stations, could very well result in greater local control and design of the public storytelling.

Southern patterns of speech and language, essential ingredients in the vision of distinctiveness, have also been modified by recent events. The net in-migration of almost four million new residents during the past two decades brought new accents to the region, and native Southern children are learning new speech patterns from network television and Sesame Street as well as from their new neighbors. "The tone and quality of life of a society are apparent in its language. Today the dominant speech of the radio and television is culturally almost a foreign language to the South," complained one group of Southerners concerned about the trend toward standardization of the region's speech. In calling for an academic effort to preserve traditional speech and for formation of an organization to coordinate that effort, they said, "the cultural heritage of the South includes distinctive qualities of speech which have been admired and emulated beyond the region itself. Hardly recognized by many, a pronounced change, destructive of these qualities, has taken place within one or two decades. Distinctions of cultured Southern speech have almost disappeared on the radio and television and in much of the common speech. The change is spreading and threatens to destroy that kind of expression." While the social value of diversity of accents might be subject to question, the fact that the national media act to standardize pronunciation and expression is undeniable. In a larger sense, as McLuhan observed, "A language is . . . little affected by the use individuals make of it; but, on the other hand, it almost entirely patterns the character of what is thought, felt, and said by those using it. And it can be utterly changed by the intrusion of another language as speech was changed by writing, and radio by television."[19]

The media's impact on storytelling, too, has been lamented by many Southerners. Alice Walker charged that the value of black folk tales was destroyed by Joel Chandler Harris and Walt Disney, who she said had stolen a part of her black heritage. She recalled having gone to see Disney's *Song of the South* as a child in Eaton, Georgia, and feeling quite disillusioned by the new meanings given to the stories she had heard at home. She then realized, "I was separated from my own folk culture by an invention." Richard Dorsen, a noted folklore scholar who acknowledged the shift from folklore to "the fake lore of industrial man," was also critical of the impact of Disney's Davy Crockett and other "assembly-line demigods" which resulted from cultural packaging by the mass media for popular consumption.[20]

John Egerton has bemoaned the loss of both the forum and the form of rhetoric in the contemporary South. "All talk is dying. No more porch talk because no more porches. Air conditioning and television have taken us inside to be passive voyeurs of a fake world made in Hollywood and New York," he said. "I yearn to hear a good stem-winding preacher, but in Nashville this week I observed Billy Graham made over into a media personality. Billy Sunday must be turning in his grave." If Sunday and Graham were Corporate Christians, as has been suggested, they at least had a more personal and more engaging rhetorical style than the "tube theology" being broadcast by contemporary Southern religious figures such as Jerry Falwell, Oral Roberts, Pat Robertson, and James Bakker. Egerton also lamented the substitution of slick political commercials for political oratory. "Political rhetoric is dying a slow and unnatural death," he said. "I long to hear one more florid politician on the stump, but there are none, and I regret that Kissing Jim Folsom has to suffer listening to his successors making a mockery of the art. I'd give anything to hear just one half-way decent storyteller in public life, but Jimmy Carter, Southerner or not, can't do it. No, friends, I'm afraid the South has had it." Reese Cleghorn, a fair storyteller in his own right, also surveyed the changing South and likewise concluded, "more than porch talk and verandas are gone."[21]

Arguments can also be made that the role of the national media as gatekeeper and opinion-maker has increased with the pervasiveness of network influence and the trend toward concentration of ownership. Lyndon Johnson, in making his decision to run for president in 1964, thought that it might be impossible for any

Southerner to be elected because "the metropolitan press of the Eastern Seaboard would never permit it." In forming that conclusion, he perceived a bias against the region that went beyond his personal qualities. As he later said, "I was not thinking just of the derisive articles about my style, my clothes, my manner, my accent, and my family—although I admit I received enough of that kind of treatment in my first few months as President to last a lifetime." Larry King chastised the national media for its biases. For example, he said, "take the way y'all treated ol' Lyndon Johnson. Maybe he *did* hoo-haw right much and ate too much barbeque sauce and tugged up his shirt to show his belly scar after his operation, but hellfire, if he'd been from anywhere but Down Home then y'all would of stopped at calling him eccentric."[22]

David Underhill, a Southerner who had worked in the New York CBS newsroom, found a distinct bias among the staff against Southern accents, Southern sources, and Southern stories, and he felt that their stereotypical perceptions of the South prevented serious attention to legitimate coverage of the region. Others, however, have contended that the negative images of the South portrayed on network television might be an advantage. The sparse coverage of the South by major media between 1965 and 1975 allowed the Southern mythmakers greater rhetorical latitude to redefine their own regional vision, and one writer has suggested that negative images on television might act to deter regional in-migration, thereby leaving "just that much more of our forests, clean air and natural resources and beauty that will be available to 'we all.'"[23]

Despite the alleged bias of the national press, some Southerners contend that the news media, both local and national, have also played an active role in establishing the new mythology. At the national level, for example, *The New York Times* in 1947 became the first major newspaper to employ a Southern correspondent when the editors assigned John Popham to cover the region. At that time, said Popham, "you couldn't find a soul in the North who knew

there was such a thing as the South. They saw the South as a mono-
lith. I knew better." In reflecting upon his success in reporting on
the region, Popham, a native of Virginia, said, "I was able to use
the language, to understand it, and you have to have a feel for the
language. . . . You have to understand the language and the people."
Those traits were shared by Claude Sitton, who followed Popham
in 1958, and Roy Reed, who followed Sitton and who covered the
South for the *Times* from 1965 to 1978. Harold Fleming, former director of the Southern Regional Council, credited Popham with
helping his organization gain national attention. "He had a sense
of institution building, an understanding that the South had to
build new institutions to help usher it into the 20th century. And he
was a key figure in the building of several. . . . He knew that what
the *Times* paid attention to could not be long ignored by the region's press, so he interpreted and communicated unsparingly on
our behalf. He lobbied articles onto the front page of the *Times*."[24]

Zeke Segal, CBS Atlanta Bureau Chief since 1972, admits coming
to the South in 1968 with many misconceptions. He said LeRoy Collins' speech at the 1964 Democratic National Convention had begun
to change the media's perception of Southern society, but George
Wallace later stole the spotlight and became the stereotypical
Southerner in the nation's mind. Segal believes that television is
acting as a cultural leveler, making the regions more homogenous,
but he also feels that it has been an active force in presenting a
more positive image of the South to the national audience. As support, he cited the fact that between 1973 and 1978 the Atlanta bureau, trying to show positive changes in the region, filed and aired
more stories on the CBS Evening News than any other bureau.[25]

In addition to the increasing coverage by CBS and *The New York
Times*, Southerners also gained greater access to the local media.
Ranging from a plethora of underground and alternative newspapers, of which Tom Forcade of the Underground Press Syndicate
said the South had more per capita than the rest of the nation in

the 1970s, to the new variety of state and metropolitan magazines, progressive Southerners found new outlets and wider audiences for social and political reporting and commentary. These channels were relatively new means of communication for Southerners, having been nonexistent during the last two-thirds of the nineteenth century and dominated by academic, financial, or political elites during the first two-thirds of the twentieth century.[26]

On the other end of the technological spectrum, the decade of the seventies also saw the beginning of Southern-originated satellite broadcasting, with Ted Turner's WTBS Super Station and Cable News Network in Atlanta, both covering stories about the South and transmitting the signals to a national audience. The advent of these new media have, therefore, served a positive function in redefining the image and encouraging the new cultural mythology of the contemporary South.

The debate over the impact of new media forms on myths and communication systems has not yet been fully resolved, although almost all observers and participants agree that a relationship exists. The old mythology of the South maintained its hegemony in large part because it was quite easy for the keepers of the myth to control the images and symbols available to the public. Kenneth Boulding, confirming this point, observed, "As long as a subculture is isolated from the rest of the world, with all its lines of communication lying within, its image tends to be self-supporting and self-perpetuating. All the messages which are received by the individuals participating confirm the images which they have, because to a large extent the messages originate in these images." As access to the new media increased during the 1960s and 1970s, it became possible for new mythic themes to circulate throughout the South, receive consideration, and gain new adherents. Undoubtedly, the televised scenes of white intransigence and brutality to blacks during the late 1950s and early 1960s helped create a new reality for both blacks and whites in the South and throughout the nation, wrenching control of reality and mythology from those who had controlled it for years.

Whether the new media will facilitate stability of the new visions which have replaced the old mythology or merely result in mythic confusion remains to be seen. Marshall McLuhan has warned of the possibility of mythic obliteration and a dysfunctional amythic culture "unless we choose to restrain the operation of form on form by due study and strategy. We now stand at this point with regard to all myth and media. We can, perhaps we must, become the masters of cultural and historical alchemy. And to this end, we can, I suggest, find means in the study of media as languages and languages as myth. For our experience with the grammar and syntax of languages can be made available for the direction and control of media old and new." It seems that the contemporary mythmakers of the South have taken McLuhan's advice, and they have exhibited an understanding of both myth and media. Louis Rubin has contended, contrary to the prognostications of those who predict the end of porch talk and social gossip, that the personal folksiness of Southern communication has defied and adapted to the new media. He cites, as one example, the phenomenon of citizen band radio gossip among truckers, the majority of whom are native or transplanted Southerners mastering a new medium for traditional purposes, and it also seems that country music is a similar indigenous mass communication system which has been able to preserve the art of storytelling and to remain under the control of Southern songwriters and singers.[27]

Conclusion

In this study I have tried to demonstrate the rhetorical nature of public myths, to show that the South has developed a new mythology to define and explain contemporary reality, and to lay bare the relationship between myth and media. I hope that my work has demonstrated the utility of myth analysis for contemporary society and that it will serve to further the efforts of those working for a progressive South and a progressive Southern mythology. The mass media should not be viewed as destructive of those ends or of the rhetorical power of mythology, for as Harry Levin has suggested, "In this part of the latter twentieth century, face to face with a decline in the literate arts and a rise in the extraliterary and audiovisual media, myth should be more influential than ever."[28] This being the case, contemporary Southern mythmakers should have an even greater opportunity to define and redefine reality for the benefit of the region as well as the rest of the nation.

Notes and References

INTRODUCTION

1. Edwin M. Yoder, Jr., Foreword, *The Enduring South: Subcultural Persistence in Mass Society*, by John Shelton Reed (Lexington: D. C. Heath, 1972) xv–xvi.

2. George B. Tindall, "Mythology: A New Frontier in Southern History, " in *Myth and Southern History*, eds. Patrick Gerster and Nicholas Cords (Chicago: Rand McNally, 1974): 2.

3. Tom Wolfe, *The Kandy-Kolored Tangerine-Flake Streamline Baby* (New York: Pocket Books, 1966): 106.

4. H. Brandt Ayres, "You Can't Eat Magnolias," in *You Can't Eat Magnolias*, ed. H. Brandt Ayers and Thomas Naylor (New York: McGraw-Hill, 1972): 5.

CHAPTER ONE

1. George B. Tindall, "Mythology: A New Frontier in Southern History," in *Myth and Southern History*, eds. Patrick Gerster and Nicholas Cords (Chicago: Rand McNally, 1974): 2.

2. T. Harry Williams, *Romance and Realism in Southern Politics* (Athens: University of Georgia Press, 1964): 3; W. J. Cash, *The Mind of the South* (New York: Alfred A. Knopf, 1941): 46; and Clement Eaton, *The Freedom of Thought Struggle in the Old South* (New York: Harper and Row, 1964): 47. See also Clement Eaton, *The Mind of the Old South* (Baton Rouge: Louisiana State University Press, 1964): 181–201.

3. Cash 48, 4.

4. John Richard Alden, *The First South* (Baton Rouge: Louisiana State University Press, 1961): 7–11.

5. Charles Sydnor, *The Development of Southern Sectionalism, 1819–1848* (Baton Rouge: Louisiana State University Press, 1948): 32; Eaton, *The Freedom of Thought Struggle in the Old South* 32.

6. Alden 132–133; John M. Anderson, ed., *Calhoun: Basic Documents* (State College: Pennsylvania State University Press, 1952): 15.

7. Sydnor 335, 332. Williams 8.

8. Lewis M. Killian, *White Southerners* (New York: Random House, 1970): 40, 5; Williams 9.

9. Cash 62; Eaton, *The Freedom of Thought Struggle in the Old South* 46–47; Sydnor ix.

10. Owen Peterson, "Speaking in the Southern Commercial Conventions, 1837–1859," in *Oratory in the Old South*, ed. Waldo W. Braden (Baton Rouge: Louisiana State University Press, 1970): 191–192.

11. Donald W. Zacharias, "The Know-Nothing Party and the Oratory of Nativism," in *Oratory in the Old South* 232.

12. Ralph T. Eubanks, "The Rhetoric of the Nullifiers," in *Oratory in the Old South* 54; William W. Freehling, *Prelude to Civil War: The Nullification Controversy in South Carolina, 1816–1836* (New York: Harper & Row, 1966): xii.

13. Bert E. Bradley and Jerry L. Tarver, "John C. Calhoun's Rhetorical Method in Defense of Slavery," in *Oratory in the Old South* 170. Sydnor 336.

14. C. Vann Woodward, *The Burden of Southern History* (Baton Rouge: Louisiana State University Press, 1968): 200–201. See also Eubanks 21; Sydnor 335; and Williams 10, for identical conclusions.

15. Bradley and Tarver 184. Sydnor 220–221.

16. Eaton, *The Freedom of Thought Struggle in the Old South* 35. See also Cash 62–63; Woodward, *Burden of Southern History* 201–202; and Williams 9.

17. Eaton, *The Freedom of Thought Struggle in the Old South* 162; Peterson 210; Waldo W. Braden, "Three Southern Readers and Southern Oratory," *Southern Speech Journal*, 32 (1966): 31–33.

18. Cash 47.

19. Cash 63.

20. Eaton, *The Mind of the Old South* 182; Cash 64, 67–68.

21. Eaton, *The Freedom of Thought Struggle in the Old South* 48; Eaton, *The Mind of the Old South* 186.

22. Cash 65; Sydnor 306–312; Eaton, *The Freedom of Thought Struggle in the Old South* 49–50; Eaton, *The Mind of the Old South* 181–201.

23. Eaton, *The Mind of the Old South* 222–224; Eubanks 31; Eaton, *The Freedom of Thought Struggle in the Old South* 5. See also Daniel R. Hundley, *Social Relations in Our Southern States* (New York: H. B. Price, 1860); and William R. Taylor, *Cavalier and Yankee* (New York: George Braziller, 1961).

24. Anne Firor Scott, *The Southern Lady: From Pedestal to Politics, 1830–1930* (Chicago: University of Chicago Press, 1970): 4; Cash 89.

25. Scott 15; Cash 87; Eaton, *The Mind of the Old South* 11–12.

26. Francis Pendleton Gaines, *The Southern Plantation: A Study in the Development and Accuracy of a Tradition* (New York: Columbia University Press, 1925). See also Eaton, *The Mind of the Old South* 222–227. John Pendleton Kennedy, *Swallow Barn*, 2nd ed. (New York: G. P. Putnam & Co., 1851): 8

27. Eaton, *The Mind of the Old South* 227–233; Sydnor 334.

28. Bradley and Tarver 177; Eaton, *The Freedom of Thought Struggle in the Old South* 155–156; Eaton, *The Mind of the Old South* 331.

29. Sydnor 338. For a detailed critique of this view, see Anthony Hillbruner, "Inequality, the Great Chain of Being, and Ante-Bellum Southern Oratory," *Southern Speech Journal*, 25 (1960): 172–189.

30. Eaton, *The Freedom of Thought Struggle in the Old South* 32–35; Eaton, *The Mind of the Old South* 101–102.

31. Annette Shelby, "The Southern Lady Becomes an Advocate," in *Oratory in the New South*, ed. Waldo W. Braden (Baton Rouge: Louisiana State University Press, 1979): 212; Eaton, *The Mind of the Old South* 233.

32. Robert G. Gunderson, "The Southern Whigs," in *Oratory in the Old South* 110; Ulrich Bonner Phillips, *Life and Labor in the Old South* (Boston: Little, Brown & Co., 1929): 110.

33. Cash 64.

34. Richard Taylor, *Destruction and Reconstruction* (New York: D. Appleton & Co., 1879): 14; David A. Thomas, "Secession and Slavery: Jefferson Davis' Rhetorical Vision of the South," Southern Speech Communication Association convention, Biloxi, 13 April 1979; E. Merton Coulter, *The Confederate States of America, 1861–1865* (Baton Rouge: Louisiana State University Press, 1950): 105.

35. Coulter 482–519.

36. Frank E. Vandiver, "The Confederate Myth," *Southwest Review*, 46 (1961): 199–204.

37. Joel Chandler Harris, *Life of Henry W. Grady* (New York: Cassell Publishing Company, 1890): 86–87.

38. W. Stuart Towns, "Ceremonial Orators and National Reconciliation," in *Oratory in the New South* 117; Waldo W. Braden, "'Repining Over an Irrevocable Past?': The Ceremonial Orator in a Defeated Society, 1865–1900," in *Oratory in the New South* 10; Howard Dorgan, "Rhetoric of the United Confederate Veterans: A Lost Cause Mythology in the Making," in *Oratory in the New South* 171.

39. C. Vann Woodward, *Origins of the New South, 1877–1913* (Baton Rouge: Louisiana State University Press, 1951): 137; Dorgan 171; Braden, "'Repining Over An Irrevocable Past?'" 12.

40. Cash 126–127; Woodward, *Origins of the New South* 157.

41. Cash 130.

42. Bradley T. Johnson, "Placing Principle Above Policy," *Confederate Veteran*, 4 (1896), 507–508.

43. Rollin G. Osterweis, *The Myth of the Lost Cause, 1865–1900* (Hamden, Conn.: Archon Books, 1973): 10.

44. "Constitution of the United Daughters of the Confederacy," reprinted in Osterweis, 93.

45. Cash 146.

46. James Oliver Robinson, *American Myth, American Reality* (New York: Hill and Wang, 1980): 88; Henry Savage, Jr., *Seeds of Time: The Background of Southern Thinking* (New York: Henry Holt and Company, 1959): 198; Osterweis 3, 101. For an example of the revised myth see Richard M. Weaver, *The Southern Tradition at Bay* (New Rochelle, N. Y.: Arlington House, 1968): 47–98.

CHAPTER TWO

1. Harold D. Mixon, "Henry Grady as a Persuasive Strategist," in *Oratory in the New South*, ed. Waldo W. Braden (Baton Rouge: Louisiana State University Press, 1979): 74–116. An article which questions both the power of the New South myth and the artistry of its proponents is J. Louis Campbell, III, "In Search of the New South," *Southern Speech Communication Journal*, 47 (1982): 361–388. This phenomenon is described in William B. Hesseltine and Henry L. Ewbanks, Jr., "Old Voices in the New South," *Quarterly Journal of Speech*, 39 (1953), 451–458.

2. Paul M. Gaston, *The New South Creed: A Study in Southern Mythmaking* (New York: Alfred A. Knopf, 1970): 221.

3. Gaston 221. An example of this white supremacy posture can be found in Grady's speech, "The South and Her Problems," delivered on October 26, 1887, at Dallas, Texas.

4. Henry Savage, Jr., *Seeds of Time: The Background of Southern Thinking* (New York: Henry Holt and Co., 1959): 212.

5. W. J. Cash, *The Mind of the South* (New York: Alfred A. Knopf, 1941): 174.

6. *Manufacturers' Record*, 18 August 1929, 53–54. Lewis M. Killian, *White Southerners* (New York: Random House, 1970): 31.

7. *I'll Take My Stand: The South and the Agrarian Tradition* (New York: Harper and Brothers, 1930): 1; Virginia Rock, "The Making and Meaning of *I'll Take My Stand*: A Study in Utopian Conservatism, 1925–1939," Diss. Minnesota 1961, 20, cited in F. Garvin Davenport, Jr., *The Myth of Southern History* (Nashville: Vanderbilt University Press, 1970): 47.

8. Owsley 79–81; Andrew Nelson Lytle, "The Hind Tit," in *I'll Take My Stand* 244.

9. Robert B. Downs, *Books That Changed the South* (Totowa, N. J.: Littlefield, Adams & Co., 1977): 229–236; Davenport 63.

10. Eastland quoted in Jack Bass and Walter DeVries, *The Transformation of Southern Politics: Social Change and Consequence Since 1945* (New York: New American Library, 1977): 5; Howard W. Odum, *Race and Rumors of Race* (Chapel Hill: University of North Carolina Press, 1943); C. Vann Woodward, *The Strange Career of Jim Crow* (New York: Oxford University Press, 1966): 119.

11. Charles P. Roland, *The Improbable Era: The South Since World War II* (Lexington: University of Kentucky Press, 1975): 59; V. O. Key Jr., *Southern Politics in State and Nation* (New York: Alfred A. Knopf, 1949): 338.

12. Key 340; Roland 60.

13. Key 9–10, 671, 11.

14. Numan V. Bartley, *The Rise of Massive Resistance* (Baton Rouge: Louisiana State University Press, 1969): 345; C. Vann Woodward, "From the First Reconstruction to the Second," *Harper's*, April 1965, 128–129; Reese Cleghorn, *Radicalism: Southern Style* (Atlanta: Southern Regional Council, 1968): 6; Tindall, "Mythology: A New Frontier in Southern History," 2; George B. Tindall, "The Benighted South: Origins of a Modern Image," *Virginia Quarterly Review*, 40 (1964): 281.

15. Francis M. Wilhoit, *The Politics of Massive Resistance* (New York: George Braziller, 1973): 56.

16. Wilhoit 74.

17. James O. Eastland, "We've Reached an Era of Judicial Tyranny," in *The American South in the Twentieth Century*, ed. Robert L. Brandfon (New York: Thomas Y. Crowell Co., 1967): 47.

18. Wilhoit 123–124.

19. Wilhoit 127–128.

20. Wilhoit 100.

21. For an account of these methods and their effectiveness see James W. Silver, *Mississippi: The Closed Society* (New York: Harcourt, Brace & World, 1966); and Waldo W. Braden, "The Rhetoric of a Closed Society," *Southern Speech Communication Journal*, 45 (1980): 333–351.

22. Woodward, *The Strange Career of Jim Crow* 3; James Branch Cabell, *Let Me Lie* (New York: Farrar, Straus and Co., 1947): 74; Davenport viii.

23. Williams 6; Dewey W. Grantham, ed., *The South and the Sectional Image* (New York: Harper and Row, 1967): 39–40.

24. Darden Asbury Pyron, "Gone With the Wind: Southern History and National Popular Culture," *Studies in Popular Culture*, 3 (1980): 19.

25. Osterweis x–xi.

26. Gaston 223–224.

CHAPTER THREE

1. J. Earl Williams, *Plantation Politics: The Southern Economic Heritage* (Austin: Futura Press, 1972); Guion Griffis Johnson, "The Ideology of White Supremacy," in *The South and the Sectional Image*, ed. Dewey W. Grantham (New York: Harper and Row, 1967); David M. Landry, "A Socio-economic View of Politics in Mississippi," *Southern Quarterly*, 13 (1975): 217–228; and Thomas H. Naylor and James Clotfelter, *Strategies for Change in the South* (Chapel Hill: University of North Carolina Press, 1975).

2. T. Harry Williams, "Trends in Southern Politics," in *The Idea of the South: Pursuit of a Central Theme*, ed. Frank E. Vandiver (Chicago: University of Chicago Press, 1964): 2.

3. Frank E. Vandiver, "The Southerner as Extremist," in *The Idea of the South*,

46; Lewis M. Killian, *White Southerners* (New York: Random House, 1970): 5; John Hope Franklin, "The Great Confrontation: The South and the Problem of Change," *Journal of Southern History*, 38 (1972): 3–20; T. Harry Williams, "Trends in Southern Politics" 61; Charles Lerche, *The Uncertain South* (Chicago: Quadrangle, 1964): 243.; and Edgar T. Thompson, "The South and the Second Emancipation," in *Change in the Contemporary South*, ed. Allen P. Sindler (Durham, N.C.: Duke University Press, 1963): 112.

4. T. Harry Williams, "Trends in Southern Politics" 61; T. Harry Williams, *Romance and Realism in Southern Politics* (Athens: University of Georgia Press, 1963): 7; Rollin G. Osterweis, *The Myth of the Lost Cause, 1865–1900* (Hamden, Conn.: Archon Books, 1973): 143–144.

5. C. Vann Woodward, *The Strange Career of Jim Crow*, 2nd ed. (New York: Oxford University Press, 1966): 10; Thomas S. Frentz and Thomas B. Farrell, "Conversion of American Consciousness: The Rhetoric of *The Exorcist*," *Quarterly Journal of Speech*, 61 (1975): 42; Leslie W. Dunbar, "The Changing Mind of the South," in *The South and the Sectional Image* 163.

6. George B. Tindall, *The Emergence of the New South, 1913–1945* (Baton Rouge: Louisiana State University Press, 1967): 390. See also Dewey W. Granthan, *The Democratic South* (Athens: University of Georgia Press, 1963): and V. O. Key, Jr., *Southern Politics in State and Nation* (New York: Alfred A. Knopf, 1949): 645.

7. W. J. Cash, *The Mind of the South* (New York: Alfred A. Knopf, 1941: 377–378.

8. Woodward 165–166.

9. F. Garvin Davenport, Jr., *The Myth of Southern History* (Nashville: Vanderbilt University Press, 1970): 81.

10. Tindall, *Emergence of the New South* 170–175.

11. Stephen Larsen, *The Shaman's Doorway* (New York: Harper and Row, 1976): 7–8.

12. Robert Penn Warren, *The Legacy of the Civil War: Meditations on the Centennial* (New York: Random House, 1961): 57; Richard E. Yates, "The Heavens Are Still There: The Errors of Our Ways," *Arkansas Democrat*, 19 August 1979, 7A.

13. Social scientific support for this proposition is quite extensive. See Herbert C. Kelman, "Compliance, Identification, and Internalization: Three Processes of Attitude Change," *Journal of Conflict Resolution*, 2 (1958): 51–60; Richard M. Johnson, *The Dynamics of Compliance* (Evanston: Northwestern University Press, 1967); Milton Rokeach, *Beliefs, Attitudes and Values* (San Francisco: Jossey-Bass, 1968); C. A. Kiesler, R. E. Nisbett, and M. P. Zanna, "On Inferring One's Beliefs from One's Behavior," *Journal of Personality and Social Psychology*, 4 (1969): 321–327; Daryl J. Bem, *Beliefs, Attitudes and Human Affairs* (Belmont, Calif.: Brooks-Cole Publishing Company, 1970; James W. Prothro, "Stateways Versus Folkways Revisited: An Error in Prediction," *Journal of Politics*, 34 (1972): 352–364; and Harrell R. Rogers, Jr., and Charles S. Bullock, III, *Law and Social Change: Civil Rights Laws and Their Consequences* (New York: McGraw-Hill, 1972).

14. Jack Bass and Walter DeVries, *The Transformation of Southern Politics: Social Change and Political Consequence Since 1945* (New York: Basic Books, 1976): 110–111.

15. Thomas Naylor, "The L. Q. C. Lamar Society," *New South* 25 (1970): 24–25; Edgar T. Thompson, ed., *Perspectives on the South: Agenda for Research* (Durham: Duke University Press, 1967): xii; Woodward 65; and Dunbar 173.

16. Woodward 141; United States Commission on Civil Rights, *The Voting Rights Act: Ten Years After* (Washington: Government Printing Office, 1975): 40–52; Hugh Stephen Whitaker, "A New Day: The Effect of Negro Enfranchisement in Selected Mississippi Counties," Diss. Florida State 1965; Voter Education Project, *Black Elected Officials in the Southern States* (Atlanta: Southern Regional Council, 1969; Steve Suitts and Alexis Barrett, *The Segregated Governments in the South* (Atlanta: Southern Regional Council, 1979): 1; Stephen A. Smith, "Southern Senators and the Continuing American Revolution: The Voting Rights Act of 1975," Southern Speech Communication Association convention, San Antonio, April 1976, provides an analysis of the changing rhetorical and axiological positions of Southern Senators during the debates in 1965 and 1975; Jimmy Carter, *Speech Delivered at the Martin Luther King Hospital, Los Angeles, June 1, 1976* (Atlanta: Democratic Presidential Campaign Committee, 1976): 1.

17. "SWC's First Black Met Opposition, Hatred," *Arkansas Democrat*, 27 July 1977, 1B; "Rebel Flag at Ole Miss Now Symbolizes New Horizons, Not Lost Causes," *Arkansas Gazette*, 14 October, 1976, 14A. Willie Morris, *The Courting of Marcus Dupree* (New York: Doubleday, 1984).

18. Paul M. Gaston, *The New South Creed: A Study in Southern Mythmaking* (New York: Alfred A. Knopf, 1970): 237–238.

19. George B. Tindall, *The Ethnic Southerner* (Baton Rouge: Louisiana State University Press, 1976): 214.

20. Henry Savage, Jr., *Seeds of Time: The Background of Southern Thinking* (New York: Henry Holt and Co., 1959): 200.

21. Chaim Perelman and L. Olbrechts-Tyteca, *The New Rhetoric*, trans. John Wilkinson and Purcell Weaver (Notre Dame: University of Notre Dame Press, 1969): 332.

22. John T. Marcus, "The World Impact of the West," in *Myth and Mythmaking*, ed. Henry A. Murray (New York: George Braziller, 1960): 224.

23. Quoted in Mark Schorer, "The Necessity of Myth," in *Myth and Mythmaking* 355.

24. Henry A. Murray, "The Possible Nature of a Mythology to Come," in *Myth and Mythmaking* 344.

25. Stephen A. Smith, "The Old South Myth as a Contemporary Southern Commodity," *Journal of Popular Culture*, 16, No. 3 (1983): 22–29; Stephen A. Smith, "Selling the South: The Rhetoric of Southern Tourism Promotion," Midwest Modern Language Association convention, St. Louis, November 1976; Carol Barrington, "Louisiana's Antebellum Mansions Offer a Rare Chance to Sample History . . . and

to Live Like Scarlett O'Hara," *Chicago Tribune*, 18 April 1982, Sect. II, 8–9; Randy Mink, "Old South and Its Heroes Linger in Historic Lexington," *Chicago Tribune*, 18 April 1982, Sect. II, 6; Four Winds Travel, Inc., *The South* (New York: Four Winds Travel, 1982).

CHAPTER FOUR

1. Samuel DuBois Cook, "Keynote Address," in *The People of the South: Heritages and Futures*, ed. William C. Havard and Jane Crater (Nashville: Southern Regional Conference on the Humanities, 1976): 24. Personal interview with Samuel DuBois Cook, Atlanta, 12 January 1981.

2. H. Brandt Ayers, "The L. Q. C. Lamar Society," in *You Can't Eat Magnolias*, ed. H. Brandt Ayers and Thomas H. Naylor (New York: McGraw-Hill, 1972): 368; Thomas Naylor, "The L. Q. C. Lamar Society," *New South*, 25 (1970): 21–25.

3. C. Vann Woodward, "New South Fraud is Papered by Old South Myth," *Washington Post*, 9 July 1961, E3; Harry S. Ashmore, *An Epitaph for Dixie* (New York: W. W. Norton & Company, 1957); Frank E. Smith, *Look Away from Dixie* (Baton Rouge: Louisiana State University Press, 1963).

4. Personal interview with Ray Thornton, Fayetteville, Ark., 5 October 1976. Mr. Thornton was a Congressman from southern Arkansas at the time of the interview, and is presently serving as President of the University of Arkansas. See also, Carl N. Degler, *The Other South* (New York: Harper & Row, 1974).

5. Quoted in John Pennington, "Is There a New South?" *Atlanta Journal and Constitution Magazine*, 20 February 1972, 18; Terry Sanford, "The End of the Myths: The South Can Lead the Nation," in *You Can't Eat Magnolias* 318.

6. Jack Temple Kirby, *Media-Made Dixie* (Baton Rouge: Louisiana State University Press, 1975): 119–123, 141–147; Janice Hocker Rushing and Thomas E. Frentz, "The Rhetoric of 'Rocky': A Social Value Model of Criticism," *Western Journal of Speech Communication*, 41 (1978): 64. See also, James McBride Dabbs, *Civil Rights in Recent Southern Fiction* (Atlanta: Southern Regional Council, 1969).

7. Martin Luther King, Jr., *Stride toward Freedom: The Montgomery Story* (New York: Harper and Brothers, 1958); *Where Do We Go from Here: Chaos or Community?* (New York: Harper & Row, 1957); *Why We Can't Wait* (New York: Harper & Row, 1964); *The Trumpet of Conscience* (New York: Harper & Row, 1968); F. Garvin Davenport, *The Myth of Southern History* (Nashville: Vanderbilt University Press, 1970): 197.

8. Jack Bass, *Unlikely Heroes: The Southern Judges Who Made the Civil Rights Revolution* (New York: Simon and Schuster, 1981): 15.

9. Kirby 138, 149–150.

10. Wayne King, "Rapidly Growing Arkansas Turns to Liberal Politicians," *The New York Times*, 14 May 1978, 26; Erick Black, "Good Ol' Boys Fall from Grace in Arkansas Politics," *Minneapolis Tribune*, 16 April 1978, 11.

11. Francis M. Wilhoit, *The Politics of Massive Resistance* (New York: George Braziller, 1973): 118.

12. Editorial, "The South of the Future," *New South*, 19 (1964): 28. A concise history of the efforts and the rhetoric of the Southern Regional Council is the 35th anniversary editorial entitled "The State of the South," *The Southern Regional Council Annual Report, 1979* (Atlanta: Southern Regional Council, 1980). I am also indebted to Paige Crosland for granting a personal interview in Atlanta, 2 May 1977.

13. Ayres, "The L. Q. C. Lamar Society" 370.

14. Personal Interview with Sue Thrasher, Atlanta, 2 May 1977; *Southern Exposure*, 1, No. 1 (1973): cover 2.

15. Julian Bond to Dear Brothers and Sisters, Multilith Letter, October 1966: 1.

16. Institute for Southern Studies, *Facing South* (Chapel Hill: Institute for Southern Studies, 1979).

17. William J. Starosta, "The Use of Traditional Entertainment Forms to Stimulate Social Change," *Quarterly Journal of Speech*, 60 (1974): 306–312; Wimal Dissanayake, "New Wine in Old Bottles: Can Folk Media Convey Modern Messages?" *Journal of Communication*, 27, No. 2 (1977): 122–124; John O'Neal, "Art and the Movement," *Southern Exposure*, 9, No. 1 (1981): 80; "We Became Visible, Our Image Was Enlarged," *Southern Exposure*, 9, No. 1 (1981): 5.

18. Pat Watters, "It's Been 20 Long Years," *Southern Voices*, May–June 1974: 5.

19. "Just Schools," *Southern Exposure*, 7, No. 2 (1979); Jimmy Carter, "Remarks at a White House Observance of the 25th Anniversary of the Supreme Court Decision *Brown v. Board of Education*," *Weekly Compilation of Presidential Documents*, 21 May 1979, 883–885. See also Betty Norwood Chaney, "Interchange," *Southern Changes*, May 1979: 2; Tom Gilmore, "The South is Rising Again—In Living Colors," in *The Rising South: Issues and Changes*, ed. Donald R. Noble and Joab L. Thomas (University: University of Alabama Press, 1976): 54–55.

20. Reubin Askew, "Remarks of the New Chairman," Southern Growth Policies Board, Pinehurst, N. C., 13 November 1975, 1–5.

21. Chris Mayfield, "The Middle Ground Turns to Quicksand," *Southern Exposure*, 7, No. 2 (1979): 40.

22. David Pryor, "Address to Little Rock Central High School Honors Assembly," 20 May 1975, 2, reading copy in possession of the author; "Ex-governor, Black Central Graduate, Recall 1957," *Arkansas Gazette*, 1 April 1977, 7A; "A History Marker at the School Where It Was Made," *Arkansas Gazette*, 26 November 1982, 3A.

23. Wayne Flint, "The Ethics of Democratic Persuasion and the Birmingham Crisis," *Southern Speech Journal*, 35 (1969): 40–53; "A City Reborn," *Time*, 27 September 1976, 55–56.

24. Rex Thomas, "Selma Marked End of an Era in Deep South," *Northwest Arkansas Times*, 16 March 1975, 7A; *Voter Education Project 1975 Annual Report* (Atlanta: Voter Education Project, 1976): 22.

25. *Congressional Quarterly Almanac, 1965* (Washington: Congressional Quar-

terly, Inc., 1966): 538; Selma as a media event is developed by David J. Garrow, *Protest at Selma: Martin Luther King, Jr., and the Voting Rights Act of 1965* (New Haven: Yale University Press, 1979).

26. Tom Mathews, "The Southern Mystique," *Newsweek*, 19 July 1976: 30, 33; Larry L. King, "We Ain't Trash No More: How Jimmy Carter Led the Rednecks from the Wilderness," *Esquire*, November 1976, 88.

27. Bob Hall, "Jimmy Carter: Master Magician," *Southern Exposure*, 5, No. 1 (1977): 43–44; Larry L. King, "We Ain't Trash No More" 154–155; Stephen A. Smith, "The Laying-On of Hands," *Grapevine*, 24 September 1976, 3.

28. "How Southern Is He?" *Time*, 27 September 1976, 47.

29. Anthony Lewis, "The South's Place in American Politics '76," *Arkansas Gazette*, 1 October 1976, 6A; letter received from Jimmy Carter, 14 August 1975.

30. "Hodding Carter, Vice President," (Memphis: Hodding Carter for Vice President, 1972).

31. Walker Percy, "Emerging from the Great Southern Obsession—Where Now?" *Southern Exchange*, March 1979, 49; H. Brandt Ayres, "We've Got to Stop Meeting Like This," Commission on the Future of the South, Atlanta, 12 January 1981.

32. "Blocking of Door Not Racial Matter, Wallace Asserts," *Arkansas Gazette*, 8 December 1978, 19A.

33. Elizabeth A. Harris, "Charlie Daniels: Southern Music at the White House?" *Arkansas Gazette*, 3 October 1976, 11E.

34. "Mathews Advises New Strategy for Mainstream South," *Southern Growth: Problems & Promise*, 4 (Spring-Summer 1977): 5.

35. Quoted in John Egerton, *School Desegregation: A Report Card from the South* (Atlanta: Southern Regional Council, 1976): 50.

36. Larry L. King, "We Ain't Trash No More" 88.

37. Personal interview with Vance Packard, Fayetteville, Ark., 26 October 1976; Jerry Jones, "Race Problems Now in Great Cities of the North, Ashmore Declares," *Arkansas Gazette*, 17 May 1979, 1A, 5A; Harry S. Ashmore, "The *Brown* Decision in Retrospect, 1954–1976," *Arkansas Gazette*, 26 September 1976, 5E; Editorial, "Boston's Own Image-Makers," *Arkansas Gazette*, 20 November 1977, 2E; "South Ahead in Changes, Judge Believes," *Arkansas Gazette*, 17 April 1978, 13A; David Hawkins, "Southerners Should Feel a Little Bit More Superior," *Arkansas Democrat*, 14 August 1977, 25A; John Egerton, "Hello, Boston, This is Little Rock Calling," *Charlotte Observer*, 5 June 1976, 18A; David Niven, "The Issue," *Southern Journal*, 4 (1976), 2.

38. Janet Papke and Patricia Dusenbury, eds., *A Profile of the Southern States: Data Book II* (Research Triangle Park, N.C.: Southern Growth Policies Board, 1981), 14–15; "Why More Blacks Are Moving South," *U. S. News & World Report*, 26 February 1973, 53–55; Bernard E. Garnett, "Going Home: More Black Americans Return to South from 'Exile' in North," *Wall Street Journal*, 10 November 1972, 1, 13; Mary E. Mebane, "And Blacks Go South Again," *The New York Times*, 4 July 1972, 17;

Thomas Bevier, "Dear Dixie: You're Looking Better Every Day," *Chicago Tribune Magazine*, 13 February 1972, 64–67; Joseph Boyce, "Reverse Migration," *Time*, 27 September 1976, 50.

39. Leslie Dunbar, "The End of the Myth and the Renewal of Man," *New South*, 22 (1967): 66.

40. Steve Suitts, "Renewal and Endurance: A Personal View," *Southern Changes*, April 1979: 5.

41. Askew 13A, 21–22.

42. John Lewis, "Statement," Atlanta, 13 January 1966, 2; Niven 2; Sanford 327–328.

43. Bobby Braddock, *I Believe the South Is Gonna Rise Again* (Nashville: Tree Publishing Co., 1973).

CHAPTER FIVE

1. C. Vann Woodward, *The Burden of Southern History*, 2nd ed. (Baton Rouge: Louisiana State University Press, 1968): 6.

2. Editorial, "A New Magazine: Our Creed and Hopes," *Southern Changes*, September 1978, 2; Dale Bumpers, "The New South," Hattiesburg, Mississippi, 10 December 1976, 3–4; Dale Bumpers, "The New South," Brunswick, Maine, 13 December 1976, 4–6; Phil Patton, "Interview: James Dickey," *Sky*, July 1977, 44.

3. George B. Tindall, "Onward and Upward with the Rising South," in *The Rising South: Issues and Changes*, ed. Donald R. Noble and Joab L. Thomas (University: University of Alabama Press, 1976): 12; Harry S. Ashmore, "An Effort to Define South's Philosophy," *Arkansas Gazette*, 2 May 1976, 2E. See also Sheldon Hackney, "The South as a Counterculture," *American Scholar*, 42 (1973): 283–293; Reese Cleghorn, "Southern Consciousness," *South Today* 1, No. 2 (1969): 1, 7; George B. Tindall, "The Resurgence of Southern Identity," in *The American South: Portrait of a Culture*, ed. Louis D. Rubin, Jr. (Baton Rouge: Louisiana State University Press, 1980): 161–168; Rennard Strickland, "The Southern Tradition in Quest for Contemporary Values," Speech Communication Association convention, Chicago, 28 December 1972; Carl N. Degler, *Place Over Time: The Continuity of Southern Distinctiveness* (Baton Rouge: Louisiana State University Press, 1977); and *Why the South Will Survive* (Athens: University of Georgia Press, 1981).

4. John Shelton Reed, *The Enduring South: Subcultural Persistence in Mass Society* (Chapel Hill: University of North Carolina Press, 1974): 33; Charles P. Roland, "The Ever Vanishing South," *Journal of Southern History*, 47 (1982): 20. See also David Bertelson, *The Lazy South* (New York: Oxford University Press, 1967).

5. Charles P. Roland, *The Improbable Era: The South since World War II* (Lexington: University of Kentucky Press, 1975): 189.

6. Editorial, "Facing South," *Southern Exposure*, 3, No. 4 (1976), cover 2.

7. Mike Royko, "Now They'll Focus on the Glook of the South," *Arkansas Gazette*, 28 November 1976, 3E. See also Ernie Deane, "A Southerner Views Carter," *Springdale News*, 7 November 1976, 1C.

8. "*Southern Exposure* sees the South as it is . . . and can still become" (Chapel Hill: Institute for Southern Studies, 1977).

9. Gary McCalla to Dear Former Subscriber, Multilith Letter, 1981.

10. Alan Dundes, "Folk Ideas as Units of World View," in *Toward New Perspectives in Folklore*, ed. Americo Paredes and Richard Bauman (Austin: University of Texas Press, 1972): 96; Lynwood Montell, "Folklore and Rhetoric: A State-of-the-Art Report," Southern Speech Communication Association convention, Tallahassee, April 1975, 5. See also Carl Kell, "Rhetoric and Folklore: A State-of-the-Art Report," Southern Speech Communication Association convention, Tallahassee, April 1975; Raymond S. Rodgers, "The Rhetorical Criticism of Folklore and Intercultural Communication Research," Southern Speech Communication Association convention, Biloxi, April 1979; and Richard M. Dorsen, "Theories of Myth and the Folklorist," in *Myth and Mythmaking*, ed. Henry A. Murray (New York: George Braziller, 1960): 76–89.

11. Patti Carr Black and William R. Ferris, "The Shotgun, the Dogtrot, and the Row House," *Southern Voices*, May-June 1974, 28.

12. Cyrus Sutherland, "Arkansas' Architectural Heritage: Focus on the Vernacular," Historic Preservation Alliance of Arkansas meeting, Hot Springs, Arkansas, 13 October 1981; Black and Ferris 29. See also Andrea Kirsten Mullen, "Preservation in the Black Community: A Growing Commitment," *Historic Preservation*, January–February 1982, 38–43.

13. Steve Taylor, "Are Y'all from Dixie? Y'all Wear Shoes?" *Arkansas Democrat*, 20 August 1979, 5A; Jesse Hill Ford, "The Southerner as a Scottish Problem," *Southern Voices*, August–September 1974, 19; Ernie Deane, "The Way We Talk," *Springdale News*, 20 July 1975, 1B; Bill Dwyer, *Southern Sayin's for Yankees and Other Immigrants* (Highlands, N. C.: Merry Mountaineers, 1976).

14. Larry L. King, "We Ain't Trash No More: How Jimmy Carter Led the Rednecks from the Wilderness," *Esquire*, November 1976, 155; Richard K. Thomas, "How to Tell You're in the South," *Southern Changes*, September 1978, 15.

15. B.C. Hall, "How to Talk to a Yankee," *Arkansas Times*, September 1977, 22, 24.

16. Jesse G. Delia, "Dialects and the Effects of Stereotypes on Interpersonal Attraction and Cognitive Processes in Impression Formation," *Quarterly Journal of Speech*, 58 (1972): 297; Robert Hopper and Frederick Williams, "Speech Characteristics and Employability," *Speech Monographs*, 40 (1973): 296–302; Dale T. Miller, "The Effects of Dialect and Ethnicity on Communicator Effectiveness," *Speech Monographs*, 42 (1975): 69–74; Jesse G. Delia, "Regional Dialect, Message Acceptance, and Perceptions of the Speaker," *Central States Speech Journal*, 26

(1975): 188–194; Sara T. Bryan, Peter A. Carmichael, and Charles D. Perry, "Sumpn Hawrble," Letter, *Southern Voices*, October–November 1974, 6.

17. Frye Gaillard, "Sour Notes at the Grand Ole Opry," *Southern Voices*, May–June 1974, 48–49.

18. Paul Johnson, "Dig Southern Rock? Capricorn Has It in 'South's Greatest Hits," *Arkansas Gazette*, 22 September 1977, 7D. See also Bill C. Malone, "Elvis, Country Music, and the South," *Southern Quarterly*, 18 (1979): 123–134; Steve Cummings, "Southern Rock 'n Roll," *Southern Exposure*, 2, No. 1 (1974), 23–26; "Tucker Boys Attract the Kinky Side of the New South," *Arkansas Democrat*, 11 July 1977, 9A; Courtney Hayden, "Dixie Rock: The Fusion's Still Burning," *Southern Exposure*, 5, No. 2 & 3 (1977): 36–43; *The South's Greatest Hits*, Capricorn Records, CP0187, 1977; *The South's Greatest Hits, Volume II*, Capricorn Records, CPN 0209, 1978.

19. "Another Piece of Fried Chicken, Please," *Southern Living*, July 1982, 72; Bill Terry; "Arkansas' Great Movable Feast: A Catfish Journal," *Arkansas Times*, May 1982, 14.

20. Terry 14; Paul Greenberg, "Of Medeas, Medusas, and the Media," *Arkansas Times*, August 1981: 23–24.

21. Roy Bode, "Georgians May Restore Southern Ethos to Capitol," *Arkansas Gazette*, 28 November 1976, 22A. See also Michael Demarest, "A Home Grown Elegance," *Time*, 27 September 1976, 66–67. For a discussion of the rhetorical nature of food, see Stephen A. Smith, "Food for Thought: Comestible Communication and Contemporary Southern Culture," in *American Material Culture* edited by Edith Mayo (Bowling Green, Ohio: Bowling Green State University Popular Press, 1984): 208–217.

22. Redding S. Sugg, Jr., "A Treatise upon Cornbread," *Southern Voices*, October–November 1974, 41; Kathleen Zobel, "Hog Heaven: Barbecue in the South," *Southern Exposure*, 5, No. 2 & 3 (1977): 58. See also Marilyn Wyrick, "Where There's Smoke There's Barbecue," *Southern Living*, September 1977, 84.

23. Gary D. Ford, "The South Burns for Barbeque," *Southern Living*, May 1982, 121, 125.

24. Gorham Kindem, "Southern Exposure: *Kudzu* and *It's Grits*," *Southern Quarterly*, 19 (1981), 199–206; Ernie Deane, "Grits and Blackeyed Peas," *Springdale News*, 28 November 1976, 1C; Linda Welch, "Cornbread: Break Off a Piece of Southern Heritage," *Southern Living*, November 1981, 102–103; Sugg 39; Tom Mathews, "The Southern Mystique," *Newsweek*, 19 July 1976, 30.

25. Bill Finger, "Just Another Ball Game," *Southern Exposure*, 7, No. 2 (1979): 74–81.

26. Peter Schrag, "A Hesitant New South: Fragile Promise on the Last Frontier," *Saturday Review*, 12 February 1972, 55; Willie Morris, "Misty, Water-Colored Memory of My First College Football Game," *Southern Living*, September 1982, 10; "Eat 'Em Up, Get 'Em," *Time*, 27 September 1976, 81.

27. Paul Hemphill, "Vaudeville's Last Outpost," *South Today*, 2, No. 10 (1971): 9; Randall Williams, "Tonight, the Hulk vs. Ox Baker," *Southern Exposure*, 7, No. 2 (1979): 30–35.

28. Pat Watters, "Cock Fight," *South Today*, 1, No. 7 (1970): 6; Harold Herzog and Pauline B. Cheek, "Grit and Steel: The Anatomy of Cockfighting," *Southern Exposure*, 7, No. 2 (1979): 36–40; James Seay, "The Southern Outdoors: Bass Boats and Bear Hunts," in *The American South: Portrait of a Culture* 118–128.

29. "Just Like Whiskey," *Time*, 27 September 1976, 82. See also Sylvia Wilkinson, "Red Necks on Wheels: The Stock Car Culture," in *The American South: Portrait of a Culture* 129–139; Tom Wolfe, "Last American Hero is Junior Johnson," *Esquire*, March 1965, 68–75; Paul Hemphill, "Hot Cars on the Dirt Track," *South Today*, 1, No. 2 (1970): 1, 7; Jonathan Ingram, "The Battle of the Independents," *Southern Exposure*, 7, No. 2 (1979): 93–99.

30. Susanne Langer, *Philosophy in a New Key: A Study in the Symbolism of Reason, Rite, and Art* (Cambridge: Harvard University Press, 1951): 181–185; Ray B. Browne, "Epilogue," in *Heroes of Popular Culture*, ed. Ray B. Browne, Marshall Fishwick, and Michael T. Marsden (Bowling Green: Bowling Green State University Popular Press, 1972): 186.

31. Pat Derian, "Mayflies No More: A Fresh Look at the Southern Woman," in *The Rising South* 60.

32. Reynolds Price quoted in McKern, 3; Personal interview with James Whitehead, Fayetteville, Arkansas, 2 December 1982; Derian 65.

33. McKern xiv–xv, 129–154; "The Belle: Magnolia and Iron," *Time*, 27 September 1976, 94. See also Florence King, *Southern Ladies and Gentlemen* (New York: Alfred A. Knopf, 1973); Lydel Sims, "Fare Thee Well, Southern Belle," *South Today*, 1, No. 4 (1970): 7; Sara Murphy, "Women's Lib in the South," *New South*, 27 (1972): 45; John N. Popham, "A Recession Would Have Lightest Impact in S. E.," *Arkansas Gazette*, 15 July 1979, 1E, 4E; Jimmie Rogers, "Images of Women in the Messages of Loretta Lynn," *Studies in Popular Culture*, 5 (1982): 42–49; Ruth A. Banes, "Southern Women in Country Songs," *Journal of Regional Culture*, 1, No. 2 (1981): 57–70; Margaret Wolfe Ripley, "The Southern Lady: Long Suffering Counterpart of the Good Ole Boy," *Journal of Popular Culture*, 11, No. 2 (1977): 18–27; Blanche McCrary Boyd, *The Redneck Way of Knowledge: Down-Home Tales* (New York: Alfred A. Knopf, 1981).

34. Billy Carter, *Redneck Power: The Wit and Wisdom of Billy Carter*, ed. Jeremy Rifkin and Ted Howard (New York: Bantam, 1977): 12; Larry L. King, *Of Outlaws, Con Men, Whores, Politicians, and Other Artists* (New York: Penguin Books, 1981): 6. The image of the redneck is fully developed in Raymond S. Rodgers, "The Rhetoric of Redneck Rock: Persuasive Strategies of a Contemporary Myth in the Making," Conference on Rhetoric of the Contemporary South, Boone, North Carolina, 21 August 1977, and Raymond S. Rodgers, "Images of Rednecks in Country Music: The

Lyrical Persona of a Southern Superman," *Journal of Regional Culture*, 1, No. 2 (1981): 71–81.

35. Bonnie Angelo, "Those Good Ole Boys," *Time*, 27 September 1976: 47; Jack Temple Kirby, *Media-Made Dixie* (Baton Rouge: Louisiana State University Press, 1975): 149. See also, Wade Austin, "The Real Beverly Hillbillies," *Southern Quarterly*, 19 (1981): 83–94; Michael Adams; "How Come Everybody Down Here Has Three Names?: Martin Ritt's Southern Films," *Southern Quarterly*, 19 (1981): 143–155; Paul Hemphill, *The Good Old Boys* (Garden City: Doubleday, 1974); Dick West, "Hello Rednecks, Goodby Chivalry," *Arkansas Gazette*, 25 February 1982, 11A.

36. Irving J. Rein, *Rudy's Red Wagon* (Glenview, Ill.: Scott, Foresman, and Company, 1972): 17–32; George P. Boss, "The Stereotype and Its Correspondence in Discourse to the Enthymeme," *Communication Quarterly*, 27 (1979): 27.

37. Travel Department, Mississippi A & I Board, "Missinformed," *Southern Living*, March 1976, 76; Travel Department, Mississippi A & I Board, "Missimpression," *Southern Living*, April 1976, 31; Travel Department, Mississippi A & I Board, "Missunderstood," *Southern Living*, May 1976, 4C.

CHAPTER SIX

1. Louis B. Wright, *The Colonial Search for a Southern Eden* (University: University of Alabama Press, 1953); Frank E. Smith, "Land Use," in *The Peoples of the South: Heritages and Futures*, ed. William C. Havard and Jane Crater (Nashville: Southern Regional Conference on the Humanities, 1976): 125; Reubin Askew, "Remarks of the New Chairman," Southern Growth Policies Board, Pinehurst, N.C., 13 November 1975, 11.

2. Carl Kell, "Toward a Theory of Rhetoric: The Contemporary South, 1954–1975," Conference on Rhetoric of the Contemporary South, Bowling Green, Kentucky, June 1975, 3–5; Carl Kell, "A Rhetoric of Community: *Southern Living* Magazine," American Culture Association Convention, Toronto, March 1984; Carl Kell and James A. Pearce, "A Rhetoric of Southerness: Screening the Soul of the South," Popular Culture in the South convention, Tampa, October 1975; for other critiques of *Southern Living*, see Allen Tullos, "Azalea Death Trip," *Southern Changes*, July 1979, 6–10, 32; Chester Goolrick, "One Way to Succeed in Sunbelt Is Simply to Sing Its Praises," *Wall Street Journal*, 23 November 1981, 1, 19.

3. Alabama, "My Home's in Alabama," *My Home's in Alabama*, RCA, AHK1-3644, 1980; Stephen A. Smith, "Sounds of the South: The Rhetorical Saga of Country Music Lyrics," *Southern Speech Communication Journal*, 45 (1980): 169–170; Askew 23–24.

4. *Washington Post*, 19 October 1977, B8; Bob Graham, "Inaugural Address," Tallahassee, Florida, 2 January 1979, 2, 8–9. Typescript copy in possession of the author.

5. Editorial, "The South: Can It Avoid Mistakes of Other Areas," *Springdale News*, 30 May 1975, 2; Editorial, "New Warning for South to Proceed with Caution," *Springdale News*, 6 April 1976, 2; Ernie Deane, "Warning to the South," *Springdale News*, 11 April 1976, 21; John Egerton, *The Americanization of Dixie: The Southernization of America* (New York: Harper's Magazine Press, 1974); John Shelton Reed, "Instant Grits and Plastic-Wrapped Crackers: Southern Culture and Regional Development," in *The American South: Portrait of a Culture*, ed. Louis D. Rubin, Jr. (Baton Rouge: Louisiana State University Press, 1980): 27–37.

6. David R. Godschalk, Bruce J.M. Knopf, and Seth G. Weissman, *Guiding Growth in the South* (Research Triangle Park, N.C.: Southern Growth Policies Board, 1978): 20; James Hunt, "Remarks of the New Chairman," Southern Growth Policies Board, Atlanta, November 1978; Askew 25.

7. "Governor Boren Pays Tribute to Askew for His Leadership," *Southern Growth: Problems & Promises*, 4 (1977): 2.

8. Commission on the Future of the South, *The Future of the South* (Research Triangle Park: Southern Growth Policies Board, 1974): 14; H. Brandt Ayres, "We've Got to Stop Meeting Like This," 1980 Commission on the Future of the South, Atlanta, 12 January 1981; Dale Bumpers, "The New South," University of Southern Mississippi, Hattiesburg, 10 December 1976, 5; Dolly Parton, quoted in Sharon McKern, *Redneck Mothers, Good Ol' Girls, and Other Southern Belles* (New York: Viking Press, 1979): 53.

9. Emory Cunningham, "Introduction to the Future of the South," *Southern Living*, January 1976, 32; Carl Kell, "The 'Southernization' of America: A Rhetorical Perspective," Speech Communication Association convention, Chicago, 28 December 1972, 1–2.

10. Anthony J. Gagliano, "Report of the Panel on Urbanization," in *The Peoples of the South* 147.

11. Southern Growth Policies Board, "Directions for the Eighties: A Proposal to the National Endowment for the Humanities," June 1980, 1; Bill Clinton, letter to Joseph D. Duffey, 22 February 1980, 1.

12. Richard W. Riley, "Inaugural Address," Columbia, South Carolina, 10 January 1979, 5; Edward M. Penick, "From Cotton to Carter: Discovering the South," *Arkansas Business and Economic Review*, 10 (Winter 1977): 7.

13. Frank E. Smith, "Land Use" 127; Mike Sarka, "Tourism is the South's Top Industry," *Southern Living*, January 1978, 34s–37s; "Dollars Marching South," *The SOUTH Magazine*, January–February 1976, 20–23.

14. Clare A. Gunn, "Southern Tourism: Will There Be a Place to Go?" *Southern Living*, January 1977, 82.

15. Editorial, "To Use the Land and Not Destroy It," *Southern Living*, January 1979, 3s; Norman K. Johnson and Glenn Morris, "The Vanishing Rural Landscape," *Southern Living*, January 1979, 21s. See also Frank E. Smith, "Improving the Southern Environment," *New South*, 25 (1970): 63–69; Frank E. Smith, "Making Dixie's

Land Livable," in *You Can't Eat Magnolias*, ed. H. Brandt Ayres and Thomas H. Naylor (New York: McGraw-Hill, 1972): 195–207; Michael Frome, "To Save Our Natural Heritage, Time Is Short and Running Fast," *Southern Living*, January 1976, 14a–16a.

16. William D. Workman, Jr., and Willis P. Whichard, "On Using Land Well," *Southern Living*, January 1977, 28a–32a. Workman was a Republican candidate for governor in South Carolina, and Whichard is a judge and former state senator from North Carolina.

17. Editorial, "A New Magazine: Our Creed and Hopes," *Southern Changes*, September 1978, 3; Editorial, "Our Promised Land," *Southern Exposure*, 2, No. 2 & 3 (1974), cover 2.

18. Commission on the Future of the South, *The Future of the South*, 22; Southern Growth Policies Board, *Profile of the Southern States: Data Book II* (Research Triangle Park, N.C.: Southern Growth Policies Board, 1981): 5–7; *Report of the 1980 Commission on the Future of the South* (Research Triangle Park, N.C.: Southern Growth Policies Board, 1981): 34–45; Reuben Anderson, "The Future of Southern Cities," Southern Growth Policies Board, Dorado Beach, Puerto Rico, 28 September 1981, 1.

19. Joel L. Fleishman, "The Southern City: Northern Mistakes in Southern Settings," in *You Can't Eat Magnolias*, 170; Editorial "Facing South," *Southern Exposure*, 3, No. 4 (1976), cover 2; E. Blaine Liner, "Director's Report," in *The South in the Seventies: Annual Report, 1977* (Research Triangle Park, N.C.: Southern Growth Policies Board, 1978): 5.

20. "Southern Cities," *Southern Exposure*, 3, No. 4 (1976): 17; David Bowman, "Memphis, Tennessee: How to Stop the Developers," *Southern Exposure*, 3, No. 4 (1976): 18–24; Carl Abbott, "Norfolk, Virginia: From Honky Tonk to Honky Glitter," *Southern Exposure*, 3, No. 4 (1976): 31–34; Tom Huth, "Should Charleston Go New South?" *Historic Preservation*, July–August 1979, 32–38; Carl Sussman, "Moving the City Slickers Out," *Southern Exposure*, 2, No. 2 & 3 (1974), 99–107; Allen Tullos, "Plans for a New South," *Southern Exposure*, 2, No. 2 & 3 (1974): 91–93.

21. Pat Watters, "Introduction," *Report of the 1980 Commission on the Future of the South*, 12; Alice Walker, "Staying Home in Mississippi," *The New York Times Magazine*, 26 August 1973, 62. See also C. Vann Woodward, "The South Tomorrow," *Time*, 27 September 1976, 99; Charles P. Roland, *The Improbable Era: The South Since World War II* (Lexington: University of Kentucky Press, 1975): 154–156; Rosalind Massow, "Atlanta: A Once and Present Queen" *Sky*, May 1977, 49–55; Edgar and Patricia Cheatham, "A Tale of Four Cities: Southern Style," *Sky*, December 1979, 30–36; James Reston, "The 'Americanization' of the Southern Region," *Arkansas Gazette*, 15 October 1976, 6A.

22. Joseph Kane, "Small Town Soul," *Time*, 27 September 1976, 56; Philip Morris, "Five Southern Towns Change and Stay the Same," *Southern Living*, January 1978, 3s; Philip Morris, "Once and Future Cities," *Southern Living*, January 1976, 5a.

23. *Report of the 1980 Commission on the Future of the South*, 45. See also Philip Morris, "Shaping Livable Southern Cities," *Southern Living*, January 1980, 3s–14s; Bill Schemmel, "Romance with a Neighborhood," *The SOUTH Magazine*, January–February 1976, 35; Philip Morris, "The Great Neighborhood Revival," *Southern Living*, November 1976, 69.

24. "Facing South," *Southern Exposure*, 3, No. 4 (1976), cover 2.

25. Linda Goldstein, "The South as a Real Estate Frontier," *SOUTH Business*, March 1981, 20–21; Hot Springs Mobile Home Estates, "Real Southern Living," *Hot Springs and Diamond Lakes Guide* (Hot Springs: Hot Springs-Diamond Lakes Travel Association, 1982): 26; James Branscome and Peggy Matthews, "Selling the Mountains," *Southern Exposure*, 2, No. 2 & 3 (1974): 122–129; Frank O'Neill, "Greatest Menace Yet to Southern Mountains," *Southern Voices*, May–June 1974, 73–78; Anita Parlow, "Pikeville, Kentucky: Millionaires and Mobile Homes," *Southern Exposure*, 3, No. 4 (1976): 25–30; Watters, 10–11.

26. The survival of the myth of Antaeus is discussed in William R. Brown, "The Prime-Time Television Environment and Emerging Rhetorical Visions," *Quarterly Journal of Speech*, 62 (1976), 389–399.

CHAPTER SEVEN

1. George B. Tindall, "Onward and Upward With the Rising South," in *The Rising South: Changes and Issues*, ed. Donald R. Nobel and Joab L. Thomas (University of Alabama Press, 1976): 12; David Mathews, "Coming to Terms with Another New South," in *The Rising South* 96.

2. Emory Cunningham, "Introduction to a Special Feature on the Future of the South," *Southern Living*, January 1977, 3a. See also Susan Wiles, "Scanning Visions of the Southern Future," *Arkansas Gazette*, 2 April 1981, 19A; C. Vann Woodward, "The South Tomorrow," *Time*, 27 September 1976, 98–99; "A Charter for the Southern Future," *Southern Changes*, April 1979; and "1980 Commission: Framing a Positive Agenda for the South," *Southern Growth: Problems & Promise*, 8 (1981), 1.

3. David Mathews, "Coming to Terms with Another New South," in *The Rising South*, 101.

4. Willard B. Gatewood, Jr., "The South, the State University, and Regional Promise," Fayetteville, Arkansas, 14 May 1977, 7; Willard B. Gatewood, Jr., "Arkansas: Newest Symbol in the New South," in *Arkansas Humanities in Perspective*, ed. A. M. Belmont and Robert S. Kay (Little Rock: Arkansas Endowment for the Humanities, n.d.): 35–36; Mathews, 101. Dr. Gatewood is Chancellor and Distinguished Professor of History at the University of Arkansas, Fayetteville.

5. Melvin L. DeFleur and Sandra Ball-Rokeach, *Theories of Mass Communication*, 4th ed. (New York: Longman, 1982): 135–140, 207–208, 223–229; 131, 138, 139–140.

6. DeFleur and Ball-Rokeach 226.

7. DeFleur and Ball-Rokeach 226–227.

8. Joseph Campbell, *The Flight of the Wild Gander* (New York: Viking Press, 1969): 6; Kenneth Boulding, *The Image* (Ann Arbor: University of Michigan Press, 1957): 7. See also Lester Thonssen, A. Craig Baird and Waldo W. Braden, *Speech Criticism*, 2nd ed. (New York: Ronald Press, 1970): 11.

9. Cunningham 3a.

10. George B. Tindall, "History and the Future of the South," University of Florida, Gainesville, 18 May 1981, 6; Paul Hemphill, *The Good Old Boys* (Garden City: Doubleday, 1974): 13.

11. Joseph B. Doughty, Jr., "One Student's Perspective," in *The Rising South*, 120; Gatewood, "Arkansas: Newest Symbol of the New South" 36.

12. Tindall, "Onward and Upward" 24; Joel Fleishman, "The Southern City: Northern Mistakes in Southern Settings," in *You Can't Eat Magnolias*, ed. H. Brandt Ayres and Thomas H. Naylor (New York: McGraw-Hill, 1972): 194.

13. Carl Kell, "Continuity and Change—The South in 1978," Conference on Rhetoric of the Contemporary South, New Orleans, 1 July 1978, 8; "Special Issue: The New South," *The Economist*, 3 March 1979; David M. Berg, "Rhetoric, Reality, and Mass Media," *Quarterly Journal of Speech*, 58 (1972): 263.

14. James Dickey quoted in "The Good Life," *Time*, 27 September 1976, 32.

15. Phil Patton, "Interview: James Dickey," *Sky*, July 1977, 44; Jack Tharpe, "Interview with Erskine Caldwell," *Southern Quarterly*, 20 (1981), 70; Michael P. Dean, "W. J. Cash's *The Mind of the South*: Southern History, Southern Style," *Southern Studies*, 20 (1981): 297–302; Willis P. Whichard, "A Letter to Walter Hines Page," Conference on Rhetoric of the Contemporary South, Bowling Green, Kentucky, 29 June 1979; Reece Cleghorn, "My Grandfather and the Cyclone," in *You Can't Eat Magnolias* 25–37; Roy Reed, "A Letter to My Grandfather," *Arkansas Times*, July 1984, 36–38, 78–86.

16. Editorial, *Southern Exposure*, 2, No. 4 (1975), cover 2.

17. John Egerton, "John N. Popham—Making Southern History Real, Making a Little History Himself," *Southern Voices*, October–November 1974, 65.

18. Personal interview with Harry Ashmore, 26 April 1976; Walter J. Ong, "Literacy and Orality in Our Times," *Journal of Communication*, 30, No. 1 (1980): 197–204; Gary Granzberg, "Television as Storyteller: The Algonkian of Central Canada," *Journal of Communication*, 32, No. 1 (1982): 48; Elihu Katz, "Can Authentic Cultures Survive the New Media?" *Journal of Communication*, 27, No. 2 (1977), 117.

19. Sara T. Bryan, Peter A. Carmichael, and Charles D. Perry, "Sumpn Hawrble," Letter, *Southern Voices*, October–November 1974, 6; Marshall McLuhan, "Myth and Mass Media," in *Myth and Mythmaking*, ed. Henry A. Murray (New York: George Braziller, 1960): 290.

20. Bob Brinkmeyer, "A Return Visit: Joel Chandler Harris," *Southern Exposure*,

5, No. 2 & 3 (1977): 214–215; Alice Walker, "Uncle Remus, No Friend of Mine," *Southern Exposure*, 9, No. 2 (1981): 30; Richard M. Dorsen, "Theories of Myth and the Folklorist," in *Myth and Mythmaking*, 85–86.

21. John Egerton, "The Americanization of Dixie—An Update," Conference on Rhetoric of the Contemporary South, Bowling Green, Kentucky, 29 June 1979, 5; Bob Arnold, "Billy Graham Superstar," *Southern Exposure*, 4, No. 3 (1976): 76–82; Bob Hall, "Jimmy Carter: Master Magician," *Southern Exposure*, 5, No. 1 (1977): 43–44; Cleghorn, 33.

22. Lyndon B. Johnson, *The Vantage Point* (New York: Holt, Rinehart, and Winston, 1971): 95; Larry L. King, "We Ain't Trash No More: How Jimmy Carter Led the Rednecks from the Wilderness," *Esquire*, November 1976, 88. See also T. Harry Williams, "Now, Maybe, We Can Begin to Appreciate Lyndon Baines Johnson," *Southern Voices*, May–June 1974, 66–71, and Jimmy Carter, *Keeping Faith* (New York: Bantam, 1982): 22–23.

23. David Underhill, "Yukking It up at CBS," *Southern Exposure*, 2, No. 4 (1975): 68–71; Steve Taylor, "Are Y'all from Dixie? Y'all Wear Shoes?" *Arkansas Democrat*, 20 August 1979, 5A.

24. John Egerton, "John N. Popham—Making Southern History Real" 63–65.

25. Zeke Segal, "The South Talks—The Nation Listens," Conference on Rhetoric of the Contemporary South, New Orleans, 30 June 1978.

26. David Doggett, "Underground in Mississippi," *Southern Exposure*, 2, No. 4 (1975): 86–95; Steve Hoffius, "Tracking the Alternative Media," *Southern Exposure*, 2, No. 4 (1975): 96–107; Faye McDonald Smith, "Minorities in Southern Television," *Southern Changes*, July 1979, 3, 26–29; Larry Noble, "Southern Newspapers: Watching the Watchdogs," *Southern Changes*, July 1979: 19–23.

27. McLuhan 229; Louis D. Rubin, Jr., "The American South: The Continuity in Self-Definition," in *The American South: Portrait of a Culture*, ed. Louis D. Rubin, Jr. (Baton Rouge: Louisiana State University Press, 1980): 19–20.

28. Harry Levin, "Some Meanings of Myth," in *Myth and Mythmaking*, 114.

Bibliography

BOOKS

Alden, John Richard. *The First South*. Baton Rouge: Louisiana State University Press, 1961.

Anderson, John M., ed. *Calhoun: Basic Documents*. State College: Pennsylvania State University Press, 1952.

Ashmore, Harry S. *An Epitaph for Dixie*. New York: W. W. Norton & Company, 1957.

Ayres, H. Brandt, and Thomas H. Naylor, eds. *You Can't Eat Magnolias*. New York: McGraw-Hill, 1972.

Bartley, Numan V. *The Rise of Massive Resistance*. Baton Rouge: Louisiana State University Press, 1969.

Bartley, Numan V., and Hugh D. Graham. *Southern Politics and the Second Reconstruction*. Baltimore: Johns Hopkins University Press, 1975.

Bass, Jack. *Unlikely Heroes: The Southern Judges Who Made the Civil Rights Revolution*. New York: Simon and Schuster, 1981.

Bass, Jack, and Walter DeVries. *The Transformation of Southern Politics: Social Change and Political Consequence Since 1945*. New York: Basic Books, 1976.

Belmont, A. M., and Robert S. Kay, eds. *Arkansas Humanities in Perspective*. Little Rock: Arkansas Endowment for the Humanities, n. d.

Bem, Daryl J. *Beliefs, Attitudes and Human Affairs*. Belmont, Calif.: Brooks-Cole Publishing Company, 1970.

Berger, Peter L., and Thomas Luckmann. *The Social Construction of Reality: A Treatise on the Sociology of Knowledge*. Garden City: Doubleday and Company, 1966.

Bertelson, David. *The Lazy South*. New York: Oxford University Press, 1967.

Bitzer, Lloyd F., and Edwin Black, eds. *The Prospect of Rhetoric*. Englewood Cliffs: Prentice-Hall, 1971.

Black Elected Officials in the Southern States. Voter Education Project. Atlanta: Southern Regional Council, 1969.

Boorstin, Daniel J. *The Americans: The Colonial Experience*. New York: Random House, 1966.

———. *The Image: A Guide to Pseudo-Events in America*. New York: Atheneum, 1973.

Boulding, Kenneth. *The Image: Knowledge in Life and Society*. Ann Arbor: University of Michigan Press, 1957.

Boyd, Blanche McCrary. *The Redneck Way of Knowledge: Down-Home Tales*. New York: Alfred A. Knopf, 1981.

Braden, Waldo W., ed. *Oratory in the New South*. Baton Rouge: Louisiana State University Press, 1979.

———, ed. *Oratory in the Old South*. Baton Rouge: Louisiana State University Press, 1970.

Brandfon, Robert L., ed. *The American South in the Twentieth Century*. New York: Thomas Y. Crowell Co., 1967.

Bridenbaugh, Carl. *Myths and Realities*. Baton Rouge: Louisiana State University Press, 1952.

Broder, David. *Changing of the Guard*. New York: Simon and Schuster, 1980.

Browne, Ray B., Marshall Fishwick, and Michael T. Marsden, eds. *Heroes of Popular Culture*. Bowling Green: Bowling Green University Popular Press, 1972.

Cabell, James Branch. *Let Me Lie*. New York: Farrar, Straus and Co., 1947.

Campbell, Joseph. *The Flight of the Wild Gander*. New York: Viking Press, 1969.

Carter, Billy. *Redneck Power: The Wit and Wisdom of Billy Carter*. Edited by Jeremy Rifkin and Ted Howard. New York: Bantam, 1977.

Carter, Jimmy. *Keeping Faith*. New York: Bantam, 1982.

Cash, W. J. *The Mind of the South*. New York: Alfred A. Knopf, 1941.

Cleghorn, Reese. *Radicalism: Southern Style*. Atlanta: Southern Regional Council, 1968.

Congressional Quarterly Almanac, 1965. Washington: Congressional Quarterly, Inc., 1966.

Cooper, John Milton, Jr. *Walter Hines Page: The Southerner as American.* Chapel Hill: University of North Carolina Press, 1977.

Coulter, E. Merton. *The Confederate States of America, 1861–1865.* Baton Rouge: Louisiana State University Press, 1950.

Craven, Wesley Frank. *The Southern Colonies in the Seventeenth Century, 1607–1689.* Baton Rouge: Louisiana State University Press, 1949.

Dabbs, James McBride. *Civil Rights in Recent Southern Fiction.* Atlanta: Southern Regional Council, 1969.

———. *A Hundred Years Later.* Atlanta: Southern Regional Council, 1962.

Davenport, F. Garvin. *Myth and Southern History.* Nashville: Vanderbilt University Press, 1970.

DeFleur, Melvin L., and Sandra Ball-Rokeach. *Theories of Mass Communication,* 4th ed. New York: Longman, 1982.

Degler, Carl N. *The Other South.* New York: Harper & Row, 1974.

———. *Place Over Time: The Continuity of Southern Distinctiveness.* Baton Rouge: Louisiana State University Press, 1977.

Dollard, John. *Caste and Class in a Southern Town.* New Haven: Yale University Press, 1937.

Downs, Robert B., ed. *Books That Changed the South.* Totowa, N. J.: Littlefield, Adams & Co., 1977.

Duncan, Hugh Dalziel. *Communication and Social Order.* New York: Oxford University Press, 1968.

Dwyer, Bill. *Southern Sayin's for Yankees and Other Immigrants.* Highlands, N. C.: Merry Mountaineers, 1970.

Dykeman, Wilma, and James Stokeley. *Seeds of Southern Change: The Life of Will Alexander.* Chicago: University of Chicago Press, 1962.

Eaton, Clement. *The Freedom of Thought Struggle in the Old South.* New York: Harper and Row, 1964.

———. *The Mind of the Old South.* Baton Rouge: Louisiana State University Press, 1964.

Egerton, John. *The Americanization of Dixie: The Southernization of America.* New York: Harper's Magazine Press, 1974.

———. *A Mind to Stay Here.* New York: Macmillan, 1970.

———. *School Desegregation: A Report Card from the South.* Atlanta: Southern Regional Council, 1976.

Flint, J. Wayne. *Dixie's Forgotten People: The South's Poor Whites.* Bloomington: Indiana University Press, 1979.

Freedman, Leon, ed. *The Civil Rights Reader: Basic Documents of the Civil Rights Movement.* New York: Walker, 1968.

Freehling, William W. *Prelude to Civil War: The Nullification Controversy in South Carolina, 1816–1836*. New York: Harper & Row, 1966.

Gaines, Francis Pendleton. *The Southern Plantation: A Study in the Development and Accuracy of a Tradition*. New York: Columbia University Press, 1925.

Gallup, George. *The Gallup Poll* Vol. 3. New York: Random House, 1972.

———. *The Gallup Poll: Public Opinion, 1978*. Wilmington, Del.: Scholarly Resources, Inc., 1979.

Garrow, David J. *Protest at Selma: Martin Luther King, Jr., and the Voting Rights Act of 1965*. New Haven: Yale University Press, 1979.

Gaston, Paul M. *The New South Creed: A Study in Southern Mythmaking*. New York: Alfred A. Knopf, 1970.

Gerster, Patrick, and Nicholas Cords, eds. *Myth and Southern History*. Chicago: Rand-McNally, 1974.

Godschalk, David R., Bruce J. M. Knopf, and Seth G. Weissman. *Guiding Growth in the South*. Research Triangle Park, N.C.: Southern Growth Policies Board, 1978.

Grantham, Dewey W. *The Democratic South*. Athens: University of Georgia Press, 1963.

———, ed. *The South and the Sectional Image*. New York: Harper and Row, 1967.

Harris, Joel Chandler. *Life of Henry W. Grady*. New York: Cassell Publishing Company, 1890.

Havard, William C., ed. *The Changing Politics of the South*. Baton Rouge: Louisiana State University Press, 1972.

Havard, William C., and Jane Crater, eds. *The Peoples of the South: Heritages and Futures*. Nashville: Southern Regional Conference on the Humanities, 1976.

Helper, Hinton Rowan. *The Impending Crisis of the South*. New York: A. B. Burdick, 1857.

Hemphill, Paul. *The Good Old Boys*. Garden City: Doubleday and Co., 1974.

Highsaw, Robert B., ed. *The Deep South in Transformation: A Symposium*. University: University of Alabama Press, 1964.

Hofstadter, Richard. *The Age of Reform: From Bryan to F. D. R.* New York: Vintage Books, 1955.

Hundley, Daniel R. *Social Relations in Our Southern States*. New York: H. B. Price, 1860.

I'll Take My Stand: The South and the Agrarian Tradition. New York: Harper and Brothers, 1930.

Johnson, Lyndon B. *The Vantage Point.* New York: Holt, Rinehart, and Winston, 1971.

Johnson, Richard M. *The Dynamics of Compliance.* Evanston: Northwestern University Press, 1967.

Kalven, Harry, Jr. *The Negro and the First Amendment.* Chicago: University of Chicago Press, 1966.

Kennedy, John Pendleton. *Swallow Barn,* 2nd ed. New York: G. P. Putnam & Co., 1851.

Key, V. O., Jr. *Southern Politics in State and Nation.* New York: Vintage Books, 1949.

Killian, Lewis M. *White Southerners.* New York: Random House, 1970.

King, Florence. *Southern Ladies and Gentlemen.* New York: Stein and Day, 1975.

King, Larry L. *Of Outlaws, Con Men, Whores, Politicians, and Other Artists.* New York: Penguin Books, 1981.

King, Martin Luther, Jr. *Stride Toward Freedom: The Montgomery Story:* New York: Harper and Brothers, 1958.

———. *The Trumpet of Conscience.* New York: Harper & Row, 1968.

———. *Where Do We Go From Here: Chaos or Community?* New York: Harper & Row, 1957.

———. *Why We Can't Wait.* New York: Harper & Row, 1964.

Kirby, Jack Temple. *Media-Made Dixie.* Baton Rouge: Louisiana State University Press, 1978.

Kluger, Richard. *Simple Justice.* New York: Alfred A. Knopf, 1976.

Krueger, Thomas A. *And Promises to Keep: The Southern Conference for Human Welfare, 1938–1948.* Nashville: Vanderbilt University Press, 1967.

Lander, Ernest M., Jr., and Richard J. Calhoun, eds. *Two Decades of Change: The South Since the Supreme Court Desegregation Decision.* Columbia: University of South Carolina Press, 1975.

Langer, Susanne. *Philosophy in a New Key: A Study in the Symbolism of Reason, Rite, and Art.* Cambridge: Harvard University Press, 1951.

Larsen, Stephen. *The Shaman's Doorway.* New York: Harper & Row, 1976.

Lerche, Charles. *The Uncertain South.* Chicago: Quadrangle, 1964.

Main, Jackson Turner. *The Social Structure of Revolutionary America.* Princeton: Princeton University Press, 1965.

Malinowski, Bronislaw. *Sex, Culture, and Myth.* New York: Harcourt, Brace, and World, 1961.

Malone, Bill C. *Country Music, U. S. A.* Austin: University of Texas Press, 1968.

———. *Southern Music/American Music.* Lexington: University of Kentucky Press, 1979.

Marx, Leo. *The Machine in the Garden: Technology and the Pastoral Ideal in America.* New York: Oxford University Press, 1964.

Mayo, Edith, ed. *American Material Culture.* Bowling Green, Oh.: Bowling Green State University Popular Press, 1984.

McKern, Sharon. *Redneck Mothers, Good Ol' Girls, and Other Southern Belles.* New York: Viking Press, 1979.

Morland, John Kenneth, ed. *The Not So Solid South: Anthropological Studies in a Regional Subculture.* Athens: University of Georgia Press, 1971.

Morris, Willie. *The Courting of Marcus Dupree.* New York: Doubleday, 1984.

———. *Terrains of the Heart and Other Essays on Home.* Oxford, Miss.: Yoknapatawpha Press, 1981.

———. *The Last of the Southern Girls.* New York: Alfred A. Knopf, 1973.

———, ed. *The South Today: One Hundred Years After Appomattox.* New York: Harper & Row, 1965.

Mowry, George. *Another Look at the Twentieth Century South.* Baton Rouge: Louisiana State University Press, 1973.

Murray, Henry A., ed. *Myth and Mythmaking.* New York: George Braziller, 1960.

Muse, Benjamin. *Ten Years of Prelude: The Story of Integration Since the Supreme Court's 1954 Decision.* New York: Viking Press, 1964.

Myrdal, Gunnar. *An American Dilemma.* New York: Harper and Brothers, 1944.

Naylor, Thomas H., and James Clotfelter. *Strategies for Change in the South.* Chapel Hill: University of North Carolina Press, 1975.

Nimmo, Dan D. *Popular Images of Politics.* Englewood Cliffs: Prentice-Hall, 1974.

Noble, Donald R., and Joab L. Thomas, eds. *The Rising South: Changes and Issues.* University: University of Alabama Press, 1976.

Odum, Howard W. *Race and Rumors of Race.* Chapel Hill: University of North Carolina Press, 1943.

Osborne, John. *The Old South.* New York: Time-Life Books, 1968.

Osterweis, Rollin G. *The Myth of the Lost Cause, 1865–1900.* Hamden, Conn.: Archon Books, 1973.

Owsley, Frank L. *Plain Folk of the Old South.* Baton Rouge: Louisiana State University Press, 1949.

Papke, Janet, and Patricia Dusenbury, eds. *A Profile of the Southern States: Data Book II*. Research Triangle Park, N.C.: Southern Growth Policies Board, 1981.

Parades, Americo, and Richard Bauman, eds. *Toward New Perspectives in Folklore*. Austin: University of Texas Press, 1972.

Peltason, J. W. *Fifty-Eight Lonely Men: Southern Federal Judges and School Desegregation*. Urbana: University of Illinois Press, 1971.

Perelman, Chaim, and L. Olbrechts-Tyteca. *The New Rhetoric*. Translated by John Wilkinson and Purcell Weaver. Notre Dame: University of Notre Dame Press, 1969.

Phillips, Ulrich Bonner. *Life and Labor in the Old South*. Boston: Little, Brown & Co., 1929.

Plato. *The Republic of Plato*. Trans. Allan Bloom. New York: Basic Books, 1968.

Reed, John Shelton. *One South: An Ethnic Approach to Regional Culture*. Baton Rouge: Louisiana State University Press, 1982.

———. *The Enduring South: Subcultural Persistence in Mass Society*, 1972 rpt. Chapel Hill: University of North Carolina Press, 1974.

Rein, Irving J. *Rudy's Red Wagon: Communication Strategies in Contemporary Society*. Glenview, Ill.: Scott, Foresman and Company, 1972.

Robinson, James Oliver. *American Myth, American Reality*. New York: Hill & Wang, 1980.

Rogers, Harrell R., Jr., and Charles S. Bullock, III. *Law and Social Change: Civil Rights Laws and Their Consequences*. New York: McGraw-Hill, 1972.

Rokeach, Milton. *Beliefs, Attitudes and Values*. San Francisco: Jossey-Bass, 1968.

Roland, Charles P. *The Improbable Era: The South Since World War II*. Lexington: University of Kentucky Press, 1975.

Rubin, Louis D., Jr., ed. *The American South: Portrait of a Culture*. Baton Rouge: Louisiana State University Press, 1980.

Savage, Henry, Jr. *Seeds of Time: The Background of Southern Thinking*. New York: Henry Holt and Company, 1959.

Scott, Anne Firor. *The Southern Lady: From Pedestal to Politics, 1830–1930*. Chicago: University of Chicago Press, 1970.

Sherrill, Robert. *Gothic Politics in the Deep South: Stars of the New Confederacy*. New York: Grossman Publishers, 1968.

Silver, James W. *Mississippi: The Closed Society*. New York: Harcourt, Brace & World, 1966.

Simkins, Francis Butler. *The Everlasting South*. Baton Rouge: Louisiana State University Press, 1963.

Sindler, Allen P., ed. *Change in the Contemporary South*. Durham: Duke University Press, 1963.

Smith, Frank E. *Look Away From Dixie*. Baton Rouge: Louisiana State University Press, 1963.

Smith, Henry Nash. *Virgin Land: The American West as Symbol and Myth*. Cambridge: Harvard University Press, 1950.

Suitts, Steve, and Alexis Barrett. *The Segregated Governments in the South*. Atlanta: Southern Regional Council, 1979.

Sydnor, Charles P. *The Development of Southern Sectionalism, 1819–1848*. Baton Rouge: Louisiana State University Press, 1948.

Taylor, Richard. *Destruction and Reconstruction*. New York: D. Appleton & Co., 1879.

Taylor, William R. *Cavalier and Yankee*. New York: George Braziller, 1961.

Thompson, Edgar T., ed. *Perspectives on the South: Agenda for Research*. Durham: Duke University Press, 1967.

Thonssen, Lester, A. Craig Baird, and Waldo W. Braden. *Speech Criticism*, 2nd ed. New York: Ronald Press, 1970.

Tillinghast, Pardon. *The Specious Past*. Reading, Mass.: Addison-Wesley Publishing Co., 1972.

Tindall, George B. *The Emergence of the New South, 1913–1945*. Baton Rouge: Louisiana State University Press, 1967.

———. *The Ethnic Southerner*. Baton Rouge: Louisiana State University Press, 1976.

Turner, Arlin, ed. *The Negro Question: A Selection on Civil Rights by George W. Cable*. Garden City: Doubleday & Company, 1958.

Vandiver, Frank E., ed. *The Idea of the South: Pursuit of a Central Theme*. Chicago: University of Chicago Press, 1964.

Warren, Robert Penn. *The Legacy of the Civil War: Meditations on the Centennial*. New York: Random House, 1961.

———. *A Place to Come To*. New York: Random House, 1977.

Weaver, Richard M. *The Southern Tradition at Bay*. New Rochelle: Arlington House, 1968.

Why the South Will Survive. Athens: University of Georgia Press, 1981.

Wilhoit, Francis M. *The Politics of Massive Resistance*. New York: George Braziller, 1973.

Williams, J. Earl. *Plantation Politics: The Southern Economic Heritage*. Austin: Futura Press, 1972.

Williams, T. Harry. *Romance and Realism in Southern Politics*. Athens: University of Georgia Press, 1964.

Wolfenstein, Martha, and Nathan Leites. *Movies: A Psychological Study*. Glencoe, Ill.: Free Press, 1950.

Woodward, C. Vann. *The Burden of Southern History*, 2nd ed. Baton Rouge: Louisiana State University Press, 1968.

———. *Origins of the New South, 1877–1913*. Baton Rouge: Louisiana State University Press, 1951.

———. *The Strange Career of Jim Crow*, 2nd ed. New York: Oxford University Press, 1966.

Wright, Louis B. *The Colonial Search for a Southern Eden*. University: University of Alabama Press, 1953.

Yarbrough, Tinsley B. *Judge Frank Johnson and Human Rights in Alabama*. University: University of Alabama Press, 1981.

REPORTS AND PROPOSALS

Commission on the Future of the South. *The Future of the South*. Research Triangle Park: Southern Growth Policies Board, 1975.

Commission on the Future of the South. *Report of the 1980 Commission on The Future of the South*. Research Triangle Park: Southern Growth Policies Board, 1981.

"Directions for the Eighties: A Proposal to the National Endowment for the Humanities." Southern Growth Policies Board, June 1980.

The South in the Seventies: Annual Report, 1977. Research Triangle Park: Southern Growth Policies Board, 1978.

The Southern Regional Council Annual Report, 1979. Atlanta: Southern Regional Council, 1980.

Voter Education Project 1975 Annual Report. Atlanta: Voter Education Project, Inc., 1976.

GOVERNMENT DOCUMENTS AND DECISIONS

Brown v. Board of Education. 347 U. S. 483. 1954.

Carter, Jimmy. "Remarks at a White House Observance of the 25th Anniversary of the Supreme Court Decision *Brown v. Board of Education*." *Weekly Compilation of Presidential Documents*, 21 May 1979, 883–885.

Congressional Record. 26 May 1955, 7124.

Congressional Record. 21 July 1975, S13084.

Nixon v. Herndon. 273 U. S. 536. 1927.

Plessy v. Ferguson. 163 U. S. 537. 1896.

Smith v. Allwright. 321 U. S. 649. 1944.

Twenty Years After Brown: The Shadows of the Past. United States Commission on Civil Rights. Washington: Government Printing Office, 1974.

The Voting Rights Act: Ten Years After. United States Commission on Civil Rights. Washington: Government Printing Office, 1975.

JOURNAL ARTICLES

Abbott, Carl. "Norfolk, Virginia: From Honky Tonk to Honky Glitter." *Southern Exposure*, 3, No. 4 (1976): 31–34.

Adams, Michael. "How Come Everybody Down Here Has Three Names? Martin Ritt's Southern Films." *Southern Quarterly*, 19 (1981): 143–155.

Arnold, Bob. "Billy Graham Superstar." *Southern Exposure*, 4, No. 3 (1976): 76–82.

Austin, Wade. "The Real Beverly Hillbillies." *Southern Quarterly*, 19 (1981): 83–94.

Ayres, H. Brandt. "Weaknesses and Strengths." *Southern Journal*, 4, No. 4 (1976): 19, 21–22.

Banes, Ruth A. "Southern Women in Country Songs." *Journal of Regional Culture*, 1, No. 2 (1981): 57–70.

Berg, David M. "Rhetoric, Reality, and Mass Media." *Quarterly Journal of Speech*, 58 (1972): 255–263.

Blount, Roy, Jr. "Sports Integration: Football as Radicalism." *South Today*, 1, No. 9 (1970): 1, 10–12.

Bormann, Ernest G. "Fantasy and Rhetorical Vision: The Rhetorical Criticism of Social Reality." *Quarterly Journal of Speech*, 58 (1972): 396–407.

Boss, George P. "The Stereotype and Its Correspondence in Discourse to the Enthymeme." *Communication Quarterly*, 27 (1979): 22–27.

Bowman, David. "Memphis, Tennessee: How to Stop the Developers." *Southern Exposure*, 3, No. 4 (1976): 18–24.

Braden, Waldo W. "The Emergence of the Concept of Southern Oratory." *Southern Speech Journal*, 26 (1961): 173–183.

———. "Myths in a Rhetorical Context." *Southern Speech Communication Journal*, 40 (1975): 113–126.

———. "The Rhetoric of a Closed Society." *Southern Speech Communication Journal*, 45 (1980): 333–351.

———. "Three Southern Readers and Southern Oratory." *Southern Speech Journal*, 32 (1966): 31–40.

Branscome, James, and Peggy Matthews. "Selling the Mountains." *Southern Exposure*, 2, No. 2 & 3 (1974): 122–129.

Breen, Myles, and Farrell Corcoran. "Myth in Television Discourse." *Communication Monographs*, 49 (1982): 127–136.

Brinkmeyer, Bob. "A Return Visit: Joel Chandler Harris." *Southern Exposure*, 5, No. 2 & 3 (1977): 214–215.

Brown, William R. "The Prime-Time Television Environment and Emerging Rhetorical Visions." *Quarterly Journal of Speech*, 62 (1976): 389–399.

Campbell, J. Louis, III. "In Search of the New South." *Southern Speech Communication Journal*, 47 (1982): 361–388.

Carey, John J. "The Paradoxical Faces of the South." *The Bulletin of the Center for the Study of Southern Culture and Religion*, 1, No. 2 (1977): 1–9.

Cleghorn, Reese. "Southern Consciousness." *South Today*, 1, No. 2 (1969): 1, 7.

Coles, Robert. "Is There a Mind of the South?" *New South*, 21 (1966): 39–41.

Cotterill, Robert S. "The Old South to the New." *Journal of Southern History*, 15 (1949): 3–8.

Cummings, Steve. "Southern Rock 'n' Roll." *Southern Exposure*, 2, No. 1 (1975): 23–26.

Dean, Michael P. "W. J. Cash's *The Mind of the South*: Southern History, Southern Style." *Southern Studies*, 20 (1981): 297–302.

Delia, Jesse G. "Dialects and the Effects of Stereotypes on Interpersonal Attraction and Cognitive Processes in Impression Formation." *Quarterly Journal of Speech*, 58 (1972): 285–297.

———. "Regional Dialect, Message Acceptance, and Perceptions of the Speaker." *Central States Speech Journal*, 26 (1975): 188–194.

Dickey, Dallas C. "Were They Ephemeral and Florid?" *Quarterly Journal of Speech*, 22 (1946): 16–20.

Dissanayake, Wimal. "New Wine in Old Bottles: Can Folk Media Convey Modern Messages?" *Journal of Communication*, 27, No. 2 (1977): 122–124.

Doggett, David. "Underground in Mississippi." *Southern Exposure*, 2, No. 4 (1974): 86–95.

Dunbar, Leslie. "The End of the Myth and the Renewal of Man." *New South*, 22 (1967): 60–67.

Editorial. *Southern Exposure*, 1, No. 1 (1973): cover 2.

Editorial. *Southern Exposure*, 2, No. 4 (1975): cover 2.

"Facing South." Editorial. *Southern Exposure*, 3, No. 4 (1976): cover 2.

Finger, Bill. "Just Another Ball Game." *Southern Exposure*, 7, No. 2 (1979): 74–81.

Flint, Wayne. "The Ethics of Democratic Persuasion and the Birmingham Crisis." *Southern Speech Journal*, 35 (1969): 40–53.

"Folklife Resources." *Southern Exposure*, 5, No. 2 & 3 (1977): 178–207.

Franklin, John Hope. "The Great Confrontation: The South and the Problem of Change." *Journal of Southern History*, 38 (1972): 3–20.

Frentz, Thomas S., and Thomas B. Farrell. "Conversion of American Consciousness: The Rhetoric of *The Exorcist*." *Quarterly Journal of Speech*, 61 (1975): 40–47.

Granzberg, Gary. "Television as Storyteller: The Algonkian of Central Canada." *Journal of Communication*, 32, No. 1 (1982): 43–52.

Hackney, Sheldon. "The South as a Counterculture." *American Scholar*, 42 (1973): 283–293.

Hall, Bob. "Jimmy Carter: Master Magician." *Southern Exposure*, 5, No. 1 (1977): 43–44.

Hayden, Courtney. "Dixie Rock: The Fusion's Still Burning." *Southern Exposure*, 5, No. 2 & 3 (1977): 36–43.

Heath, Robert. "Black Rhetoric: An Example of the Poverty of Values." *Southern Speech Communication Journal*, 39 (1973): 145–160.

Hemphill, Paul. "Hot Cars on the Dirt Track." *South Today*, 1, No. 2 (1970): 1, 7.

———. "Vaudeville's Last Outpost." *South Today*, 2, No. 10 (1971): 9.

Herzog, Harold, and Pauline B. Cheek. "Grit and Steel: The Anatomy of Cockfighting." *Southern Exposure*, 7, No. 2 (1979): 36–40.

Hesseltine, William B., and Henry L. Ewbank, Jr. "Old Voices in the New South." *Quarterly Journal of Speech*, 39 (1953): 451–458.

Hillbrunner, Anthony. "Inequality, the Great Chain of Being, and Ante-Bellum Southern Oratory." *Southern Speech Journal*, 25 (1960): 172–189.

Hoffius, Steve. "Tracking the Alternative Media." *Southern Exposure*, 2, No. 4 (1974): 96–107.

Holt, George. "Tales and Tellers: Storytelling in the South." *Southern Exposure*, 9, No. 2 (1981): 25.

Hopper, Robert, and Frederick Williams. "Speech Characteristics and Employability." *Speech Monographs*, 40 (1973): 296–302.

Ingram, Jonathan. "The Battle of the Independents." *Southern Exposure*, 7, No. 2 (1979): 93–99.

Jamieson, Kathleen. "The Rhetorical Manifestations of *Weltanschauung*." *Central States Speech Journal*, 27 (1976): 4–14.

Johnson, Bradley T. "Placing Principle Above Policy." *Confederate Veteran*, 4 (1896): 507–509.

Katz, Elihu. "Can Authentic Cultures Survive the New Media?" *Journal of Communication*, 27, No. 2 (1977): 113–121.

Kelman, Herbert C. "Compliance, Identification and Internalization: Three Processes of Attitude Change." *Journal of Conflict Resolution*, 2 (1958): 51–60.

Kiesler, C. A., R. E. Nisbett, and M. P. Zanna. "On Inferring One's Beliefs From One's Behavior." *Journal of Personality and Social Psychology*, 4 (1969): 321–327.

Kindem, Gorham. "Southern Exposure: *Kudzu* and *It's Grits*." *Southern Quarterly*, 19 (1981): 199–206.

King, Richard. "The Mind of the South: Narcissus Grown Analytical." *New South*, 27 (1972): 15–27.

Landry, David M. "A Socio-economic View of Politics in Mississippi." *Southern Quarterly*, 13 (1975): 217–228.

Lave, James H. "The Movement, Negro Challenge to the Myth." *New South*, 18 (1963): 9–17.

Link, Arthur S. "The Progressive Movement in the South, 1870–1914." *North Carolina Historical Review*, 23 (1946): 172–195.

Malone, Bill C. "Elvis, Country Music, and the South." *Southern Quarterly*, 18 (1979): 123–134.

Mayfield, Chris. "The Middle Ground Turns to Quicksand." *Southern Exposure*, 7, No. 2 (1979): 40–44.

Mayo, Amory Dwight. "Is There a New South?" *Social Economist*, 5 (1983): 200–208.

Miller, Dale T. "The Effects of Dialect and Ethnicity on Communicator Effectiveness." *Speech Monographs*, 42 (1975): 69–74.

Murphy, Sara. "Women's Lib in the South." *New South*, 27 (1972), 42–46.

Naylor, Thomas H. "The L. Q. C. Lamar Society." *New South*, 25 (1970): 21–25.

Niven, David. "The Issue." *Southern Journal*, 4, No. 4 (1976): 2–5.

Nixon, H. Clarence. "The South After the War." *Virginia Quarterly Review*, 20 (1944): 321–334.

Okun, Tema, and Peter Wood. "Through the Hoop." *Southern Exposure*, 7, No. 2 (1979): 1.

O'Neal, John. "Art and the Movement." *Southern Exposure*, 9, No. 1 (1981): 80–83.

Ong, Walter J. "Literacy and Orality in Our Times." *Journal of Communication*, 30, No. 1 (1980): 197–204.

"Our Promised Land." Editorial. *Southern Exposure*, 2, No. 2 & 3 (1974), cover 2.

Oxendine, Jill. "Kathryn Windham: Something I Want to Tell You." *Southern Exposure*, 9, No. 2 (1981): 33–35.

Parlow, Anita. "Pikeville, Kentucky: Millionaires and Mobile Homes." *Southern Exposure*, 3, No. 4 (1976): 25–30.

Penick, Edward M. "From Cotton to Carter: Discovering the South." *Arkansas Business and Economic Review*, 10 (Winter, 1977): 1–8.

Philipsen, Gerry. "Navajo World View and Culture Patterns of Speech: A Case Study in Ethnorhetoric." *Speech Monographs*, 39 (1972): 132–139.

Prothro, James W. "Stateways Versus Folkways Revisited: An Error in Prediction." *Journal of Politics*, 34 (1972): 352–364.

Pryor, Peggie J. "Myth as an Aspect of Persuasion in the Rhetorical Act." *Journal of the Illinois Speech and Theatre Association*, 27 (1973): 54–59.

Pyron, Darden Asbury. "Gone With the Wind: Southern History and National Popular Culture." *Studies in Popular Culture*, 3 (1980): 11–19.

Ripley, Margaret Wolfe. "The Southern Lady: Long Suffering Counterpart of the Good Ole Boy." *Journal of Popular Culture*, 11, No. 2 (1977): 18–27.

Rodgers, Raymond S. "Images of Rednecks in Country Music: The Lyrical Persona of a Southern Superman." *Journal of Regional Culture*, 1, No. 2 (1981): 71–81.

Rogers, Jimmie N. "Images of Women in the Messages of Loretta Lynn." *Studies in Popular Culture*, 5 (1982): 42–49.

Roland, Charles P. "The Ever-Vanishing South." *Journal of Southern History*, 47 (1982): 3–20.

———. "The South, America's Will-o'-the-Wisp Eden." *Louisiana History*, 11 (1970): 101–119.

Rushing, Janice Hocker, and Thomas S. Frentz. "The Rhetoric of 'Rocky': A Social Value Model of Criticism." *Western Journal of Speech Communication*, 41 (1978): 63–72.

Saxon, John D. "Contemporary Southern Oratory: A Rhetoric of Hope, Not Desperation." *Southern Speech Communication Journal*, 40 (1975): 262–274.

Scott, Robert L. "Diego Rivera at Rockefeller Center: Fresco Painting and Rhetoric." *Western Journal of Speech Communication*, 41 (1977): 70–82.

Sims, Lydel. "Fare Thee Well, Southern Belle." *South Today*, 1, No. 4 (1970): 7.

Smith, Frank E. "Improving the Southern Environment." *South Today*, 25 (1970): 63–69.

Smith, Stephen A. "The Old South Myth as a Contemporary Southern Commodity." *Journal of Popular Culture*, 16, No. 3 (1983): 22–29.

———. "Sounds of the South: The Rhetorical Saga of Country Music Lyrics." *Southern Speech Communication Journal*, 45 (1980): 164–172.

"The South of the Future." Editorial. *New South*, 19 (1964): 28.

"Southern Cities." *Southern Exposure*, 3, No. 4 (1976): p. 17.

Starosta, William J. "The Uses of Traditional Entertainment Forms to Stimulate Social Change." *Quarterly Journal of Speech*, 60 (1974): 306–312.

Stuart, Charlotte L. "Architecture in Nazi Germany: A Rhetorical Perspective." *Western Journal of Speech Communication*, 37 (1973): 253–263.

Sussman, Carl. "Moving the City Slickers Out." *Southern Exposure*, 2, No. 2 & 3 (1974): 99–107.

Sykes, A. J. M. "Myth and Attitude Change." *Human Relations*, 18 (1965): 323–337.

———. "Myth in Communication." *Journal of Communication*, 20, No. 1 (1975): 17–31.

Tharp, Jack. "Interview with Erskine Caldwell." *Southern Quarterly*, 20 (1981): 64–74.

Tindall, George B. "The Benighted South: Origins of a Modern Image." *Virginia Quarterly Review*, 40 (1964): 281–294.

Tullos, Allen. "Plans for a New South." *Southern Exposure*, 2, No. 2 & 3 (1974): 91–93.

Underhill, David. "Yukking It Up at CBS." *Southern Exposure*, 2, No. 4 (1975): 68–71.

Vandiver, Frank E. "The Confederate Myth." *Southwest Review*, 46 (1961): 199–204.

Veninga, Robert. "The Functions of Symbols in Legend Construction . . . Some Exploratory Comments." *Central States Speech Journal*, 22 (1971): 161–170.

Walker, Alice. "The Black Writer and the Southern Experience." *New South*, 25 (1970): 23–26.

———. "Uncle Remus, No Friend of Mine." *Southern Exposure*, 9, No. 2 (1981): 29–31.

Watters, Pat. "Cock Fight." *South Today*, 1, No. 7 (1970): 6.

"We Became Visible, Our Image Was Enlarged." *Southern Exposure*, 9, No. 1 (1981): 5.

Williams, Randall. "Tonight, The Hulk vs. Ox Baker." *Southern Exposure*, 7, No. 2 (1979): 30–35.

Yeomans, G. Allen. "Southern Oratory and the Art of Storytelling: A Case Study." *Southern Speech Journal*, 32 (1967): 251–260.

Zobel, Kathleen. "Hog Heaven: Barbecue in the South." *Southern Exposure*, 5, No. 2 & 3 (1977): 58–61.

MAGAZINES

Angelo, Bonnie. "Those Good Ole Boys." *Time*, 27 September 1976: 47.

"Another Piece of Fried Chicken, Please." *Southern Living*, July 1982: 72–73.

"The Belle: Magnolia and Iron." *Time*, 27 September 1976: 94–97.

Bevier, Thomas. "Dear Dixie: You're Looking Better Every Day." *Chicago Tribune Magazine*, 13 February 1972: 64–67.

Black, Patti Carr, and William R. Ferris. "The Shotgun, the Dogtrot, and the Row House." *Southern Voices*, May-June 1974: 28–32.

Boyce, Joseph. "Reverse Migration." *Time*, 27 September 1976: 50.

Chaney, Betty Norwood. "Interchange." *Southern Changes*, May 1979: 2.

Cheatham, Edward, and Patricia Cheatham. "A Tale of Four Cities: Southern Style." *Sky*, December 1979: 30–36.

"A City Reborn." *Time*, 27 September 1976: 55–56.

Cunningham, Emory. "Introduction to the Future of the South." *Southern Living*, January 1976: 32.

Davidson, Ralph P. "A Letter from the Publisher." *Time*, 27 September 1976: 3.

Demarest, Michael. "A Home Grown Elegance." *Time*, 27 September 1976: 66–67.

"Dollars Marching South." *The SOUTH Magazine*, January-February 1976: 20–23.

"Eat 'Em up, Get 'Em." *Time*, 27 September 1976: 81.

Egerton, John. "John N. Popham—Making Southern History Real, Making a Little History Himself." *Southern Voices*, October-November 1974: 62–65.

———. "The Man Who Cried Impeachment First." *Southern Voices*, May-June 1974: 11–16.

Ford, Gary D. "The South Burns for Barbeque." *Southern Living*, May 1982: 120–129.

Ford, Jesse Hill. "The Southerner as a Scottish Problem." *Southern Voices*, August-September 1974: 19.

Frome, Michael. "To Save Our Natural Heritage, Time is Short and Running Fast." *Southern Living*, January 1976: 14a–16a.

Goldstein, Linda. "The South as a Real Estate Frontier." *SOUTH Business*, March 1981: 20–21.

"The Good Life." *Time*, 27 September 1976: 32–39.

Greenberg, Paul. "Of Medeas, Medusas, and the Media." *Arkansas Times*, August 1981: 23–25.

Greene, Melissa. "The Storytellers." *Country Journal*, October 1981: 46–53.

Gunn, Clare A. "Southern Tourism: Will There Be a Place to Go?" *Southern Living*, January 1977: 4a–8a.

Hall, B. C. "How to Talk to a Yankee." *Arkansas Times*, September 1977: 22–24.

"How Southern Is He?" *Time*, 27 September 1976: 46–47.

Huth, Tom. "Should Charleston Go New South?" *Historic Preservation*, July-August 1979: 32–38.

Johnson, Norman K., and Glenn Morris. "The Vanishing Rural Landscape." *Southern Living*, January 1979: 20s–23s.

"Just Like Whiskey." *Time*, 27 September 1976: 82.

Kane, Joseph. "Small Town Soul." *Time*, 27 September 1976: 56.

King, Larry L. "We Ain't Trash No More: How Jimmy Carter Led the Rednecks From the Wilderness." *Esquire*, November 1976: 87–90, 152–156.

Massow, Rosalind. "Atlanta: A Once and Present Queen." *Sky*, May 1977: 49–55.

Mathews, Tom. "The Southern Mystique." *Newsweek*, 19 July 1976: 30–33.

Morris, Philip. "Five Southern Towns Change and Stay the Same." *Southern Living*, January 1978: 3s–12s.

———. "The Great Neighborhood Revival." *Southern Living*, November 1976: 69–77.

———. "Once and Future Cities." *Southern Living*, January 1976: 5a–13a.

————. "Shaping Livable Southern Cities." *Southern Living*, January 1980: 3s–14s.

Morris, Willie. "Misty, Water-Colored Memory of My First College Football Game." *Southern Living*, September 1982: 10–15.

Mullen, Andrea Kirsten. "Preservation in the Black Community: A Growing Commitment." *Historic Preservation*, January-February 1982: 38–43.

"A New Magazine: Our Creed and Hopes." Editorial. *Southern Changes*, September 1978: 2–3.

Noble, Larry. "Southern Newspapers: Watching the Watchdogs." *Southern Changes*, July 1979: 19–23.

O'Neill, Frank. "Greatest Menace Yet to Southern Mountains." *Southern Voices*, May-June 1974: 73–78.

Patton, Phil. "Interview: James Dickey." *Sky*, July 1977: 26, 42–44.

Pennington, John. "Is There a New South?" *Atlanta Journal and Constitution Magazine*, 20 February 1972: 18, 28.

Percy, Walker. "Emerging from the Great Southern Obsession—Where Now?" *Southern Exchange*, March 1979: 36–39, 49.

Reed, Roy. "A Letter to My Grandfather." *Arkansas Times*, July 1984: 36–38, 78–86.

Sarka, Mike. "Tourism is the South's Top Industry." *Southern Living*, January 1978: 34s–37s.

Schemmel, Bill. "Romance with a Neighborhood." *The SOUTH Magazine*, January-February 1976: 34–35.

Schrag, Peter. "A Hesitant New South: Fragile Promise on the Last Frontier." *Saturday Review*, 12 February 1972: 51–56.

Smith, Faye McDonald. "Minorities in Southern Television." *Southern Changes*, July 1979: 2, 26–29.

"Special Issue: The New South." *The Economist*, 3 March 1979.

Sugg, Redding S., Jr. "A Treatise Upon Cornbread." *Southern Voices*, October-November 1974: 38–43.

Suitts, Steve. "Renewal and Endurance: A Personal View." *Southern Changes*, April 1979: 4–5.

Terry, Bill. "Arkansas' Great Moveable Feast: A Catfish Journal." *Arkansas Times*, May 1982: 14–32.

Thomas, Richard K. "How to Tell You're in the South." *Southern Changes*, September 1978: 13–15.

"To Use the Land and Not Destroy It." Editorial. *Southern Living*, January 1979: 3s.

Tullos, Allen. "Azalea Death Trip." *Southern Changes*, July 1979: 6–10, 32.

Walker, Alice. "Staying Home in Mississippi." *The New York Times Magazine*, 26 August 1973: 9, 49, 52–53, 58, 60, 62.

Watters, Pat. "It's Been 20 Long Years." *Southern Voices*, May-June 1974: 5–6, 8.

Welch, Linda. "Cornbread: Break Off a Piece of Southern Heritage." *Southern Living*, November 1981: 102–103.

White, Otis. "The Future of the South." *SOUTH Business*, January 1981: 29–35.

"Why More Blacks Are Moving South." *U. S. News & World Report*, 26 February 1973: 53–55.

Williams, T. Harry. "Now, Maybe, We Can Begin to Appreciate Lyndon Baines Johnson." *Southern Voices*, May-June 1974: 66–71.

Wolfe, Tom. "Last American Hero Is Junior Johnson." *Esquire*, March 1965: 68–75.

Woodward, C. Vann. "From the First Reconstruction to the Second." *Harper's Magazine*, April 1965: 127–133.

———. "The South Tomorrow." *Time*, 27 September 1976: 98–99.

Workman, William D., Jr., and Willis P. Whichard. "On Using Land Well." *Southern Living*, January 1977: 28a–32a.

Wyrick, Marilyn. "Where There's Smoke There's Barbecue." *Southern Living*, September 1977: 84.

NEWSPAPERS

Ashmore, Harry S. "The *Brown* Decision in Retrospect, 1954–1976." *Arkansas Gazette*, 26 September 1976: 5E.

———"An Effort to Define South's Philosophy." *Arkansas Gazette*, 2 May 1976: 2E.

Barrington, Carol. "Louisiana's Antebellum Mansions Offer a Rare Chance to Sample History . . . and to Live Like Scarlett O'Hara." *Chicago Tribune*, 18 April 1982, Sec. 2: 8–9.

Black, Eric. "Good Ol' Boys Fall From Grace in Arkansas Politics." *Minneapolis Tribune*, 16 April 1978: 11.

"Blocking of Door Not Racial Matter, Wallace Asserts." *Arkansas Gazette*, 8 December 1978: 19A.

Bode, Roy. "Georgians May Restore Southern Ethos to Capitol." *Arkansas Gazette*, 26 November 1976: 22A.

"Boston's Own Image Makers." Editorial. *Arkansas Gazette*, 20 November 1977: 2E.

"Commendable Choice for the FBI." Editorial. *Arkansas Gazette*, 18 August 1977: 20A.

Deane, Ernie. "Grits and Blackeyed Peas." *Springdale News*, 28 November 1976: 1C.

———. "A Southerner Views Carter." *Springdale News*, 7 November 1976: 1C.

———. "Warning to the South." *Springdale News*, 11 April 1976: 21.

———. "The Way We Talk." *Springdale News*, 20 July 1975: 1B.

Dumas, Ernest. "Major Symbolism in Pryor's Appointments." *Arkansas Gazette*, 13 November 1977: 3E.

Editorial. *Manufacturers' Record*. 18 August 1929: 53–54.

Egerton, John. "Hello, Boston, This is Little Rock Calling." *Charlotte Observer*, 5 June 1976: 18A.

"Ex-governor, Black Central Graduate, Recall 1957." *Arkansas Gazette*, 1 April 1977: 7A.

Garnett, Bernard E. "Going Home: More Black Americans Return to South from 'Exile' in North." *Wall Street Journal*, 10 November 1972: 1, 13.

Goolrick, Chester. "One Way to Succeed in Sunbelt is Simply to Sing Its Praises." *Wall Street Journal*, 23 November 1981: 1, 19.

Harris, Elizabeth A. "Charlie Daniels: Southern Music at the White House?" *Arkansas Gazette*, 3 October 1976: 11E.

Hawkins, David. "Southerners Should Feel a Little Bit More Superior." *Arkansas Democrat*, 14 August 1977: 25A.

"A History Marker at the School Where It Was Made." *Arkansas Gazette*, 26 November 1982: 3A.

Johnson, Paul. "Dig Southern Rock? Capricorn Has it In 'South's Greatest Hits.'" *Arkansas Gazette*, 22 September 1977: 7D.

Jones, Jerry. "Race Problems Now in Great Cities of the North, Ashmore Declares." *Arkansas Gazette*, 17 May 1979: 1A, 5A.

King, Wayne. "Rapidly Growing Arkansas Turns to Liberal Politicians." *The New York Times*, 14 May 1978: 26.

Lewis, Anthony. "The South's Place in American Politics '76." *Arkansas Gazette*, 1 October 1976: 6A.

Mebane, Mary E. "And Blacks Go South Again." *The New York Times*, 4 July 1972: 17.

"Middle Class Blacks in North Move South for Better Lifestyle." *Arkansas Gazette*, 16 March 1976: 18B.

Mink, Randy. "Old South and Its Heroes Linger in Historic Lexington." *Chicago Tribune*, 18 April 1982, Sec. 2: 6.

"New Warning for South to Proceed With Caution." Editorial. *Springdale News*, 6 April 1976: 2.

Popham, John N. "A Recession Would Have Lightest Impact in S. E." *Arkansas Gazette*, 15 July 1979: 1E, 4E.

Raines, Howell. "The South's New Reform-Minded Governors." *Louisville Courier-Journal*, 4 March 1979: D1.

———. "Success of 'Different' Politicians Reflects New Attitudes in the South." *The New York Times*, 3 July 1978: 1, 8.

"Rebel Flag at Ole Miss Now Symbolizes New Horizons, Not Lost Causes." *Arkansas Gazette*, 14 October 1976: 14A.

Reston, James. "The 'Americanization' of the Southern Region." *Arkansas Gazette*, 15 October 1976: 6A.

Roberts, Steven V. "New Breed of Arkansas Officials Taking Race Out of Politics." *The New York Times*, 14 December 1978: A 26.

Royko, Mike. "Now They'll Focus on the Glook of the South." *Arkansas Gazette*, 28 November 1976: 3E.

Smith, Stephen A. "The Laying On of Hands." *Grapevine*, 24 September 1976: 3.

"South Ahead in Changes, Judge Believes." *Arkansas Gazette*, 17 April 1978: 13A.

"The South: Can It Avoid Mistakes of Other Areas." Editorial. *Springdale News*, 30 May 1975: 2.

"SWC's First Black Met Opposition, Hatred." *Arkansas Democrat*, 27 July 1977: 1B.

Taylor, Steve, "Are Y'all From Dixie? Y'all Wear Shoes?" *Arkansas Democrat*, 20 August 1979: 5A.

Thomas, Rex. "Selma Marked End of an Era in Deep South." *Northwest Arkansas Times*, 16 March 1975: 7A.

"Tucker Boys Attract Kinky Side of New South." *Arkansas Democrat*, 11 July 1977: 9A.

West, Dick. "Hello Rednecks, Goodbye Chivalry." *Arkansas Gazette*, 25 February 1981: 11A.

Wicker, Tom. "Johnson: The Law Against the Order." *Arkansas Gazette*, 25 May 1977: 21A.

————. "South Carolina Politics Has Changed." *Arkansas Gazette*, 5 April 1978: 19A.

Wiles, Susan. "Scanning Visions of the Southern Future." *Arkansas Gazette*, 2 April 1981: 19A.

Woodward, C. Vann. "New South Fraud Is Prepared by Old South Myth." *Washington Post*, 9 July 1961: E3.

Yates, Richard E. "The Heavens are Still There: The Errors of Our Ways." *Arkansas Democrat*, 19 August 1979: 7A.

NEWSLETTERS

"Askew Lists SGPB Priorities for Regional Leadership Role." *Southern Growth: Problems & Promise*, 3 (1976): 2.

"Governor Boren Pays Tribute to Askew for His Leadership." *Southern Growth: Problems & Promise*, 4 (1977): 2.

"Mathews Advises New Strategy for Mainstream South." *Southern Growth: Problems & Promise*, 5 (1977): 5.

"1980 Commission: Framing a Positive Agenda for the South." *Southern Growth: Problems & Promise*, 8 (1981): 1.

RECORDINGS

Alabama. "My Home's in Alabama." *My Home's in Alabama*. RCA, AHK1–3644, 1980.

Braddock, Bobby. *I Believe the South is Gonna Rise Again*. Nashville: Tree Publishing Co., 1973.

The South's Greatest Hits. Capricorn Records, CP 0187, 1977.

The South's Greatest Hits, Volume II. Capricorn Records, CPN 0209, 1978.

PAMPHLETS

The Center for South Folklore. Memphis: Center for Southern Folklore, 1977.

Facing South. Chapel Hill: Institute for Southern Studies, 1979.

Hodding Carter, Vice President. Memphis: Hodding Carter for Vice President, 1972.

The South. New York: Four Winds Travel, Inc., 1982.

Southern Exposure sees the South as it is . . . and can still become. Chapel Hill: Institute for Southern Studies, 1977.

ADVERTISEMENTS

Hot Springs Mobile Home Estates. "Real Southern Living." *Hot Springs and Diamond Lakes Guide*. Hot Springs: Hot Springs-Diamond Lakes Travel Association, 1982: 26.

Travel Department, Mississippi A & I Board. "Missimpression." *Southern Living*, April 1976: 31.

Travel Department, Mississippi A & I Board. "Missinformed." *Southern Living*, March 1976: 76.

Travel Department, Mississippi A & I Board. "Missunderstood." *Southern Living*, May 1976: 4C.

DISSERTATIONS

Clayton, Bruce Lynn. "Southern Critics of the New South, 1890–1914." Diss. Duke 1966.

Gaston, Paul M. "The New South Creed, 1865–1900." Diss. North Carolina 1961.

Hoban, James Leon. "The Structure of Myth in Rhetorical Criticism." Diss. Illinois 1971.

Whitaker, Hugh Stephen. "A New Day: The Effect of Negro Enfranchisement in Selected Mississippi Counties." Diss. Florida State 1965.

PAPERS

Anderson, Ruben. "The Future of Southern Cities." Southern Growth Policies Board, Dorado Beach, Puerto Rico. 28 September 1981.

Braden, Waldo W. "Problems and Prospects in the Study of the Rhetoric of the Contemporary South." Conference on Rhetoric of the Contemporary South, Boone, N. C. 18 June 1974.

Dorgan, Howard. "The Mountain Metaphor of Senator Sam." Southern Speech Communication Association convention, Tallahassee. April 1975.

Egerton, John. "The Americanization of Dixie—An Update." Conference on Rhetoric of the Contemporary South, Bowling Green, Kentucky. 29 June 1979.

Heath, Robert L. "Perfect Political Myth as Substance for Social Movement Vulnerability." Speech Communication Association convention, San Antonio. November 1979.

Kell, Carl. "Continuity and Change—The South in 1978." Conference on Rhetoric of the Contemporary South, New Orleans. 1 July 1978.

——. "Rhetoric and Folklore: A State-of-the-Art Report." Southern Speech Communication Association convention, Tallahassee. April 1975.

——. "A Rhetoric of Community: *Southern Living* Magazine." American Culture Association convention, Toronto. March 1984.

——. "The Southernization of America: A Rhetorical Perspective." Speech Communication Association convention, Chicago. 28 December 1972.

——. "Towards a Theory of Rhetoric: The Contemporary South." Conference on Rhetoric of the Contemporary South, Bowling Green, Kentucky. 27 June 1975.

Kell, Carl, and James A. Pearce. "A Rhetoric of Southernness: Screening the Soul of the South." Popular Culture in the South convention, Tampa. October 1975.

Logue, Calvin M. "Public Address as Myth." Speech Communication Association convention, Chicago. 28 December 1972.

Montell, Lynnwood. "Folklore and Rhetoric: A State-of-the-Art Report." Southern Speech Communication Association convention, Tallahassee. April 1975.

Rodgers, Raymond S. "The Rhetoric of Redneck Rock: Persuasive Strategies of a Contemporary Myth in the Making." Conference on Rhetoric of the Contemporary South, Boone, N. C. 21 August 1977.

——. "The Rhetorical Criticism of Folklore and Intercultural Communication." Southern Speech Communication Association convention, Biloxi. April 1979.

Segal, Zeke. "The South Talks—the Nation Listens." Conference on Rhetoric of the Contemporary South, New Orleans. 30 June 1978.

Smith, Stephen A. "Culture and Commerce: The Image of the Ozark Hillbilly." Popular Culture Association convention, Chicago. April 1976.

——. "Food for Thought: Comestible Communication and Gastronomical Geography." Popular Culture Association convention, Wichita. April 1983.

——. "New Myths in the Rhetoric of the Contemporary South." Conference on Rhetoric of the Contemporary South, Pensacola. 13 August 1976.

——. "Selling the South: The Rhetoric of Southern Tourism Promotion."

Midwest Modern Language Association convention, St. Louis. November 1976.

———. "Southern Senators and the Continuing American Revolution: The Voting Rights Act of 1975." Southern Speech Communication Association convention, San Antonio. April 1976.

Strickland, Rennard. "The Southern Tradition in Quest for Contemporary Values." Speech Communication Association convention, Chicago. 28 December 1972.

Sutherland, Cyrus. "Arkansas' Architectural Heritage: Focus on the Vernacular." Historic Preservation Alliance of Arkansas, Hot Springs. October 1981.

Thomas, David A. "Secession and Slavery: Jefferson Davis' Rhetorical Vision of the South." Southern Speech Communication Association convention, Biloxi. 13 April 1979.

Whichard, Willis P. "A Letter to Walter Hines Page." Conference on Rhetoric of the Contemporary South, Bowling Green, Kentucky. 29 June 1979.

SPEECHES

Askew, Reubin. Remarks of the New Chairman. Southern Growth Policies Board, Pinehurst, N. C., 13 November 1975.

Ayres, H. Brandt. "We've Got to Stop Meeting Like This." Commission on the Future of the South, Atlanta, 12 January 1981.

Bumpers, Dale. "The New South." Bowdoin College, Brunswick, Maine. 13 December 1976.

———. "The New South." University of Southern Mississippi, Hattiesburg, 10 December 1976.

Carter, Jimmy. Speech delivered at the Martin Luther King Hospital, Los Angeles, June 1, 1976. Atlanta: Democratic Presidential Campaign Committee, 1976.

Gatewood, Willard B., Jr. "The South, The State University, and Regional Promise." University of Arkansas, Fayetteville. 14 May 1977.

Graham, Bob. Inaugural address. Tallahassee, 2 January 1979.

Hunt, James. Remarks of the New Chairman. Southern Growth Policies Board, Atlanta, November 1978.

James, Forrest H., Jr. Inaugural Address. Montgomery, Al., 15 January 1979.

Lewis, John. Statement. Voter Education Project, Atlanta, 13 January 1977.
McGovern, George. "The Southern Strategy." San Antonio, 26 June 1972.
Pryor, David. Address to Little Rock Central High School honors assembly. Little Rock, 20 May 1975.
Riley, Richard W. Inaugural Address. Columbia, S. C., 10 January 1979.
Sanford, Terry. Address to the Planning Group Considering a Southern Regional Growth Board. Durham, N. C., 3 October 1971.
Tindall, George B. History and the Future of the South. University of Florida, Gainesville. 18 May 1981.

INTERVIEWS

Ashmore, Harry S. Personal interview. 26 April 1976.
Collins, Leroy. Personal interview. 19 October 1980.
Cook, Samuel DuBois. Personal interview. 12 January 1981.
Crosland, Paige. Personal interview. 2 May 1977.
Packard, Vance. Personal interview. 26 October 1976.
Thornton, Ray. Personal interview. 5 October 1976.
Thrasher, Sue. Personal interview. 2 May 1977.
Whitehead, James. Personal interview. 2 December 1982.

LETTERS

Bond, Julian. Letter to Dear Brothers and Sisters. October 1977.
Bryan, Sara T., Peter A. Carmichael, and Charles D. Perry. "Sumpn Hawrble." Letter. *Southern Voices*, October-November 1974: 6.
Carter, Jimmy. Letter to author. 14 August 1975.
Clinton, Bill. Letter to Joseph D. Duffey. 22 February 1980.
McCalla, Gary. Letter to Dear Former Subscriber. 1981.

Index